D1048479

THE PETA
PRACTICAL
GUIDE
TO ANIMAL
RIGHTS

ALSO BY INGRID NEWKIRK

One Can Make a Difference

Making Kind Choices

Let's Have a Dog Party

50 Awesome Ways Kids Can Help Animals

250 Ways to Make Your Cat Adore You

Free the Animals!

Simple Acts of Kindness to Help Animals in Trouble

THE PETA
PRACTICAL
GUIDE
TO ANIMAL
RIGHTS

INGRID NEWKIRK

*President of People for
the Ethical Treatment of Animals*

ST. MARTIN'S GRIFFIN
NEW YORK

THE PETA PRACTICAL GUIDE TO ANIMAL RIGHTS. Copyright © 2009 by Ingrid Newkirk. Foreword copyright © 2009 by Bill Maher. All rights reserved. Printed in the United States of America. For information, address St. Martin's Press, 175 Fifth Avenue, New York, N.Y. 10010.

www.stmartins.com

Book design by Ellen Cipriano

Grateful acknowledgment is given for permission to reprint the following material:

"The Master Listens" by Thomas D. Murray. Reprinted with permission of *The Wall Street Journal*, copyright © 1995, Dow Jones & Company, Inc. All rights reserved.

The poem "Look Mommy, isn't he cute?" by Paul Haggard. Reprinted by permission of the author.

An excerpt from the poem "Meantime (or How I Spent My Summer Vacation)" by Paulette Callen. Reprinted by permission of the author.

LIBRARY OF CONGRESS CATALOGING-IN-PUBLICATION DATA

Newkirk, Ingrid.
    The PETA practical guide to animal rights : simple acts of kindness to help animals in trouble / Ingrid Newkirk.
        p.   cm.
    Includes bibliographical references and index.
    ISBN-13: 978-0-312-55994-6
    ISBN-10: 0-312-55994-1
    1. Animal rights.   2. Animal welfare.   3. Human-animal relationships.   4. People for the Ethical Treatment of Animals.   I. Title.
    HV4708.N485   2009
    179'.3—dc22

                                                                        2009006904

First Edition: June 2009

Printed on recycled paper

10 9 8 7 6 5 4 3 2 1

Dedication

In addition to everyone who says and does anything to make this world a kinder place, this book is dedicated to two special women who have inspired many others: Nanci Alexander and the late Linda McCartney. Each has recognized the power of her own voice, her resources, and her life, and the similarities are striking:

Aware that a wonderful way to reach people's hearts is through their stomachs, Nanci opened an international gourmet restaurant in Fort Lauderdale called Sublime. What a stunning introduction to a humane way of eating—discovering that the "caviar" and the "quiche" on the menu are 100 percent vegan (no animal bits and pieces in them), as is everything else. As for Linda, she was the pioneer of frozen vegetarian food in the

U.K., the first person to bring to the supermarket vegetarian "fish" sticks and "bangers" (sausages). It was a revolutionary idea that really took hold.

Neither of these women has ever hesitated to speak out. Fully aware that giving animals a voice is the most vital and powerful gift to them, Linda would ask everyone she met, from electricians to royals (and she met a few!), whether backstage at Paul's concerts or out walking in the countryside, the bald-faced question, "Are you veggie?" And if they answered no, or hemmed and hawed a bit (after all, this was a Beatle's wife!), Linda would tell them in graphic detail exactly what happens to animals in slaughterhouses. It would have been impossible for them to fail to think twice before ordering that next chicken limb.

Nanci never misses a chance to open people's eyes and minds, from the "Remember—animals have rights" message on her answering machine to buttonholing a politician at a fundraiser or politely bending the ear of a guest at a social function. She founded the Animal Rights Foundation of Florida, which distributes footage from fur farms and pig factories, from laboratories and circuses, so that no one will be able to say that they don't know what animals endure. Linda used video too. She persuaded Paul to show PETA undercover footage to fans at every concert on his world tours, exposing millions to the animal rights message.

I dedicate this book to these two true angels for animals and pioneers for animal rights.

Contents

Acknowledgments

Thanks to everyone at PETA, past and present, staff member, member, supporter, volunteer, or intern, who offered ideas and helped with this special book. Special mention goes to Joel Bartlett, Carla Bennett, Patti Breitman, Kathy Guillermo, Starza Kolman, Paula Moore, Alisa Mullins, Mary Ann Naples, Karen Porreca, Robyn Wesley, and Anna West.

Foreword

My job is listening to people's opinions. I know that when four people discuss any topic, they're likely to agree on only one thing: everyone else is wrong. This, I've found, is the human condition. Each of us tends to see the world from our own perspective, planting our flag on our individual hill and defending our point of view as if it's a democratic territory under siege by the evil empire.

Rarely is the human perspective more self-serving than when dealing with animals. We can be altruistic; many people love their canine companions and let their cats sleep on their best bedspreads. But we don't like to be made uncomfortable. Just ask a friend who's about to cut into a slab of sirloin steak if he's ever been to a slaughter-house.

If you fall into this category (most of us normal folks do to some extent), this book may make you squirm just a bit. But you won't be able to put it down. Who knew that macaws could play practical jokes on people? That an octopus could unscrew the lid from a jar? That animals are capable of acts so brave and so selfless that they should inspire humans to greater deeds? After reading these pages, you'll no longer think of animals as mere experimental subjects or livestock breeds or garden pests.

And thinking of animals as the remarkable individuals they are will change your life. Because once you do, you'll want to do something about it.

That's where Ingrid Newkirk gets down to business. This book is about *doing.* You can take a tiny step, a firm stride, or a great leap to change. You can start by clearing the animal-tested products from your bathroom cabinet or by coming down off the hill and handcuffing yourself to the entrance gate at a zoo. There are as many ways to make a difference in the lives of ani-mals as there are personality types in a psychology text. Just find one you're comfortable with and start. You'll probably find, as I did, that the more you read, the more you'll want to stretch, try something new, speak up more.

There are great examples here: people who put their ca-reers, even their own safety, on the line to stop an injustice against an animal. If they were embarrassed, if they were self-conscious, if they were nervous—who cares? They got past the things that often stand in the way of change. We can too. This book shows us how.

Now read and get busy!

—Bill Maher

PETA: How It All Began

People for the Ethical Treatment of Animals, (PETA) was born in a basement apartment way back in 1980, before anyone had yet coined the term "animal rights." The apartment overlooked a garden that was often filled with birds. Their antics and relationships with one another were mesmerizing: there were mother birds teaching nestlings how to survive, bird friends played in the little fountain, and on a hot day, you could almost feel the pleasure a bird felt from sipping a cool drink. Seeing their joy made me start to think how sad it was that some birds are kept in cages, indoors and all alone, as if they are mere decorations without feelings and interests. Why isn't there justice for all beings, I wondered. So, with modest ambitions and local actions in mind,

I rounded up some friends and started a group to promote the ethical treatment of animals, PETA.

As it happened, a young political science student named Alex Pacheco had recently walked into the Washington, D.C., animal shelter where I worked and offered his time. As the beleaguered person in charge, I took him up on the offer, and as he worked, he told me his story.

Only a few months earlier, he had been aboard an anti-whaling ship, *Sea Shepherd.* The vessel's captain, Paul Watson, had recruited the first group of marine mammal "warriors," Alex among them, to hunt down a pirate whaling ship called the *Sierra.* Over the years, the *Sierra* had been responsible for butchering hundreds of whales in international waters. After combing the Atlantic, Watson and the crew of the *Sea Shepherd* found the *Sierra* off the coast of Portugal. They trailed it from a distance until it berthed in Lisbon and, when its crew was safely ashore, rammed its bow. The *Sierra* went to the bottom, never to harpoon another Great Blue again.

In his backpack, Alex carried copies of Peter Singer's *Animal Liberation*, a book that had changed his way of thinking about animals and is today a must-read classic. He loaned a copy to me, and as I turned the pages, I came to realize that deep in my heart, I believed, along with the author, that animals have a worth in and of themselves, that they are not inferior to human beings but are rather just different from us. They don't exist for us nor do they belong to us. I also realized that it should not be a question simply of *how* animals should be treated within the context of their usefulness, or perceived usefulness, to us, but rather whether we have a *right* to use them at all.

I came to see that although most of us grew up knowing and believing in kindness to animals, wanting animals to be treated with decency and respect, something has gone wrong.

Luckily, we can fix the problem. After all, it is not as if we accept the psychopath who buries puppies alive in the back-yard or condone the teenager who maliciously ties a firecracker to a cat's tail. We don't. We react with outrage and horror at such violence, because we recognize that animals are vulnerable and cannot adequately defend themselves against human wrath and callousness. So when we hear of such abominations, we picket the courthouse, demand heavy sentences for the perpetrators of such acts, and call for stricter laws.

However, the problems animals face are far larger than isolated incidents of individual abuse.

We have become, mostly unwittingly, participants in heinous atrocities. These are *institutionalized* cruelties that affect billions of animals every year. We often don't know how to begin to stop them because they don't take place on the public street. They happen out of sight, on the factory farm, in the slaughterhouse and laboratory, on the trapline, behind the Big Top, in jungles and forests, and even beneath the surface of oceans and lakes. Yet these cruelties are so ghastly that, unless we learn how to reject them outright, and take action to stop them, it will be difficult for us, when we look back on our lives, not to feel ashamed of what *our* species has done to all the others.

Let's go back all the way to 1977. That's when a kind young man was charged with freeing a dolphin named Puka from a laboratory isolation tank in Hawaii and releasing him into the ocean off Maui. The man said he had been driven to this desperate act, which cost him his career, by the attitudes of those around him in the science lab where he worked.

At his trial, the man said this: "I came to realize that these dolphins were just like me. I watched the psychiatrists torment them and I watched the dolphins sink into deep depression, cut off from all that was natural and all that they had loved and wanted. I could not stand my own inaction any longer. I will go to jail with sadness that the world does not yet understand what I do, but my confinement will be nothing compared to what they have endured."

Luckily, no one has to go to jail to free animals, although some courageous people will. There are legal ways to effect a change in attitudes, in hearts, and in minds that will afford animals the dignity and respect they deserve.

My aim is to take you to places most people will never visit and to look at our interactions with animals in ways that are dramatically different for most of us. I hope to motivate and empower you to make the vital changes that must come about. For you are the most important asset the animals have: you are the voice and lifeline they depend on.

I will show you what you need to see so that you can easily understand just how important you are to animals in trouble. From the moment of birth to its invariably unsavory end, life has become a nightmare for the gentle cows, frightened dogs, and displaced elephants who now find themselves facing such hardware as debeaking machines, decapitators, restraint chairs (such as those used by NASA to keep monkeys immobile for weeks on end), mechanized knives, shock prods, martingales (shackles that keep elephants' heads chained down to their front legs), and cranial electrode implants.

For these wonderful, sensitive beings, contact with humans comes not in the form of a hand reaching out to stroke them, but a metal-tipped bull hook or a whip meeting their soft flesh. It comes when they are thrown against the side of the stainless steel cage that is their home, or when, old, sick, and broken, they are kicked into the final transport truck.

When I founded PETA, I had no idea that it would grow as much as it has, attracting millions of compassionate people who have switched from being sloppy shoppers to caring consumers. PETA members usually don't sit quietly when animals need their voices; they speak out, often politely but always firmly.

They don't accept cruelty; they openly and firmly object to it and, in many cases, get it stopped. It is thanks to them that great changes happen.

This book will link you up to a community that respects animals enough to consider their welfare when making choices. Sometimes the choices are simple, like which movie to see or which veterinarian or haircutter to patronize. Sometimes they're tougher ones, like what to do if your teacher insists that every student must dissect a frog or a cat. You will learn how to make your vote count, how to influence magazine publishers and television producers with a few taps on the keyboard or a few strokes of the pen. Thanks to you, your local mall will begin to reflect your choices by adding items to their store shelves and even subtracting unacceptable ones. And people around you will be influenced by the "new you," and you will see a change in their thinking and in their buying habits too. It's inevitable.

If you do only a few of the things suggested in this book, you should feel good about yourself. The more you do, the better you'll feel, the happier your companion animals will be, the healthier you'll become, and the more impact you'll have on the world around you. I'm positive of it.

I promise too that, after reading this book, you will be able to answer the question "What did you do, in your lifetime, to help animals?" joyfully and without a second thought.

Author's Note:
Join the Army of the Kind

Three things in human life are important. The first is to be kind. The second is to be kind. And the third is to be kind.

—HENRY JAMES

In order to be kind, we must *do*. There is no point in thinking good thoughts but not acting on them. There is no currency in wishing things were better but not rolling up one's sleeves and helping to change them. And it doesn't take much to make a huge difference.

Sometimes people tell me they feel so alone in their compassion. The fact is, we never are alone. Let me give you just two of many examples.

A friend of mine who's a doctor was vacationing in Mexico when he spotted a man wearing an animal rights T-shirt. "Great shirt!" my friend said to the man. "Oh, I love it, but I only get to wear it here," the man said. "I'm a doctor back in the States and none of my colleagues believe in animal rights." My friend said, "I'm a doctor too. Where are you from?" The man told him the name of the town. "But I know several physicians there who are animal rights advocates," my friend said, and then named them. "I can't believe it," said the other doctor. "Charlie and Richard? I had no idea they cared about animals."

On a beach in France some years ago, I saw two boys catch a crab and put him in a pail and start to poke at him. Knowing only enough French to order a room and a drink, I was about to grab the crab and run for the water with him when I saw my companion, who speaks French well, walk up to the boys and start to talk to them. A moment later, a big man approached the group. Uh-oh, I thought, that's their father. He won't like someone telling his children what to do. Suddenly, the boys ran to the water and let the crab go. When my companion returned, I asked, "What did that man say?" "Oh," said my friend, "he told them he wanted them to let the crab go!"

No matter where you are or what you are doing, there are people as interested as you are in treating animals well but who haven't said it or shown it. Often your action or words can make them see how easy it is to do the right thing.

A study on a college campus proves how vital it is to speak up for justice, no matter how awkward you might feel. In this study, a student researcher would approach a student and say, "One of the students received a letter containing racist remarks. Will you sign my petition to say we won't tolerate racism on this campus?"

Another student, actually a shill who gave the appearance of just happening to walk by, would stop to listen, and then adopt one of two attitudes. He would say either, "Well, how do we know the first student didn't provoke that remark?" Or, "Yes, we need to stop letting people be bullied because of their race."

Like it or not, in most cases when the student expressed concern and wished to sign the petition, the other student wanted to sign too. But in most cases where the student expressed doubt that there was anything wrong with the racist letter, the other student also thought it might be okay.

Our lesson is that we must be the first ones to speak up *for* animals and *against* cruelty. We will find others joining us, but we don't have to wait to be led.

In the late 1800s, the novelist John Galsworthy wrote:

> We are not living in a private world of our own. Everything we say and do and think has its effect on everything around us. If we feel and say loudly enough that it is an infernal shame to keep larks and other wild song birds in cages, we will infallibly infect a number of other people with that sentiment, and in the course of time, those people who feel as you do will become so numerous that larks, thrushes, blackbirds and linnets will no longer be caught and kept that way. How do you imagine it ever came about that bulls and bears and badgers are no longer openly encouraged to tear each other to pieces, and carthorses are no longer beaten to a pulp. When a thing exists that you really abhor, I wish you would remember a little whether in letting it strictly alone, you are minding your own business on principle, or simply because it seems more comfortable for you to do so.

In Galsworthy's lifetime, he witnessed an end to many abhorrent things done to animals. In my lifetime, I too have seen enormous changes in attitudes and behaviors toward animals. Veggie burgers are now on menus that once featured only steaks, and over seven hundred companies have stopped testing their products in rabbits' eyes or down the throats of mice. Wonderful circuses featuring human acrobats, jugglers, fire-eaters, and choreographed human performers are wowing crowds that once turned out to see tired and cruelly treated animals. It can only cheer you up to look back and recognize those advances, even when the task ahead may seem daunting.

Animal slavery will end, just as surely as women got the vote and human slavery was abolished. (Those fighting for its abolition almost unanimously believed they would never succeed.) The only question is when. The answer is that the busier we are and the greater our number, the quicker that day will dawn.

The beautiful thing is that activism is easy and takes as many forms as there are drops of water in a river. It can be quiet, practical, and incorporate seamlessly into our lives. Or it can be exciting, avant-garde, and even raucous. It takes all kinds of people and all kinds of actions to get the job done. All that matters is that if enough of us do *something*, then all the bits and pieces will come together to make one glorious success story.

Please share the What You Can Do sections in this book with your friends, family, dorm residents, co-workers, neighbors, doctor, and whoever is standing at the bus stop or wheeling a cart beside yours at the grocery store. No one needs a fancy degree to help animals (although that can certainly be put to good use!): all you need is the desire to help to make a huge difference.

Here are ten things you can do to help animals. More specific ideas are outlined in the What You Can Do section at the end of each chapter.

1. **Respect all species** and their wonderful attributes and beauty. Discover our mutual relationships and interdependencies, such as the ability to bond, feel pain, and enjoy food and physical comfort, so that as a soci-

ety we can think of and treat animals as beings, as other nations, and as fellow Earthlings, not as property to be controlled, or disposed of at whim.

2. **Become a vegan, avoiding all animal products,** thereby sparing animals from the terrible abuses of intensive rearing and the agony of the slaughterhouse, while at the same time helping to decrease factory farming pollution of rivers and streams and reduce the greenhouse gases that come from animal farming.

3. **Work for the abolition of entertainment that exploits animals,** such as the old-style animal circus and rodeo and cruel "sports" and "blood sports" such as hunting, fishing, and horse racing, so that this kind of treatment of animals can end.

4. **Educate yourself and others at school, work, home, and wherever you go.** Share online videos and facts about animals with everyone you know; write to newspapers; support stronger animal protection laws; protest cruelty wherever you find it; and speak out for animals in as many ways as you can.

5. **Get the "Look That Kills" without killing.** Embrace a fur- and skin-free wardrobe, avoiding killing for vanity and leaving the animals to enjoy the skins they were born in.

6. **Buy only household products and cosmetics that are cruelty-free,** that is, the ones that are not tested on animals, contain no animal ingredients, and are environmentally safe.

7. **Support alternatives to vivisection** (animal experimentation), such as using computer programs in laboratories rather than dissection, championing human tissue culture and high-speed computer analysis, buying only dog and cat foods tested in private homes,

and supporting only health charities that help humans rather than hurt animals.

8. **Volunteer for PETA, join PETA2's street team, help out at a humane animal shelter**, and/or donate money or tithe your income to help animals gain their rights.

9. **Practice Your ABCs (Animal Birth Control).** Make sure your dog or cat is "fixed" (sterilized, spayed, or neutered), so that you do not contribute to the over-population, homelessness, and consequent suffering of these animals. Consider helping someone else in a low-income neighborhood get their dog or cat steril-ized too. **And always adopt from a shelter** rather than buy from a pet shop or breeder.

10. **Simplify your lifestyle** by consuming less and recy-cling more, thus helping to curb development so you can help preserve wildlife habitat like rivers and shore-lines, wooded areas, and ponds near your home, na-tional forests, and even the rain forest.

From everyone at PETA, good luck in everything you do to help the animals. They need us all.

Thank you for caring and, most of all, for doing.

PART ONE
The Issues

Not "What" but
Who Are Animals?

To comprehend the organs of the horse,
is not to comprehend the horse himself.

—LIN YUTAN, CHINESE PHILOSOPHER

Let me start with a true story about a rhinoceros. These animals are hard for people to understand. They aren't furry or big-eyed or easy to pet, and a person might be forgiven for imagining that a charging rhino could flatten you like a locomotive.

Anna Merz, the founder of the Ngare Sergoi Rhino Sanctuary in Kenya, has lived with rhinos for many years. She now realizes that these enormous animals live in a completely different sphere from ours. They are the Mr. Magoos of the animal kingdom, barely able to see a thing, and their world is dominated by smell and hearing. Anna also realizes that "different" does not mean "stupid." In fact, the rhinos' communication system is quite complex. To communicate, they use body language, a wide variety of calls, and even urine or droppings as markers. Perhaps most interesting, they use a highly complicated method of regulating their breathing, a sort of Morse code, to talk to one another.

Rhinos are not alone here. Behavioral biologists have discovered "seismic communication" in elephants and mice. Male Malaysian tree frogs use their toes methodically to click out messages, and female frogs send electronic signals by vibrating the small saplings in which they live.

People may fear rhinos because they do not understand them, but Anna Merz says that fear is very much a two-way street, with most of the traffic coming from the opposite direction. "Most wild rhinos are obsessed by their *terror* of humans" because people have chased them, separated them from their calves, and slaughtered family members in front of them, cutting off their tusks for sale as aphrodisiacs.

The animals' fear makes close observation difficult. In the course of her work, however, Anna was lucky enough to raise and release a bull rhino called Makara, who had never witnessed an attack by hunters and so never learned to fear people. Over time, he actually came to regard Anna as a friend.

On one occasion, Anna was out with a tracker when the two of them saw a rhino moving very slowly toward them, looking very odd. When he got close, they saw it was Makara, and that he was completely entangled in barbed wire.

Barbed wire is terrifying to animals. When horses get tangled in even a little piece of the stuff, they invariably go wild with panic. Makara had recognized the sound of Anna's car engine and had come to her for help.

Anna got out of the car, and Makara, although trembling all over, gave her the greeting breathing. Somehow, Anna managed to get a handkerchief between Makara's eye and the jagged wire that was cutting into it, then took off her jacket and worked it under the wire that was cutting into his huge thigh. Anna and the tracker had no wire cutters with them, so the tracker used his cutlass and a flat stone to cut the wire while Anna disentangled it as it came free.

Anna talked reassuringly to the big bull rhino for the forty minutes or more it took to get the job done. The whole time Makara stood stock-still, except for the tremors that shook his body.

When the last bit of wire fell away, he breathed a grateful good-bye and moved slowly back into the bush.

Anna knew she had witnessed an act of outstanding intelligence and courage. Wire is terrifying for animals to comprehend, yet Makara had known to come for help. Still more incredible was the control he had exercised over himself while he was being slowly extricated, although the process must have been painful to him. And, although Makara knew Anna's voice well, she had never before attempted to touch him.

Perhaps if we could sit rhino hunters down and get them to see that a rhino is not just an object to line up in their sights, not just a meal or trophy on the hoof, but a living, thinking, feeling *player* in what behaviorist Dr. Roger Fouts calls the "great symphony of life in which each of us is assigned a different instrument," it might be harder for them to raise their rifles to their shoulders and blow these magnificent beings to kingdom come. Perhaps not. But lightning-quick realizations do happen.

Take, for example, a case in upstate New York one winter when the lakes and rivers were frozen solid. Two hunters, a father and his son, were out looking for "game," when they came across a deer lying on the ice in the middle of a frozen river.

Seeing them, the deer struggled to get up, but the slippery surface prevented her from rising. Every time she struggled, she fell back hard on the ice, her legs splaying out from under her. The hunters stood back and watched her trying to right herself, each time without success, until she seemed too exhausted to try again.

The father and son skated cautiously up to the doe. Like most hunters, they had never been really close to a live deer before, except to deal a final blow to their prey. The son, a man in his twenties, said later that when he bent down and put out his hand, he was afraid she would bite him. He reached out slowly, and the deer leaned forward and gently smelled the back of his hand, then looked up at him with her big eyes. The younger man began petting her.

The hunters found themselves in a predicament. Things were different. Somehow, they could not bring themselves to shoot this animal who, lying at their feet, as the son said, "looked like a big, old, sweet dog!"

The father and son found a nylon rope in one of their backpacks, and to their surprise the deer let them put it under her rump. Then, working in tandem, they started pulling the deer carefully across the ice toward the bank. It was hard work, and about every ten minutes they collapsed to rest, the three of them sitting close together on the ice until the father and son caught their breath. Then they pulled again, and the deer sat there quietly and helplessly, knowing they were all in this together.

When they finally got to the shoreline, the deer put her hoofs on the snow-covered earth, balanced herself, and stood. But now she saw the men as friends, rescuers, and was reluctant to leave. The three just stood there together, stock-still except for their labored breathing until, eventually, the hunters decided they must shoo her away.

Later, the younger hunter appeared on television, showing his home video of the incident and saying nothing could ever be the same again. He can't hunt deer any longer because he sees them differently now.

If this wonderful sort of breakthrough happened every day to people actively engaged in harming and killing animals, we would have a peaceful revolution on our hands. Hunters and slaughterhouse workers and people who steal cats to sell them to schools for dissection would not see animals as inconsequential and unfeeling commodities or as enemies. Animals might come to be viewed in the way Henry Beston, an English philosopher, saw them—as members of "other nations, caught with ourselves in the net of life and time."

Most of us can't imagine picking up a firearm to slaughter a deer or a rhino. We never meet or come to know the animals *we* ourselves harm, directly or, far more likely, through strangers. Because we haven't really thought much about it, or don't imagine there is a choice in the matter, we buy products and services that provide the funds to pay others to put harsh chemicals down beagles' throats, to castrate lambs without anesthetic, to shoot mother orangutans out of trees, and to build tiny cages in which foxes and lynx live until their necks are snapped and their pelts turned into the fur trim on winter jackets and gloves. These experiences are all very real to these animals, who aren't lulled into acceptance, as we are, by the myths about humane treatment and necessity, and who aren't distracted, as we are, by the pretty packaging, alluring descriptions, and upbeat marketing that surround almost everything we buy, from floor cleaner to circus tickets.

Although anyone who has taken Biology 101 would agree that animals are not inanimate objects, people often treat them as though they have no more feeling than a desk or a chair. Stop and look at the images of animals offered to us by fast-food companies. Animals are converted from flesh and blood into caricatures to make us feel comfortable about our complicity in their slaughter: happy chickens in little aprons dance their way merrily across the sign above the fast-food restaurant; a cute baby pig wearing a chef's hat stirs the pot. Similarly, to nip children's inquiries in the bud, the research industry sends colorful posters into schools, dishonestly depicting the rats it poisons and kills by the millions as cute cartoon creatures, snuggled up in cozy laboratory homes. And so it goes.

Walt Whitman saw things somewhat differently. He wrote:

> *I believe that a leaf of grass is no less than the journey*
> *work of the stars,*
> *And the ant is equally perfect, and a grain of sand,*
> *and the egg of the wren,*
> *And the tree-toad is a chef d'oeuvre for the highest,*
> *And the running blackberry would adorn the*
> *parlors of heaven. And the narrowest hinge*
> *in my hand puts to scorn all machinery,*
> *And the cow, crunching with depress'd head*
> *surpasses any statue,*
> *And a mouse is enough to stagger sextillions of infidels.*

To the outside observer, the human race seems not to agree. It has separated the entire animal kingdom into two parts. Humans are given the status of gods. We can do anything we please. We can take baby orcas away from their loving families at sea and put them in a SeaWorld tank for visitors to gawk at, or we can destroy scores of animals' habitats to build a new driveway or roller rink. Quite separate from us are all the other animals, be they our closest living relatives on the phylogenetic tree, the great apes, with whom we share 98 percent of our DNA, or the tiniest beetle. We see them not as whole, complete, or important in their own right. In fact, they are viewed as inconsequential, allowed to live only if their existence serves some purpose to us, if they are pretty, amusing, tasty, or strong. We debase their nature, deny their needs, and consider them to be merely cheap burglar alarms, windup toys, hamburgers, or handbags.

Some people rationalize their abuse by saying that humans are the cleverest animals on Earth, the only ones to land on the moon or write a symphony. True, but humans are also the only animals to devise an atomic bomb, invent concentration camps, and kill hitchhikers for sexual gratification. So what does it mean?

Grand and pompous statements about human superiority are reminiscent of the claims we read in history books, made by white slaveholders to defend auctioning black children after taking them away from their mothers (for more than a century, many people actually thought that slaves were incapable of maternal love), and by powerful men determined to deny women any rights whatsoever ("You might as well give asses the vote," wrote one Boston editor).

No doubt human beings, or at least some of them, are clever in ways other animals are not, although cleverness is hardly the criterion by which we decide whom to treat decently. If we did, many humans would be in deep trouble.

The fact is that animals are often amazing and awe inspiring, and their intelligence often leaves us in the dust. Long before any human sailor made the discovery, albatrosses knew the world was round because they had circumnavigated it without benefit of even a compass. The tiny desert mouse is far superior at surviving in Death Valley than the people who travel there, usually equipped with all manner of helpful gear, to test themselves against nature. These tiny rodents construct piles of stones around their burrows to collect the dew so they can take a drink when morning comes.

Name any animal, and our silly prejudices fade in the face of their feats: male Emperor penguins go without food for up to 145 days while guarding their eggs in the frozen tundra.

Fruit-eating bats act as midwives for bats who run into difficulty giving birth and have been known to bring food to ailing group members. Some birds, like indigo buntings, guide their long flights by learning the constellations; other birds fix their position by the height of the sun and, if blown off course by the wind, reset their path by the phases of the moon and the rising and setting of the stars. Turtles "read" Earth's magnetic field in order to navigate thousands of miles across vast, open oceans. Elephants mourn their relatives by cradling the bones of the dead animal in their trunks and rocking back and forth with them. Seals can absorb their own fetuses to prevent overpopulation during a time when food is scarce. Octopuses collect pretty objects and use them to decorate the walls of their subterranean caves. Chimpanzees seek out and use medicinal wild plants that have antibiotic properties. Birds make clay by mixing water and mud to harden nests or as casts for broken limbs. A type of Antarctic fish can feed under the ice because they have the highest known level of serum antifreeze in their blood; salmon know the *taste* of their ancestral rivers; whales sing their histories down through the generations, adding a "verse" every year; dolphins can "see" through the human body to detect cancers. Ants form living bridges to get their fellows across streams; orangutan babies use big leaves as umbrellas when it rains heavily, holding them over their heads to keep dry. And there are dogs who can warn of impending seizures and detect cancerous tumors in their human companions.

Some of these traits and accomplishments can be attributed to nature or instinct, but they are no less impressive because of it. After all, much of what *we* humans do is "natural" or "instinctive" too. Few people love their children or choose a mate based on careful calculation.

Ironically, animals are kind to us. Pigs have pulled children from ponds; canaries have flown into rooms where their guardians were sleeping, frantically warning them of fire; beavers have kept lost trekkers alive in the freezing forest by pressing their warm bodies against the hikers; dolphins have kept sailors afloat in shark-infested waters; and Binti, a mother gorilla, and Jambo, a giant, silverback male, both won international admiration when they guarded and protected human children who, in separate incidents, fell into concrete enclosures at a zoo. Fearing the worst, keepers ran to get tranquilizer guns with which to subdue the apes, but the apes recognized that these children needed their help and simply offered it, at personal risk.

Of course, dogs and cats, the animals we interact with perhaps more than any others, have saved our skins from everything from frozen lakes to armed attackers. They look after their own kind too. The mothers of cats and dogs will suffer burned faces and paws, crawling back into buildings to rescue their young. Take Sheba, a mother Rottweiler in Florida, who watched helplessly from her chain as her owner dug a two-foot-deep hole in the backyard, dropped her live puppies into a paper bag, and buried them. Neighbors reported that they heard the heartbroken dog howl mournfully and strain at her chain all that day and night.

Almost twenty-four hours later, Sheba managed to snap her chain, break free, and dig the pups out of their grave. Some survived, and the owner was charged with animal abuse.

Why is it then that some people still refuse to attribute feelings and emotions to animals? It is very ignorant of anyone to think that love, loneliness, grief, joy, jealousy, or the desire to cling to life are singularly human traits.

Gus, a polar bear in a New York zoo, exhibited such misery from his confinement, including swimming endless laps in his pathetic cement pool, that he was prescribed antidepressants. Other animals in zoos are not so lucky. Wendy Wood, one of the first Jane Goodall Fellows at the University of Southern

California, describes how chimpanzees develop autistic characteristics when denied opportunities to perform natural activities, like playing, fighting, and looking for food, which they cannot do in a laboratory cage or inside a trailer in a traveling sideshow. The distressed primates pull their hair out and rock endlessly, day after day.

Even octopuses, casually dismissed as "stupid invertebrates" by those who know no better, show their feelings. These mysterious sea creatures demonstrate their intelligence by learning how to unscrew a jar top to remove food, simply by watching the procedure. When given electric shocks, they show their desperation by biting into their own tentacles. Other cephalopods, including cuttlefish, can not only disguise themselves as plants on the ocean floor to avoid a prowling predatory fish, but can also fascinate a female with their displays of attractive colors and patterns on one side of their bodies while, on the other side, facing away from the female, simultaneously warning off a competitor male by showing colors and patterns that indicate aggression. Pretty fancy shooting!

Altruism too is found in the other animals. In Carl Sagan and Ann Druyan's book, *Shadows of Forgotten Ancestors*, there is a hideous true story about macaque monkeys who were fed only if they pulled a chain, electrically shocking an unrelated macaque whose agony was in plain view through a one-way mirror. Eighty-seven percent of the monkeys preferred to go hungry rather than pull the chain, and one refused to eat for fourteen days. The authors write:

> The relative social status or gender of the macaques had little bearing on their reluctance to hurt others. If asked to choose between the human experimenters offering the macaques this Faustian bargain and the macaques themselves—suffering from real hunger rather than causing pain to others—our

own moral sympathies do not lie with the scientists. But their experiments permit us to glimpse in non-humans a saintly willingness to make sacrifices in order to save others—even those who are not close kin. By conventional human standards, these macaques who have never gone to Sunday school, never heard of the Ten Commandments, never squirmed through a junior high school civics lesson—seem exemplary in their moral grounding and their courageous resistance to evil. Among the macaques, at least in this case, heroism is the norm. If the circumstances were reversed, and captive humans were offered the same deal by macaque scientists, would we do as well?

Professor Frans de Waal, a primatologist who has spent decades watching chimpanzees taken away from their natural homes and kept in captivity says, "An animal does not have to be human to be humane." De Waal's observations have taught him that chimpanzees have strong views about what is right and wrong and have a deep sense of justice. They believe in such concepts as sharing and will not usually tolerate misbehavior in the group, literally turning their backs on those who step out of line.

We don't need these extraordinary examples to derail the myth that our own species is in all ways superior to all others. Many animals have much keener senses—clearer vision, better hearing, such acute senses of smell that you wonder how they tolerate sharing a home with human beings and their cigarettes, floor cleaner, and so on. They are also much faster than we slowly trudging primates.

One of the most infuriating arguments used to deride animals is that they can't speak—which implies that they can't speak a human language. None of us, of course, can speak even a word of an animal language, but some animals have made serious headway with ours. Washoe is one such linguist. This chimpanzee mastered 132 American Sign Language signs by the age of five and had a remarkable "vocabulary." Washoe was rescued from a research laboratory by behaviorist Dr. Roger Fouts and lived for many years in a small group of other chimpanzees, including her adopted son, Loulis. Washoe spontaneously combined words to describe her experiences and desires, such as "You me hide" and "Listen dog" and invented names for her possessions, such as "Baby Mine" for her doll.

All this language among apes causes Douglas H. Chadwick to write in the *New York Times*, "Apes certainly seem capable of using language to communicate. Whether scientists are, remains doubtful."

Some people believe parrots just mimic what they hear, and they certainly do that well, but the way they can use what they have learned shows not only considerable intelligence but also skill with language use too.

A friend of mine has a rescued macaw who can imitate almost any sound he has ever heard in the house, including her husband's voice. The bird will sometimes drive her mad. As my friend runs to answer the phone, there will be a knock at the back door, then, immediately, the front doorbell will ring. A second later, not knowing which way to turn, she will hear the words, "Can you get that, dear?" Of course, the bird is fully responsible for all these sounds—the phone, the knock at the door, the bell, and the request.

I found out firsthand what a terrific sense of fun macaws have, when the Washington Humane Society asked PETA to temporarily house two who had been taken away in a raid on a badly run pet shop. Although these birds eyed us warily—they had good reason to, given what they had endured at human hands—they learned eight different laughs and greetings in a single afternoon, simply by eavesdropping. If you passed their room, you could hear them practicing to themselves.

At about three-thirty every weekday afternoon, workers from the factory below our office would start up the hill to the bus stop. Every day at that time, the birds would quietly move to the window and wait. When they spotted someone moving up the hill, two stories below them, they would start their game.

"Hello!" they would call out, just loud enough for whoever was trudging up the hill to hear. The victim would look around but see no one near him on the street. "Hello! Hello!" The birds would pick up the pace, using a slightly different tone, calling a little louder.

The man would cast about, baffled.

"Hello! Hello! Hello!" they would scream in unison.

Finally, the worker would look up, see the parrots, and, inevitably, relieved to have solved the mystery, say "Hello!" back.

The parrots would then become quiet as church mice. Whereas they had been completely intent on this game, now they concentrated closely on grooming a nail or picking at a sunflower seed.

"Hello, there. Hello, birdies!" the man would call up.

The birds ignored him.

Giving up, he would move on. Then the birds would choose one of the laughs they had adopted as their own, drop all other sham activity, resume their positions, and wait intently for their next victim.

Alex, an African grey parrot with a large vocabulary of English words, which he could use in whole sentences, used his language skills to try to save himself from unpleasantness. In one memorable moment, when he found himself about to be left behind at the vet's office, Alex urgently called out to his person, "Come here. I love you. I'm sorry. I want to go back." His death in 2007 was the subject of obituaries in major newspapers and a book by Alex's guardian, Irene Pepperberg, entitled *Alex & Me.*

Alex's avian relatives notwithstanding, most animals have throat and vocal chord structures that do not permit them to make the same sort of speech humans make, and most use very different forms of communication than ours. Dolphins, for example, use echolocation, bats use sonar, octopuses and cuttlefish use fantastic color waves and patterns that ripple through their bodies, and bees flap their wings at varying speeds to give complicated directions for locating flower beds.

Some cetacean experts believe that dolphins may transmit whole pictures of events to one another in ways more sophisticated than we can fathom. But even those animals that are commonly despised out of sheer ignorance—the animals who bear the brunt of our prejudice—communicate in ways we are only just beginning to understand. Rats and mice, like elephants, "talk" at frequencies we cannot hear. Sadly, for them, cats are tuned in to the same wavelengths. Prairie dogs' squeaks and chattering sounds are certainly components of a structured language, according to, among others, Professor Con Slobodchikoff at Northern Arizona University. Slobodchikoff converts the little rodents' sounds to sonograms, then uses a computer to correlate them to events. He has identified many dozens of words so far and realizes that prairie dogs can distinguish colors, shapes, and sizes, as well as tell a coyote from a German shepherd and a man from a woman. You can just imagine them warning one another to get back in the burrow quick, because "here's that insurance salesman from Prudential again."

E. Sue Savage-Rumbaugh, a behavioral researcher at Yerkes, a huge primate laboratory in Atlanta, Georgia, found that chimpanzees are so like us, they tell lies.

She reported that when one baby chimpanzee in a sign language study broke a toy, the student who had been watching him quietly behind a two-way glass panel entered the room.

"Who broke the toy?" she signed to the responsible infant. "He did!" the baby signed back, pointing to his innocent friend.

This story illustrates the perhaps painful fact that though animals are not inferior to us in some grand way, they also have their own load of bad behavior.

We might well ask, as did the author of this verse:

> *Coat with fur,*
> *Hat with feathers,*
> *Lobster broiled alive,*
> *Shoes and bags in sundry leathers*
> *Of animals who've died.*
>
> *Hunted, trapped, and torn apart*
> *For me to satisfy*
> *And, who am I? And what my rank?*
> *That I may live*
> *And they must die?*

Let's explore where such thoughts will take us, and see how we can stop killing and hurting animals as an incidental part of our lifestyles.

 WHAT YOU CAN DO

Respect Animals

Respect animals as individuals. Don't call them "it," but "she" and "he" and use "who" not "that." Be patient, understanding, and thoughtful around animals. Put yourself in their place.

Avoid bossing animals around. Animals are not our slaves, they have interests that should be respected, even if those interests don't always coincide with our own. Never yell or tug on your dog's neck, as if it were something stuck in a door. Never make animals beg in order to receive food or a treat. Do not tease them. And try to imagine their boredom, the lack of variety in their lives, and take the time to help give them diversions and to enjoy their lives.

Look out for animals. In everything you do, try to educate others, stop cruel behaviors, and bring about a revolution in human consciousness.

 FREQUENTLY ASKED QUESTIONS

What do you mean by "animal rights"?

People who support animal rights believe that animals are not ours to use for food, clothing, entertainment, experimentation, or any other purpose and that animals deserve consideration and what is in their best interests, regardless of whether they are cute, useful to humans, or endangered, and regardless of whether any human cares about them at all (just as a mentally challenged human has rights, even if he or she is not cute or useful and even if everyone dislikes him or her). For more information on why animals should have rights, go to PETA.org

*What is the difference between
"animal rights" and "animal welfare"?*

Supporters of the animal rights movement believe that animals are not ours, while supporters of the animal welfare movement believe that animals can be used and even killed for those purposes as long as "humane" guidelines are followed.

What rights should animals have?

Animals should have the right to equal consideration of their interests. For instance, a dog most certainly has an interest in not having pain inflicted on him unnecessarily. We must take that interest into consideration. However, animals don't always have the same rights as humans (any more than a man needs the same rights as a woman), because their interests are not always the same as ours, and some rights would be irrelevant to animals. For instance, a dog doesn't have an interest in voting and, therefore, doesn't have the right to vote because that right would be as meaningless to a dog as it is to a child.

Where do you draw the line?

The renowned humanitarian Albert Schweitzer, who accomplished so much for both humans and animals in his lifetime, would take time to stoop and move a worm from hot pavement to cool earth. Aware of the problems and responsibilities that an expanded ethic brings, he said, "A man is really ethical only when he obeys the constraint laid on him to aid all life which he is able to help. . . . He does not ask how far this or that life deserves sympathy . . . nor how far it is capable of feeling." We can't stop all suffering, but that doesn't mean that we shouldn't stop any. In today's world of virtually unlimited choices, there are plenty of kind, gentle ways for us to feed, clothe, entertain, and educate ourselves that do not involve hurting and killing animals.

Aren't you trying to tell other people what to do?

Everybody is entitled to his or her own opinion, but freedom of thought is not the same thing as freedom of action. You are free to believe whatever you want, as long as you don't hurt others. You may believe that animals should be killed, that black people should be enslaved, or that women should be beaten, but you don't always have the right to put your beliefs into practice. The very nature of reform movements is to tell others what we should stop doing—don't use humans as slaves, don't sexually harass women, etc.—and all movements initially encounter opposition from people who want to continue the criticized behavior.

Animals don't reason, don't understand rights,
and don't always respect our rights, so why
should we apply our ideas of morality to them?

An animal's inability to understand and adhere to human rules of conduct is as irrelevant as a child's. Animals are not always able to choose to change their behaviors, but adult human beings have the intelligence and ability to choose between behaviors that hurt others and behaviors that do not hurt others. When given the choice, it makes sense to choose compassion.

How can you justify spending your time helping animals
when there are human beings who need help?

It's funny that football players or dry cleaners aren't asked why they do what they do, even though there are humans that need help, but animal aid workers are! There are serious problems in the world that deserve our attention, and cruelty to animals is one of them. Helping animals is not any more or less important than helping human beings—they are both important and they are usually interconnected. Surely, everyone should be asked, "What are *you* doing to make this a kinder world in one way or the other?"

Animals are not as intelligent or as advanced as humans, so why can't we use them?

Animals are intelligent in ways we are not, but possessing superior intelligence has never entitled one human to abuse another human, so why should it entitle humans to abuse nonhumans? Might does not make right. There are animals who are unquestionably more intelligent, creative, aware, communicative, and able to use language than some humans, as is the case when a parrot is compared to a human infant. Should the more intelligent animals have rights and the less intelligent humans be denied rights?

2

How Animals
End Up as Dinner

If you ask me, now that I can look back a long way to the time when I thought eating animals was normal, meat eating is an odd and gruesome business. The only way we can continue to do it is by forgetting that animals are all "who" not "what."

Take Lucie, for instance. When Lucie was a baby chick, the size of a Ping-Pong ball, a man selling chicks under a bridge sold Lucie for a dollar to a little girl. By the time the girl got home, the chick was peeping loudly. She put him— Lucie was a rooster—in the basement in a shoe box with air holes and a tissue for a blanket, but the peeping didn't stop.

The next day, the girl's mother, Barbara Munroe, realized the chick was freezing. She made a bed in her night table drawer and fitted it with a heating pad. Finally, Lucie went to sleep.

Barbara took to carrying Lucie around in her hand. He always wanted to be with people, so she kept him with her, letting him sleep with her. "The most amazing thing to me," says Barbara, "was the way Lucie adapted to suburban life, sitting in a car like a perfect gentleman or on the sofa while the family read or watched television." (Chickens are widely reported to enjoy watching television. In a study at the University of Edinburgh, their stress was reduced when they were exposed to just one half hour of TV a day. The chickens looked forward to that half hour, and it made them "more well-rounded" as individuals and "less self-conscious.")

Leftovers were never acceptable to Lucie. When he was little, he would peck at Barbara's skirt impatiently while she made breakfast. Later, when he grew up, he would stand on a chair at the table and eat from a plate. He was always checking to see whether someone had something on their plate that he didn't have.

At about three months, Lucie went through an adolescent stage. He ran away when anyone tried to pick him up. However, he still liked to be in the same room with people and watch television with them.

Lucie used to be left outside during the day, but something must have frightened him, because he eventually preferred to stay indoors. When Barbara would come home from work, she often saw him sitting on the back of a chair in an upstairs window, watching for her. By the time she got in, he was down in the kitchen, jumping up and down, greeting her.

If people in the house raised their voices, Lucie chimed in loudly. It was almost impossible to shout over him, and usually everyone ended up laughing.

Lucie "talked" a lot. He had a lot of inflections, and his

"mom" often thought she understood what he was saying. When she called him, he didn't always come, but he always answered.

Barbara's daughter kept her bedroom door closed. Lucie hated that, as he liked to be able to go everywhere in the house. If everyone in the family was downstairs and the daughter appeared, Lucie ran upstairs to see whether she had left her door open by accident, and he would than go into her room. Every once in a while the girl forgot to close her door. Lucie would run in and jump on her bed but remain very quiet, so as not to alert her.

All chickens have the potential of Lucie or more, if allowed to live a natural life—by which I mean, uncaged—in which they interact pleasantly with others. The same is true of all animals we think of as "food." It is just that we never get to know them.

George Bernard Shaw once challenged a woman's appetite for chicken by suggesting that, instead of sitting passively and being served the dish, she slit the bird's throat herself. That is a helpful challenge to think about whenever we consider ordering Chicken McNuggets. Most of us are too kind to wield the knife, but the tragedy is that if we pay for the service, someone else will gladly wield it for us.

GIVE A LITTLE BIRD A BREAK

Chickens go from shell to hell as one of the most abused animals in the meat industry, which is truly saying something. Ducks, geese, and turkeys fare no better, but, because of sheer numbers (Americans now eat a million chickens an hour), chickens are in the soup. In fact, chicken soup is often the last resting place of their battered remains.

If you've ever known a chicken then you know that chickens are individuals, with as much personality, or lack thereof, as anyone you could ever meet. Yet, can a personality develop if a bird is squeezed with tens of thousands of other birds into a stifling warehouse, unable to find room enough to stretch a wing, never to feel a breeze or the warmth of the sun? When the only regular human "contact" the bird makes is a glimpse of the person whose job it is to check the automatic feed and water troughs and to sling out the dead every day?

The life of a "layer" is even worse than that of a "broiler" (birds raised specifically for meat) because it lasts longer and because layers' beaks are seared off with a hot wire. Red hot blades are used to both melt and cut through the beak, resulting in smoke rising from the beak. Sometimes the cut is too high up, which then makes eating normally impossible. This is done to prevent cannibalism, which can occur in birds who are denied the room to establish a pecking order. The birds also experience chronic leg pain. They are kept in constant light to fool their bodies into churning out more eggs than is normal (a single egg on the breakfast plate means at least twenty-two hours of misery for the hen), and periodic "false moltings" to kick-start more vigorous egg production mean farmers withhold *all* food from birds for up to *fourteen days*. Their hunger must be indescribable as they drop not only their feathers, but also up to 30 percent of their body weight.

A PETA investigator who worked in the chicken sheds at a major poultry farm on the Delmarva Peninsula reported sick and injured chickens everywhere. Many had missing feathers, runny wounds, painful eye and ear infections, "frosted eyes" (blindness caused by ammonia from the birds' waste that is simply left to accumulate in the sheds), badly swollen feet and knee joints, golf ball–size growths, wounds caused by sharp wires, and deformities caused by debeaking.

If workers paid any attention to "damaged" birds at all, it was to hold them by their heads and swing their bodies around to break their necks, slam them into a debeaking machine, twist their heads off, or simply step on them, breaking their backs or rupturing their internal organs.

Workers are not likely to be kind to the birds but treat them carelessly and are irritated by them. There is a cruel game called "bagpiping," in which workers forcefully squeeze out a live bird's feces and try to hit other workers with the mess. One of the supervisors observed by PETA investigators, swearing about a bird who had escaped during unloading, threw a board at the bird and missed, then kicked her four or five feet into the air. Another swore at a chicken he blamed for having made him twist his ankle, then lunged at her, throwing his whole weight on her, and punched her in the face.

Then there are the "downer birds." These are chickens who live with chronic leg pain, bent or bowed legs, brittle bones, rickets, "kinky back," or arthritis. Unable to walk to their feed and water, many die on the factory farm floor. Pain relief is never given.

When the birds reach the age of sixty-five to seventy weeks, if they are layers, their egg production usually declines, and they are auctioned off to companies like Campbell Soup Company. If they are broilers, life ends at six to eight weeks.

If they do not succumb to death when the cooling system shorts out in the summer heat, die from being pecked alive by psychotic housemates or from untreated illness or disease, "eating" or "laying" chickens' abbreviated lives come to an end after a nightmare ride. Smashed into a crate aboard a chicken truck, they will be jostled for hours in all weather to the slaughterhouse. There, the poor birds are hung upside down, screaming mightily and trying to right themselves as the conveyor belt carries them to their deaths.

Some years ago, four men accepted a $15,000 challenge from a British animal rights group to live like laying hens for a week. They didn't make it, emerging after just eighteen hours from a cage that had no provision for sanitation and which measured three feet square and six feet high. PETA has asked US poultry executives to take a similar challenge and live for just one day like the chickens they profit from. So far there have been no takers.

As for the turkey, the bird Benjamin Franklin wanted to name as America's national bird, animal protection campaigners estimate that about 7 percent never get stunned, never get cut with the knife, and are dropped alive into vats of boiling water. Once fleet of foot and lithe, turkeys are now bred by the industry to meet the demand for breast meat. So turkeys develop such unnaturally large chests that their legs cannot support them for long.

Yet, if removed from their living hell, these birds show delightful personalities and innately gentle natures. The *Miami Herald* reported about a local man named Sam Garcia who had bought a live turkey, intending to cut the bird's throat for Thanksgiving. What he got instead of a meal was "a relationship." According to Garcia, "Our family lost its stomach for a personable bird who likes children and gobbles back when you speak to him. We did call him 'dinner': but now we call him our pal."

What a wonderful lesson for those children. Needless to say, it is to the animals' detriment that everyone isn't formally introduced to their intended meals before dinner. If we were, fewer axes would fall.

A STRANGE TASTE

Some have claimed that the kiss originated when our ancestors returned from the hunt, bringing mouthfuls of chewed meat to the young, the sick, and the elderly.

Today, the taste for meat represents the kiss of death to more billions of animals every year in the United States alone.

These animals are suffering and being slaughtered not to feed the needy, who have no other options, but to have tons of their flesh discarded on hotel room service trays and into Dumpsters by the most overfed (and often obese) members of a nation that can command endless varieties of foodstuffs by picking up a phone or driving to the supermarket.

It is truly bizarre that people who love animals grow up eating them. Although many young children are often repulsed by meat, they are usually persuaded by adults that the portion of flesh and bone on their plates is somehow different from Libby the Lamb in their storybook.

After a while, we become addicted to the taste, for meat eating is habit-forming, just like smoking. If it were not, no one presented with the facts about health, the environment, or animals would say, "I don't want to know, I could *never* give up my steak!" and people who bristle at the suggestion that they are anything other than humane "animal lovers" would not eat the objects of their compassion. That phenomenon was captured in this excerpt from a poem by Paulette Callen:

Look! Cows! Stop the car!
They are so beautiful! I will
commune with cows!

and I think (not kindly, I confess):
Commune with the cow
that rots in your gut.

Commune with her.
For my car-mate
had cow for lunch.

We are slow-thinking animals. It is not entirely our fault, but we can do better. Thanks to steady sales pitches and dishonest advertising, when someone asks, "What's for dinner?" the mental image often conjured up is that of the prepared pot roast or chicken drumstick, not of what went before it. No one thinks, "A pig!" and starts imagining what it must have been like for that animal at the moment when he watched his fellows being killed by the machine or the knife just ahead of him in that strange, frightening place. We are used to a world in which we accept the Oscar Mayer jingle in which children gathered around the "Wienermobile" sing gaily about how they would like to be a hot dog: a world in which parents scream bloody murder, not at the butcher and the company exploiting their children, but at the spoilsport idealist in the pig suit clambering atop the giant hot dog on wheels with a sign saying, PIGS ARE FRIENDS, NOT FOOD. It is all quite mad.

Animals aren't one thing and meat another. Each calf and turkey and duck and pig is real, as are their experiences.

Here's a glimpse:

A truck carrying cows was unloaded at a stockyard in Kentucky one September morning. After the other animals were removed from the truck, one was left behind, unable to move, probably because she had slipped and injured herself in the crush of animals being trampled. The stockyard workers proceeded to beat and kick her in the face, ribs, and back. They used the customary electric prods in her ear to try to get her out of the truck, but still she did not move. The workers tied a rope around her head, tied the other end to a post in the ground, and drove the truck away. She was dragged along the floor of the truck and fell to the ground, where she was left with both hind legs and her pelvis broken.

The cow lay in the hot sun, crying out for the first three hours. Periodically, when she urinated or defecated, she used her front legs to drag herself along the gravel roadway to a clean spot. She also tried to crawl to a shaded area but could not move far enough, although she managed to crawl more than thirteen or fourteen yards. The stockyard employees would not allow her any drinking water; the only water she received was given to her by Jessie Pierce. Jessie, a local animal rights activist, had been contacted by a woman who had witnessed the incident. Jessie arrived at noon, giving the cow her first drink of the day. After receiving no cooperation from the stockyard workers, Jessie called the county police. A police officer arrived, but after calling his superiors, he was instructed to do nothing and left at 1 P.M.

The stockyard operator informed Jessie at 1 P.M. that he had obtained permission from the insurance company to kill the cow, but he would not do so until Jessie left. Although doubtful that he would keep his word, Jessie did leave at 3 P.M. She returned at 4:30 P.M., by which time the stockyard was deserted and three dogs were attacking the cow, who was still alive. She had suffered a number of bite wounds and her drinking water had been removed. Jessie then contacted the state police.

Four troopers arrived at about 5:30 P.M. One trooper wanted to shoot the cow but was told that a veterinarian should kill her. The two US Department of Agriculture (USDA) veterinarians at the facility would not euthanize the cow, claiming that in order to preserve the value of the meat, the cow could not be destroyed until a butcher was present. The butcher finally arrived at 7:30 P.M. and did shoot the cow—her body was purchased for $307.50. (Usually animals who are bruised, crippled, or found dead are considered unfit for human consumption and are used for pet food.)

When the stockyard operator was questioned earlier in the day by a local reporter, he stated, "We didn't do a darned thing to it," and referred to the attention given to the cow by humane workers and police as "bull crap." He laughed throughout the questioning, saying he found nothing wrong with the way the incident was handled.

The "incident" with the cow is not an isolated case; in fact, it is so common that animals in this condition are known as "downers."

There are lots of reasons to rethink what has become the standard American diet, among them the fact that producing meat uses up so much fossil fuel that it is actually more energy efficient to drive a Hummer than it is to walk—if the energy for walking comes from a meat-based diet—and that more than half of all precious freshwater used in the United States—which will one day be as precious as gold dust in the West, just as it is now in parts of Asia and Africa—goes to raise and kill animals for the table. But, for me, that cow is the most powerful one.

Her life ended as I have described, but how did it begin? Her mother was probably artificially inseminated on what farmers themselves call a "rape rack," an unpleasant metal device in a cement-floored room. After her birth, she would have been taken away from the mother who loved her, and to whom her presence brought such comfort and joy, and sold at auction.

USDA inspectors can attest to how she was handled throughout her life. Even they, who see so many horrors, are appalled that animals are kicked in the face, electrically shocked on their genitals, and have sticks rammed into their rectums to move them along. (Pigs often have their snouts broken with a stout stick or baseball bat if they hesitate on the slippery ramps to the trucks.)

If you think back, you may have seen this cow, or others like her, staring out of the slats in the transport trucks that move animals to the slaughterhouse in all weather extremes, from snow to scorching heat. (Sometimes pigs freeze to the metal sides of transport trucks and their flesh is ripped off when they are unloaded.)

By the time she reached market and before she broke her pelvis, she would probably have been one of the 80 percent of cows who already have "carcass bruises" from abuse.

What would have befallen her in the chute or on the killing floor would have been terrifying, at best. In the first slaughterhouse I ever entered, I can remember being hit by the smell of warm death, the stench of hot, steaming blood and offal. To animals, with their finely honed sense of smell, the sensation must be overwhelming.

If only our restaurants and kitchens had glass walls that allowed diners to see meals being prepared from start to finish. In Gail Eisnitz's chilling book, *Slaughterhouse*, real-life USDA inspector Steve Cockerman describes seeing plant workers cut off feet, ears, and udders of conscious cattle after stun guns failed to work properly.

"They were blinking and moving, it is a sickening thing to see," he said. In the same book, another USDA veterinarian, Lester Friedlander, tells us that most inspectors are discouraged by USDA officials from reporting the mistreatment of animals, although the inspectors are the only hope the animals have. "Sometimes the wheels of justice turn slowly," Friedlander said, "but the wheels of justice at the USDA don't even turn."

A lot of people no longer eat meat but continue to use dairy products, not realizing that the "dairy cow" ends up in the same situations as the "beef cow." There are no retirement parties and retirement homes for the worn-out dairy cow. By the time she gets to the slaughterhouse, she is often on her last legs: her teats may be sore and inflamed; just walking up the ramp may be more than she can manage. Vegans—people who don't use dairy products—are still a minority of the population, while people who boycott veal are numerous. Yet, once understood, the connection between veal and dairy would seem to dictate that ethical transitioning consumers—those awakening to ethical issues that will inform their purchases—stop buying dairy products even before they give the meat counter the cold shoulder.

When I was seven, my mother came home from the supermarket and announced that she would no longer buy or cook veal. She had run into picketers bearing photographs. In Britain, the "veal crates," which are common in North America and other countries in Europe, are now banned, but then they were just starting to become popular. The calves were to be torn away from their mothers and raised in crates inside dark sheds so that their mothers' milk could be sold for human consumption. My father, who rather liked veal cordon bleu—thin slices of white veal (white because the calf is purposely deprived of iron to induce anemia) wrapped in bacon and cheese—was the hardest hit. Of course, we all believed the suffering of veal calves was an isolated case. We never realized that our demand for *milk* products had created the nightmare, and that there is a piece of veal calf in every glass of milk.

In our cheese-on-everything society, the mother cow is reduced to a milk machine. Her only potential source of joy, her calf, is kicked aside and prodded into a crate so we can steal the milk meant for him.

In the barns, veal calves are kept in elevated wooden stalls, their heads often chained. They reek of scours, a diarrheal disease common in intensive farming operations, and their knees are raw from falling and kneeling, falling and kneeling, on the hard metal gridwork or the wooden slats. People petrify them, and they scramble up when the feeder enters the barn, bucking at their chains, slipping in their own waste, and scraping their shins on the slats.

Here's what one former dairy farmer, Paddy McGrath, had to say: "Despite the most advanced equipment and technology, which allowed less and less contact between man and beast, there were facts that could not be hidden: cows have individual personalities and feelings. They love, mourn, and feel depressed or joyous just as we do. Replacing cows' names with numbers doesn't hide their individuality. Some soon became pets and often slipped their heads through the railings for a pat."

Cows singled out as sick or low producers go to their deaths earlier than the others.

Says Paddy, "So Mary-Anne (number fifty-two) had to go. I looked at her big watery and gentle trusting eyes as she stood in the holding yard waiting for the truck to come and take her away. She called to her friends, who were making their way down the lane to the grazing paddocks. She called until they disappeared behind the dust of hundreds of hooves, and a voice inside me cried out, *Why* do we have to do this? . . . Because we have to live, don't *we*?

Paddy McGrath eventually realized he could live without killing animals. He left the industry and stopped eating meat and dairy products.

People who abandon milk products get a prize: they have a greater chance of avoiding bronchial, respiratory, and stomach complaints than do dairy consumers. A Finnish nutrition researcher, Teuvo Rantala, is among those who have also linked the indigestibility of milk proteins to autism and depression.

His own son, once withdrawn, violent, and unaffectionate, stopped having tantrums and began hugging his parents after milk products were removed from his diet. Rantala has shown that instead of breaking down into amino acids, milk proteins are partially broken down into peptides, which can leak across the gut wall into the blood and eventually penetrate the membrane that protects the brain, interfering with its development.

In Dr. Benjamin Spock's book *Baby and Child Care,* the icon of child rearing warns parents to steer clear of dairy products and to make sure their offspring get the calcium and protein they need from beans, legumes, nuts, and plenty of green leafy vegetables, not from milk. Spock, once a "meat and milk man," credited pure vegetarianism with curing him of a debilitating ailment in later life. So advocating for a calf and his mother is also a sound personal health move too.

The animals aside, it is hard to understand why the filthy habit of meat consumption persists. Converting natural resources and plants into food by shoveling them down animals' throats is extremely inefficient. It uses six to twenty times as much plant food and the energy to grow it, not to mention causing the destruction of forest land and the depletion of topsoil, than were we to eat the plants themselves and forget the cow, the pig, and the chicken. It is also a destructive habit, that has dire environmental consequences, sucking water out of aquifers and causing more waterway pollution from animal waste runoff than any other industry.

Meat eating is irrefutably linked to heart disease, cancer, stroke, high blood pressure, diabetes, and almost every other chronic disease except ingrown toenails. In some pig-producing states, like Iowa, radio stations routinely warn residents not to drink the water on certain days because of contamination from intensive hog farm waste. Even Washington, D.C., city water has made people ill when bacteria from factory farms in other areas invaded reservoirs downstream. In a country whose citizens are rightly obsessed with their unhealthy and ever expanding girths, a vegetarian diet is more than 25 percent lower in fat than a meat eater's diet. However, whether or not we draw one of the many short straws in the health lottery, the animals always do, and only because we demand satisfaction for our insane craving to chew on their flesh.

A slaughterhouse manager once told me that it's foolish to care about animals because "they are stupid and dirty." After pointing out that animals are neither, I found myself wondering aloud that, surely, only a stupid person would stick a decomposing corpse in their mouth, and only a dirty person would lick their fingers afterward.

A PIG'S LIFE CAN'T GET MUCH SADDER

One November morning, a nurse, a veterinarian, an opera singer, a construction worker, and a member of the Australian parliament met at dawn outside a pig farm in New South Wales. Part of a rescue team of thirty-six activists who had become totally frustrated at the lack of action taken by the government over abysmal living conditions for pigs kept on factory farms, they marched through the fields and into one of Australia's largest piggeries, where they promptly chained themselves to the sows' stalls.

According to Patty Mark, the group's organizer, the noise from the pigs' screams was deafening. Two hundred and thirty thousand pigs were squeezed into individual concrete and iron chambers without room to turn around. As in the United States, where such intensive farming is considered standard practice, their total confinement had caused their joints to swell and produced painful leg and foot problems.

Some pigs were weak, some were dying. Some sows had bleeding wounds infested with maggots. Many were frothing at the mouth and biting their metal stall bars, signs of extreme distress. Pigs who were about to give birth tried to do what nature had taught them to do: make a nest. They were pathetic sights, virtually wearing their hooves out scraping pointlessly at cement.

Pigs don't cope well with the standard hog industry idea that breeding sows are nothing more than pieces of machinery whose function is to pump out baby pigs. Deidre Brollo, one of the people chained to the stalls, can attest to that:

Sitting there in the dark, it's impossible to forget where you are. Feeling the cold, smelling the stench, hearing the noise of teeth on bars, but seeing nothing. And while surrounded by pigs and people, I felt extremely alone. The sound became familiar over those hours of waiting, almost like rain on a tin roof, until dawn's lights brought home the reality of the situation. Frenzied bar-biting was accompanied by anguished faces and pitiful squeals. The pigs had woken to another day of suffering. Soon we began to offer pieces of fruit and hay to the sows, something to ease the monotony and pain of their lives. Initially the sow opposite me didn't seem to understand it was food. She was happily destroying the hay, throwing it around and pushing it into the water trough. Finally she took a bite of the apple, and that was it! She wanted more! I gave her all I had and she had a marvelous time. Then she gratefully accepted a good scratch under the chin. Feeding time approached and the sows knew it. The noise became deafening as they awaited their one meal of the day. Some jumped up to put their front feet on the top bars and then struggled to get back down within the painfully small stalls. The bar-biting worsened. My sow screeched as she looked at me. Until this point I had felt numb and separated from the situation. All this came crashing down and I felt helpless, alone, and so ashamed as the sow caught my gaze. I was human. Not something to be proud of at the moment, and somehow a victim of a world that doesn't seem to listen. The shed seemed less like a prison at that moment and more like an asylum. Looking at these frantic animals, some mad, some pathetically broken, just sitting and staring, I understood the true tragedy of it all.

Because of the public demand for ham, bacon, ribs, and other animal parts, modern sows are driven beyond the breaking point. As with chickens, there is a big push to grow them as meaty as possible. All that extra weight causes painful leg problems, aggravated by brittle bones from lack of exercise.

If their teats become infected and sore or raw from rubbing against the cement, that's just how it is. No one will rush over with a tube of salve or an aspirin. Although most state laws do not technically differentiate between cruelty to a dog and cruelty to any other animal, as Peter Singer, author of *Animal Liberation*, wrote, "Anyone who kept a dog in the way in which pigs are usually kept would be liable for prosecution, but because our interest in exploiting pigs is greater than our interest in exploiting dogs, we object to the cruelty to dogs while consuming the product of cruelty to pigs."

Having seen inside dog slaughterhouses in Asia and pig slaughterhouses in the United States, I can personally say that, while all animal slaughter for food is unjustifiable, it is awkward to join the chorus of Western voices raised against dog eating when many of the protesters blithely tolerate equally hideous cruelties visited upon equally feeling animals in our own cheerfully named "packing plants."

Such thoughts led Dr. Donald Doll, a Los Angeles physician, to stop eating animals after hearing a radio station announcer blasting Vietnamese immigrants in California for eating dogs. Dr. Doll started wondering what made eating other animals right and couldn't come up with a logical answer.

This very odd dichotomy came home to me too when I was a humane officer in Maryland. My job was to bring prosecutions for cruelty to animals.

I had been called out to an abandoned farm and found the place in a mess. A dog had been left on his chain and had somehow survived, thanks to a bucket of dirty water. The horses and pigs had not. The barn was littered with broken bottles, left by the departing occupants of the farmhouse in the wake of a drunken party. In some stalls, the animals had cut their legs to ribbons on the shards before dying.

Just as I was leaving the dark barn, I saw a movement back in a corner. Stepping carefully over to the straw, I found a little pig, too frail to stand. He couldn't have weighed more than a few bags of flour. I took him in my arms and carried him out into the fresh air and, laying him down under a tree, went to the pump to get some water.

He was too weak to raise his head, but he sipped the drops of water from my fingers, making little grunting noises of what could only be gratitude and relief. I sat with him, rocking him back and forth and talking to him until the van came to take him and the dog to the veterinary clinic. I had to stay behind to look for anything pointing to the whereabouts of the people who had done this to him and his fellows, so I could charge them with cruelty.

That evening, driving home, I began to think of what I could cook for dinner. Ah, I thought, I have pork chops in the freezer. Then it hit me. How could I pay someone to hurt a pig, when here I was, trying to prosecute other people for doing the same sort of thing? I didn't know then that pigs are routinely castrated without anesthetic and that they often have their tails cut off to prevent injuries from their fellow inmates who have become enraged by confinement. I hadn't yet visited a slaughterhouse, but like anyone with a functional brain, I knew full well they must be appalling places if you happen to have been born an animal labeled "food."

For others, the revelations are more intellectual. Brigid Brophy, author of *Hackenfeller's Ape*, became a vegetarian "for the same reason I am not a cannibal. If you thought I would taste nice roasted or in a casserole, that would not give you the right to take away my life." She wrote:

> You might argue that you were not endangering my species since there are plenty of (perhaps too many) human beings. You might argue that my life is of no value or interest to you and is a pretty dim sort of life anyway.
>
> But the crucial question is not what value you set on my life and my enjoyment of it, but the value I set on them. Dim my life may be, but it is the only life I have.
>
> And, like every pig and every sheep, chicken, herring, etc., I am an individual as well as a representative of my species. The fact that my species will continue to exist doesn't compensate me for the discontinuation of me.

Some animals (but, paradoxically, not as a rule those humans kill in order to eat their corpses) kill and eat other animals. So far as we can tell, they have no choice. Humans have choice and are very proud of it. Instead of killing animals on the grounds that they are intellectually superior to the animals, humans should stop killing animals and thereby demonstrate that they have more freedom of choice than other animals.

A human who supposes that he can't do without a diet that includes consuming the dead bodies of animals is deceiving himself. He is pretending to be a slave of habit and convention, whereas he is in fact a free agent.

HOOK, LINE, AND FACTORY SHIP

The word *animal* comes from *anima*, meaning "life." How odd, then, that many people do not consider a fish, a very animated being, to be an animal at all. Some people find protests over cruelty to fish laughable, but where an animal is placed in the hierarchy of our wildly arbitrary value system should have no effect on how we treat him or her.

I suppose this blind spot is what makes whalers in Norway and Japan (and the ones who used to harpoon these great beasts off the New England coast, for that matter) think of whales as nothing more important than uncooperative blobs of gray blubber, and so find nothing wrong with thrusting a steel harpoon into them. Certainly, fish and whales all thrash around with equal vigor and desperation when the metal sinks into their bodies, and both kinds of animals try with every fiber of their being to flee for their lives. But fishers and whalers don't "get it." Impervious to the animal's perspective, they can stand about, laughing and discussing the comparative worth of their new gum boots, while agonizing dramas are being played out at their feet.

Why do people think differently about the salmon or sole they eat as opposed to the feathery lionfish, which they gaze upon with awe and have their pictures taken with underwater while scuba diving in some tropical paradise? Or the guppies they view or keep and tend to in aquariums? For most people it would be unthinkable to eat that little fellow in the tank in the living room, but aren't they all fish?

I knew a banded severum long ago who lived in an aquarium

in a country house. During the mornings, when the house was quiet, the fish spent his time at the end of the tank near the window, catching the morning sunlight on his fins and browsing among the reeds. But, at about 4:30 P.M., he swam to the other side of the tank and floated there, staring at the hallway door.

At that time of day, "his" man came home from work. Before the key turned in the lock, the fish began "pacing," swimming back and forth without letup, showing the sort of impatience you might see in a person drumming his or her fingers on a tabletop or a puppy jumping up and down in anticipation of a walk. Every few laps he paused and hung in the water, staring hopefully at the door.

Perhaps he sensed that the man loved him, as wholly inadequate as a man's love for a fish must be. In fact, the man had usually forgotten all about the fish until he reached the door, but then he remembered and rushed straight into the living room so as not to disappoint him. The fish jumped and wagged his tail like a dog, lifting about a fifth of his body clean out of the water. The man would gently scratch the fish's back, the fish offering first one side of his body to be petted, then the other, making little waves with the swishing of his fins.

The fish didn't know that, as a boy, the man had thrown cherry bombs into the creek when the carp were spawning and then killed them with blows from two-by-fours as they thrashed about on the bank. The fish didn't know that on summer days the man still caught and gutted fish from that creek and barbecued them just outside the window.

Not that the man would ever harm the fish in the tank, but like most of us, he had a compartmentalized mind. Killing fish whom you don't know is just part of our culture.

The captive severum tried to make the best of what was otherwise a plain life. He cleaned rocks by rolling them about in his mouth, swam through the hair curlers fastened together to form a jungle gym, and tickled his back in the bubbles from the aerator. Once, he swam purposefully to the west end of the tank, seized a plastic plant in his tiny jaws, and dragged it back to his corner. The next day, when the man tidied the tank and put the plant back in its "place," the fish moved it again to the new spot he had chosen for it.

The fish had a sport. When the fish saw a cat tiptoe over the bookshelves to drink from the aquarium, he would lie in wait for her in the reeds. Experience had taught the cat to peer into the depths for any sign of an ambush, but the fish knew that and stayed quiet as a mouse. Only when the cat's tongue descended did the fish burst into action, propelling himself up through the reeds like a torpedo, hell-bent on taking a chunk out of that raspy organ. If she sensed the underwater eruption, the cat might get her first lap in before tongue and fish met. No blood was ever drawn on either side, but the contest was a welcome diversion.

The fish kept to himself, taking the presence of newcomers to his tank with all the dignity and despair of a librarian who finds a group of young bikers living among the shelves. He would puff himself up and shake his fins at them and give chase if they did anything truly appalling, but he never attacked.

In the end he outlived them all. Some died of "seasickness"— the trauma of sloshing around in the bag from ocean to distributor, in the truck to the pet shop, and then in the car on the way home; others succumbed to epidemics of "ick," which destroyed their fins, sending them spinning helplessly to the bottom of the tank, tiny vestiges of their graceful selves. Still more suffocated when power failures robbed the water of oxygen.

On the Saturday the tank cracked, there were only two other fish left. They were African "elephant noses," exotic fish with trunklike protuberances. The old severum accepted their presence; he and they kept as respectful a distance from each other as fish can in a modest aquarium.

The man had been at the movies and returned to find water all over the floor and still dripping from a crack in the glass. In the inch of liquid left in the bottom of the tank, three individuals lay on their sides, dying.

Rescue had to be effected without delay. The fish was whisked into a large pot. One elephant nose went into a saucepan, the other into a coffeepot; but this last little fish struggled, caught his long nose in the spout, and suffered a terrible injury. When the substitute tank was set up, the injured elephant nose could not breathe properly or keep his balance. His companion helped keep him afloat, pushing him up against the side of the tank so he could reach food and air. But this didn't save his life. Within a week of his death, his companion died, too. After that, the old fish was alone again.

When I had first seen him, he had only been about half an inch long, and I was still eating cod roe on toast and salmon steak. But by the time the elephant noses died, he was six inches long and I had stopped eating others of his kind. As he had grown, so had my understanding that there might be something wrong with eating fish or pretending that they could be kept as living room decorations. Human amusement was not worth their barren lives and "accidental" deaths.

When the fish died, I found myself trying to imagine what his ancestral waters were like, where and how he had been captured or bred, and how sad it was that he had been robbed of his fish destiny.

Although some people fish to eat, which might be considered a necessity for bears, eagles, or certain aboriginal peoples, it is hard to imagine anything very noble about choosing to eat fish if you live in a land of a million more benign choices. Especially when one becomes aware, as was announced by behaviorists at the University of St. Andrews, that fish value friendship, choose which fish to adopt as friends (they recognize their chums by both smell and appearance), and decide to swim with them instead of with other fish.

UP FROM THE DEEP

Most consumers get their fish without ever picking up a rod and reel, of course. Table fish, in the main, come from grocery stores and supermarkets, glassy-eyed or filleted, tidily frozen or "fresh," an odd term for a body that is busy breaking down. Although an increasing amount comes from foul "fish farms," most of this fish comes from fishing boats nicknamed "the bulldozers of the seas," trawlers as big as football fields that vacuum the oceans clean of most sea life, not only the target catch, but also the "trash catch," including wonderful octopuses and cuttlefish, dogfish, turtles, and eels.

These boats–floating islands, really—use satellite communications to track their prey and then drop huge nets, sometimes many miles long. The nets snag animals of countless species, including dolphins, seals, and sea otters. An estimated one million seabirds every year become entangled in fishing nets and drown. Some fishing outfits use underwater explosives to herd dolphins away from tuna nets, causing extreme pressure to fish and making internal organs shift, split, and even explode painfully.

When nets are dragged through the water, fish are squeezed together, suffocating, and the whole mess is bounced along, together with any netted debris, like rocks. The fish rub against one another and file away sharp scales, making their flanks raw. When they are hauled aboard from the depths of the ocean, they endure excruciating decompression, which can give their eyes that popped-out appearance and push their esophagi and stomachs out their throats. Due to the change of pressure, fish can also rupture their swim bladders when they are pulled rapidly from their watery habitat.

Up on the decks, the crew stab the fish with short, spiked rods and sort them, slitting their bellies and throats. The "trash catch" is dumped back overboard, often with a pitchfork, sometimes alive, sometimes badly injured, to die slowly or be picked up by a new predator. There is nothing humane about any part of the process.

One person who stopped eating fish for ethical reasons is Sylvia Earle, a leading marine biologist and ocean explorer. She knows a thing or two about the denizens of the deep. "I never eat anyone I know personally," says Earle. "I wouldn't deliberately eat a grouper any more than I'd eat a cocker spaniel. They're so good-natured, so curious. You know, fish really are sensitive, they have personalities, they hurt when they're wounded."

Another person who stopped eating fish is Harriet Schliffer, a Canadian feminist who went fishing with her father for the first time when she was very small. As soon as she saw a fish being reeled in, she immediately understood that this was an animal being hurt. Harriet was deeply upset that her father was doing something horrid to this fish and begged him to help the animal.

Other people abandon fish eating for health reasons.

Dr. Andrew Nicholson reminds us that "fish doesn't have a speck of fiber, complex carbs, or vitamin C." Another physician, Dr. Peggy Carlson, has written of fish, "It is loaded with chemical contaminants that nobody needs!" The National Wildlife Federation report on the risks of cancer from eating freshwater fish concluded that one weekly meal of a trout from Lake Michigan poses a cancer risk of one in ten. In another study, DDT was found in fatty fish tissue at nearly all sites tested, although it was banned more than thirty years ago. PCBs, also out of production since 1977, showed up in 91 percent of sampled fish and represented the highest cancer risk to fish consumers. Mercury turned up in 92 percent of fish studied.

Raw shellfish is one of the riskiest foods you can put in your mouth. An estimated 1 in 250 people who eat raw shellfish gets sick. According to the Centers for Disease Control and Prevention, there are about seventy-five million cases of food-borne illness every year, including hundreds of thousands of hospitalizations and thousands of deaths. Seafood is the number one cause of food poisoning in the United States. Symptoms of seafood poisoning include mild to extreme discomfort, nervous system damage, and worse. The chance of contracting a digestive problem from fish is about twenty-five times greater than from beef and about sixteen times greater than from pork or poultry.

According to a report by the General Accounting Office, the seafood industry is dangerously underregulated. In fact, the Food and Drug Administration doesn't even bother to test most fish flesh for many well-known chemical and bacterial health hazards. Only 1 to 3 percent of fish imported from other countries is inspected at the border. Many segments of the industry are completely exempt from regulation, including warehouses and most shipboard processors.

As for the idea that eating fish or fish oil is somehow good for your heart, the highest levels of omega-3 fatty acids, which are believed to reduce the risk of heart disease, do not come from fish. Four grams of flaxseeds pack a whopping 2,372 milligrams of omega-3s, walnuts also beat fish cold with 2,000 milligrams per few ounces, while tuna only contains 700 milligrams. The vegetarian sources have the added advantage of not containing metals, sewage, or toxins.

FISH FARMING: SEWERS OF THE SEA

These days, a lot of the fish sold—some 30 percent or more—comes from farmed fish, which sounds all very well and good until you look, literally, beneath the surface.

Fish farms consist of series of floating cages anchored by floats near the seashore or occasionally inland. To save money, the maximum number of fish possible are crammed together in a stocking density that makes the expression "sardines in a can" seem extremely generous, with fish floating on top of one another, gill to gill, mostly unable to move.

With that "stocking density," as many as fifty thousand fish knock up against one another, causing damage to fins and scales, in an area about the size of a standard bathtub. It is no wonder that Daniel Pauly, a professor of fisheries at the University of British Columbia in Vancouver, compares industrial fish farms to "floating pig farms."

Unable to enjoy and benefit from a swim in the ocean or river currents, the fish cannot keep clean, and lice do not wash off but start infesting the group. Their own waste is not swiftly washed away either, as it would be in nature, so the fish, bullied by those larger than them, infested with parasites from filth, are jostled in their tight spaces, awaiting death and drinking in their own waste, An estimated 40 percent of them do not even survive long enough to be killed. And, like their free-living ocean and river fellows, they will not be given the courtesy of being stunned before they are killed, but will experience a frightening and painfully slow death. Some are packed in ice for long journeys while alive, many are fully aware when they are cut into fillets and steaks.

The environmental impact of fish farming is appalling: the waste produced by such a large concentration of fish kept in one place heavily pollutes the water, and farming fish upsets the fragile balance of marine life.

SNAILS, DUCK LIVER, AND OTHER INDELICACIES

"Gourmet" columnists are constantly waxing lyrical about some culinary "delight" that has invariably been painfully extracted from an animal. As if the horrors our race has dreamed up for the everyday kitchen are not enough, we are expected to drool over and to laud chefs who split open the backs of live lobsters, drip butter into their wounds, and then broil them to death. The days are gone when chefs took themselves as seriously as Monsieur Vatel, the Prince de Condé's kitchen man, who became so despondent at the prospect of preparing a dinner without the right ingredients to make lobster sauce that he ran himself through with his own sword. Some of today's "celebrity chefs" still follow in the footsteps of one of TV's first chefs, Julia Child, who used to gaily cut holes in a fish's neck so as to stick the animal's tail through its body and out of its mouth, simply for effect. Lobsters are, by the way, widely believed to be fully aware of sensation when they are frozen alive or dropped into boiling water. Invertebrate zoologists tell us that these complex crustaceans have tens of thousands of bristles on their bodies that are sensitive to touch, and they still feel pain until their nerve ganglia are destroyed, fixing the tissue.

In my youth, I once saw a bin of live snails at an Italian market and decided to try to cook them. A helpful man in an apron put a couple of little shovelfuls of them into a brown paper bag and gave me his best advice on soaking them and then sautéing then. It sounded simple enough even for a bad cook like me. Off I drove, the bag on the front passenger seat.

About half an hour later, nearing home, I began to get the feeling I was being watched. I looked over at the seat beside me, and there, peering out of the bag into the precipice below or up at giant me, were the snails. Having looked like nothing more than a cluster of shells when I bought them, the little horned beings had come to life, crawled up to the end of the bag, and managed to work their way out of it. Now they were sitting or standing there—it is hard to tell with a snail—escape weighing heavily on their minds.

I remembered the cooking directions. It said that the snails should be washed by swilling them about in a pan of warm water and then left overnight in a deep pot of cold water. The next day, I was to get the olive oil sizzling, remove their tiny bodies from their portable homes, and toss them into the pan with some garlic, sauterne, and herbs. This was now impossible.

I drove as quickly as prudence allowed, raced the snails and their open bag to the back of my garden, deposited them gently on the grass, apologized, and went into the house. So much for escargot. When I went back to the garden the next morning, they had all disappeared. From then on, any delicious garlic-wine juice would have to be sopped up with breadsticks. After all, like tofu, snails don't have much taste in and of themselves. It's all in the sauce.

John Bunyan must have had a similar experience when he wrote of the snail:

> *She goes but softly, but she goeth sure;*
> *She stumbles not, as stronger creatures do:*
> *Her journey's shorter, so she may endure*
> *Better than they which do much further go.*
>
> *She makes no noise, but stilly seizeth on*
> *The flower or herb appointed for her food,*

The which she quietly doth feed upon,
While others range, and gare, but find no good.

And though she doth very softly go,
However, 'tis not fast, nor slow, but sure;
And certainly they that do travel so,
The prize they do aim at, they do procure.

"My" snails had certainly gone, and they had procured the prize they sought: freedom.

Perhaps one of the most appalling cruelties in the name of the food business, and we certainly have enough to choose from, is in the production of foie gras, or fatty liver, scorned now by some of the best chefs although still prized by many, and more commonly used mashed up in a sandwich paste or pâté available in a can.

Konrad Lorenz, the world-renowned wildlife ethologist, called foie gras production "a shame on all Europe," although today the United States is equally shamed. Lorenz was particularly incensed because he had adopted, or been adopted by, a flock of greylag geese during his studies in Switzerland, and had slept and swum with them as part of their family. The British actor Sir John Gielgud was so appalled about the treatment of ducks and geese used for foie gras that he narrated a video for PETA, denouncing foie gras and urging chefs and restaurateurs to withhold it from their menus.

In his video, John Gielgud described the intricate relationships among ducks and their amazing abilities by telling us:

Anyone who has ever watched ducks bobbing underwater for food or skimming across a lake in a graceful landing would probably agree that these birds seem delighted to be alive. The diversity and charm of ducks are apparent in every facet of their behavior. Complex communicators, they begin early—even before hatching. Developing ducklings can be heard cheeping inside their eggs. After her ducklings hatch, mother duck devotes all her time to her young.

Ducks have elaborate courtship rituals and have been known to develop caring, steady relationships with each other. Ducks are natural athletes with remarkable physical capabilities. They are able to dive a hundred feet deep and fly more than sixty miles an hour. In the wild, they have been known to live as long as eighteen years, but on today's foie gras farms, their throats are slit when they are just three months old.

After Sir John passed away, Sir Roger Moore, famous for the high life in his character role of James Bond, offered his services. Now you can hear and see Sir Roger's video for PETA, in which he calls on chefs and consumers to be civilized enough to forgo foie gras.

What moved both these actor-advocates was a videotape filmed by a PETA investigator at a New York foie gras farm. It shows the birds being violently force-fed by machine. Workers thrust long metal pipes down the birds' throats, then used a compressor to pump 3 kilograms (6.5 pounds) of cooked corn into their stomachs. Sometimes, the birds' internal organs simply burst; other times their necks ruptured from the sheer force and manhandling. Injury is so common on such farms that the people on the force-feeding line may be given a pay bonus if they manage to kill fewer than fifty birds during the process.

In the distant past, foie gras production was limited to France and Belgium. Women living on farms would keep a duck or goose confined to their kitchen or barn, sometimes actually nailing the bird's feet to the floor or putting him in a small wooden box so he could not move.

After being blindfolded, a stick and long funnel were used to shove food down the bird's throat. Today, human ingenuity has resulted in a far more efficient, mechanized version of this abominable cruelty; we have moved thousands of geese and ducks onto factory farms, and the market is flooded with the canned livers of these dear birds.

Force-feeding isn't the only horror the birds endure. In addition to the three-times-a-day cramming (accelerated to every three hours, even throughout the night, during the last four days of the birds' lives), their wings often break when they are dragged roughly from their pens or cages, and they suffer hideous injuries, the metal pipe sometimes penetrating the neck and making terrible wounds. They are also pathetic to see, because, so deformed and sick from overfeeding (their livers expand to six, seven, or more times their normal size), most cannot walk and must push themselves along on their wings.

Luckily, many airlines that once proudly listed foie gras on their first-class cabin menus have responded to PETA's appeal and dropped it. An ever-growing number of stores have been sufficiently moved or pressured to stop stocking it, some top restaurants no longer serve it, and treating ducks and geese that way to produce foie gras is illegal in Britain, Germany, and what was at one time the third largest foie gras–producing nation of them all, Israel.

HOW GOING VEGAN CAN SAVE THE WORLD

There are many reasons vegans choose not to eat meat. Sometimes it is a dietary choice—they don't like the taste of flesh. Sometimes it is an ethical choice—be it a religious conviction or general love and respect for all life. Sometimes it is due to a worry about health. Regardless of the reason, one thing is certain—going vegan *can* help save the world.

When asked what change people could make in their lives to help the environment, Sir Paul McCartney didn't hesitate: "I think the biggest change anyone could make in their own lifestyle would be to become vegetarian," he said. McCartney, a longtime vegetarian and environmental activist, is fully aware of the meat industry's negative impact on Mother Earth.

Did you know that the cultivation of livestock for human consumption is responsible for the production of more greenhouse gases than *all* of the world's automobiles combined? It's true. Animal production produces more than just animals. It also produces harmful gases. The nitrous oxide and methane gases that are released into the atmosphere every day from the millions of cows, pigs, chickens, and other imprisoned farmed animals are the leading cause of global warming. Therefore, saying no to meat is just as important as saying yes to that new hybrid car you've had your eye on. Actually, it is more important.

The Environmental Protection Agency (EPA) has found that nitrous oxide gas is about three hundred times more dangerous and destructive than the carbon dioxide that leaks out of your car.

Meat production also translates into more air pollution. Not only do the animals themselves give off greenhouse gases, but the trucks used to haul the feed to the meat factories and haul the cattle to slaughter also give off harmful emissions, primarily carbon dioxide.

Going vegan is good for the land and sea. Animal cultivation requires a lot of land. In order to keep up with demands, animal farmers have encroached on some of Earth's most diverse and fragile ecosystems, including forests and wetlands. Greenpeace has found that in just one year more than 2.9 million acres of rain forest were destroyed in order to raise chickens for the table.

And animals degrade the land they are "raised" on because they are often forced to stay in one place. Although it is not their fault, farmed animals "lucky enough" to be outdoors at all trample the land they are forced to inhabit, and that too contributes to soil erosion and the destruction of precious topsoil.

Free, itinerant animals don't like to be around their own waste, so they make sure to relieve themselves in such a way that they leave their waste in a variety of locations. But penned-up animals have no choice but to deposit their waste in a fixed location—in their pens or other prisons. What fails to seep into the ground eventually makes its way to the water in rivers, streams, seas, and oceans, which all life-forms depend on, because water is the most basic and most important commodity that sustains all of us. A US Senate Agricultural Committee report described the consequences of introducing animal waste to our water supply. Animal waste, they determined, is "untreated and unsanitary, bubbling with chemicals and diseased organisms. . . . It goes onto the soil and into the water that many people will, ultimately, bathe in and wash their clothes with and drink." It "is poisoning rivers and killing fish and making people sick. . . . Catastrophic cases of pollution, sickness, and death are occurring in areas where livestock operations are concentrated." So there is another excellent reason to adopt a vegan diet: you can help protect the land and seas from suffering the negative environmental side effects of animal agriculture.

ACQUIRING GOOD TASTE

We are so lucky to have endless choices when it comes to food, including the luxury of enjoying countless tasty foods that cause no harm or death to animals. Baseball stadiums from one end of the country to the other now sell vegan hot dogs, but I remember serving some of the first "Not Dogs" at the Tides stadium in Norfolk, Virginia. The first men I offered a "Not Dog" to actually wrinkled their noses and looked disgusted. How amazing that the same men thought it unremarkable to buy a "real" hot dog into which has been packed blood, gristle, and the scraps of meat found around animals' noses and anuses and between their toes.

Although many new vegetarians don't want anything that reminds them of their old diet, and they eat a full, tasty, and healthful diet of dishes based on fresh vegetables, fruits, nuts, cereals, and legumes (which are foods that come in a pod, such as beans, peas, and lentils), there exists now virtually every imitation meat and dairy product anyone could imagine. There are soy "ice creams," dozens of different brands of soy, rice, or nut "milks," and faux cheese and sour cream for those who love those flavors but don't wish to contribute to animals' suffering. The veggie burger market means a good investment as well as good eating, and there is soy "bacon," "chicken," "buffalo wings," even "Tofurky" with stuffing and all the trimmings.

Some people are switching, not from meat to vegetables, but from "red meat" (cows, pigs, and lambs) to "white meat" (chickens, turkeys, and fish). I would give my eyeteeth to be able to find a way to quietly dye chickens red. Although such a switch is usually made "for health reasons," chicken is, in fact, about as far from a health food as potato chips are removed from a potato. Chicken contains exactly as much cholesterol as beef, 25 milligrams per ounce (if you think that's bad, an egg is a cholesterol *bomb*, with a whopping 213 milligrams of cholesterol), and isn't much lower in fat, even if you remove the skin. It contains no fiber at all and fills you out, not up.

It also makes bad mathematical sense, from a humane point of view, to switch from cows to chickens and turkeys, when you consider that it would take perhaps one hundred meals of beef to use up the meat from one cow, whereas only three or four meals could be made out of the flesh of a single chicken. One of PETA's provocative, tongue-in-cheek, make-you-think campaigns suggested that if any of us truly wishes to save animals but can't bring ourselves to stop eating meat, we should "Eat the Whales." After all, PETA argued, thousands of gentle birds and hundreds of sensitive mammals like cows would have to be killed to feed as many people as could be fed by one whale!

But changes in the way we eat are happening rapidly, as is evidenced by the success of umpteen varieties of veggie burger and the proliferation of veggie hot dogs in ballparks. Nevertheless, millions of animals are being bred, hurt, and killed at this very moment. Slaughterhouses may be carefully and deliberately built miles from our schools, homes, and businesses, but if we don't do our part to close them down, then as Ralph Waldo Emerson remarked, "You have just dined, and however scrupulously the slaughterhouse is concealed in the graceful distance of miles, there is complicity." That is why our actions are vital. In the pages ahead, there is a wealth of information on things we can do to help, from where to buy "phony baloney" to how to protest when the Wienermobile drives into town.

 WHAT YOU CAN DO

Help Animals Used for Food

Help Yourself!

Go Vegan! Good intentions are not good enough. It's easy to stop eating animals. Here's how: Order a Vegetarian Starter Kit from PETA by going to GoVeg.com or by calling 888-VEG-FOOD.

Subscribe to vegetarian magazines like *VegNews*, which costs about twenty dollars per year. Visit VegNews.com for more information.

Order cookbooks. Try PETA's cookbooks, *The Compassionate Cook*, *Cooking with PETA*, or *The PETA Celebrity Cookbook*, or see the book section at PETACatalog.org.

Put a FREE VEGETARIAN STARTER KIT, CALL I-888-VEG-FOOD bumper sticker on your vehicle, and on the back of your laptop.

Record an animal rights message on your answering machine or voice mail, such as "millions of animals are killed for the table every hour in the United States. For a free Vegetarian Starter Kit, visit GoVeg.com."

Put your MySpace or Facebook page to work. Post PETA videos, including *Meet Your Meat*, on your page and add PETA as a "friend."

Practice your cooking. Visit VegCooking.com for the best vegan recipes, from lunch box suggestions to sophisticated dinner party fare and everything in between.

Feed your friends. The way to a person's heart is through their stomach, they say. Cook or buy vegan treats for others and supply the recipe.

Be encouraging. Give others food for thought by wearing a proveggie button, baseball cap, or ASK ME WHY I'M A VEGAN T-shirt and providing information to those who request it.

Offer suggestions. Use blog comments and suggestion sections on Web sites to promote vegan products and lifestyle choices.

Get on food committees. If you do, you can be sure to turn menus in the direction of healthful, humane vegan foods for work, social events, and outings.

Put stickers on envelopes. On every item you mail, whether a card or a bill payment, stick a GOVEG.COM or a MEAT'S NO

TREAT FOR THOSE YOU EAT sticker on the front of the envelope. Lots of people will see it as your letter travels to its final destination.

Hand out stickers and leaflets including at school events, such as football games—PETA can provide you with it all for free.

Show a video. Show *Meet Your Meat, Nonviolence Includes Animals,* or *I Am an Animal* to school groups, friends, family, and coworkers. Both are available at PETACatalog.org. You can download additional videos at PETATV.com

Contact your local cable company about running a provegetarian video on cable public access television.

Use your license plate. Advertise your compassionate lifestyle on your license plate. Sample phrases include NO MEAT or BE VEGAN.

Ask for vegan food at ballparks. Ask your local baseball stadium concession to serve veggie dogs, veggie burgers, and other vegan food, if they don't already. The Citizens Bank Park in Philadelphia, AT&T Park in San Francisco, PETCO Park in San Diego, Harbor Park stadium in Norfolk, Virginia, and many more already offer veg options. Visit GoVeg.com for more information.

Exercise. Promote a healthy vegan diet when you exercise or compete. Don Lutz organized a pool team of vegetarians who have amassed more than two hundred titles in league and tournament competition and spread the word about animal rights everywhere they go. Put a stack of PETA's free Vegetarian Starter Kits by the StairMaster and watch people read something useful while they sweat!

Feed your legislators. Let your legislators try veggie food. Ask about hosting a vegetarian hot dog stand at lunchtime at your capitol or city council building.

Sponsor one of PETA's hard-to-ignore vegan billboards or find a company that will run one for free. Check out the media center at PETA.org for more information and contact us for help!

Raise money. Hold a yard sale, bake sale, car wash, or sell something on eBay to support PETA's work for animals killed for the table. These are easy and fun ways to raise money to run an ad or sponsor a Vegetarian Starter Kit newsstand. PETA hosts a combination yard sale/veggie hot dog and burger stand/clearance extravaganza called "Bonanza for the Beasties," in Norfolk, Virginia, in the summer, and it is always an overwhelming success. One year, sales topped $3,000.

Send your legislator books, magazines, or articles on vegetarian living and animal issues.

Be a helpful guest. Invited to a meal? Explain politely what you eat and what you don't. Many meat eaters are unaware that vegetarians eat no flesh whatsoever—no meat or chicken or fish. Let your host know this. If the dinner is very informal, you could help your host by suggesting some easily prepared, familiar meatless dishes—like a casserole or stir-fry, for example. Far better, volunteer to bring a tasty vegan entrée for all to share.

Talk to your workplace cafeteria. Ask your office cafeteria to offer vegan food. If you attend meetings where food will be served (such as a professional workshop), request ahead of time that they provide vegan food for you. Be specific about what constitutes "vegan"—many people don't know. Check out VegAdvantage.com to find menus and helpful advice for food professionals. For instance, Norm Mason, the CEO of Cat Communications, based in Roanoke, Virginia, made headlines across the country when he introduced a company cafeteria where employees dine exclusively on vegan foods—soy steaks, soy sloppy joes, veggie burgers, nachos, and other meatless, eggless, butter-free delicacies—for free!

Another company that offers vegan meals among other animal-friendly options is Holiday Systems International, a Las Vegas–based vacation planner. HSI gives its employees a free membership to PETA, provides them with free vegan lunches, and pays them to have their companion animal neutered. HSI's employee guidelines stress animal rights and green issues, promote education and awareness, and reward employees for their compassionate choices.

Request vegan benefits. If your company gives employees free holiday hams or turkeys, as early as possible before the occasion politely ask that they switch to a vegan food gift.

Organize others. Get your coworkers involved in recognition of the annual Great American MeatOut, coordinated nationally by the Farm Animal Reform Movement (FARM). Four thousand casino workers at the Trump Castle in Atlantic City enjoyed a veggie menu in their cafeteria. At a Michigan Chrysler plant, employees sampled meatless foods during a lunchtime vegetarian seminar.

Help Others!

Put free VEGETARIAN STARTER KIT cards on your grocery store bulletin boards.

Donate vegan cookbooks, animal rights books, and DVDs to libraries. Donate a copy of PETA's *Celebrity Cookbook*, *The Compassionate Cook*, *Making Kind Choices*, or the DVD of *I Am an Animal* to your local library, put them on your own bookshelf or in your own DVD collection, and lend them to friends

Welcome newcomers to your neighborhood with a vegan welcome basket, complete with vegan food, literature, stickers, and a nice letter with tips on vegetarian-friendly restaurants in town.

Feed your coworkers. If they like what you feed them, all resistance breaks down! Learn what foods appeal to those you work with and cook them up something vegan that fits the bill. Don't say, "it's vegan," just say, "free food" and break the news afterward. For recipes, visit VegCook ing.com

Feed the homeless. Call your local homeless shelter and offer to get a team together to cook a simple vegan meal.

Get Active!

Read—there's a veggie book for everyone, from the arch conservative to the starving college student. See chapter 12, "Readings and Visuals."

Defend animals; use visuals. If you hear ridicule or criticism of animal rights or a veggie diet, politely but firmly defend the validity of your concern for animals and how great eating vegan is. Point out that the circle of compassion does not start and end with *Homo sapiens* but should extend to *all* living beings who share Earth. Try to reason with the critics. Explain calmly how battery hens and veal calves are treated, and show pictures or a video (which you can download at PETATV.com) if you can. Ask, "Do you really think this is right?"

Say what you want. By telling store managers, restaurant owners, and anyone in the food business that you would like vegan food, you will be helping create a bigger market for it.

Enter competitions. Enter your vegan recipes into cooking competitions, Bake-Offs, and bake sales, and make it clear that no animal ingredients were used. Dan Handley, a Colorado businessman, won a barbecue cook-off contest with his vegan "ribs" recipe!

Act on principle. When bus driver Bruce Anderson stuck to his principles and refused to give riders coupons for free hamburgers, he was fired by the Orange County (California) Transit Authority (OCTA). Anderson was reinstated when he won a lawsuit ruling that all vegetarians and vegans are entitled to protect their beliefs and rights.

Be an armchair activist. You don't even have to leave your living room to stop animal abuse. You can do it by making phone calls, writing letters, and sending e-mails. Don't worry if you aren't a wordsmith. Just read the "Guide to Letter-Writing" on PETA.org for advice.

Contact local radio stations to run one of PETA's thirty- or sixty-second public service announcements.

Write letters to the editors of newspapers and magazines about going vegan—your comments could be read by millions!

Incorporate animal rights issues into school assignments. Write essays about vegan living or how animals get to the table whenever you have a choice of topics.

Make a display. Do a library display on how easy it is to go vegan or on factory farming issues.

Make art. Create a photographic series, a painting, a collage, etc. and use vegetarian or animal factories as your theme. Ask a school or library to display it or take pictures of it, and post it on your blog, Facebook, or MySpace page.

Volunteer

Join PETA or just sign up for PETA Action Alerts by visiting PETA.org.

Talk to PETA or your animal protection organization. If you belong to an animal protection organization that is still serving meat and dairy at their events, urge the group to adopt an ethically consistent plan. For instance, it is a bit odd to save dogs by hosting a meal that meant pigs had to suffer.

Make Easter "eggs." At Easter, look around the craft shop for all the different "eggs" you can display, "hunt," and give as gifts. Craft stores offer a variety of "eggs" made from plastic, papier-mâché, wood, even glass. To create a fun party for young children use plastic eggs and colorful stickers that are appropriate for Easter. Card shops, fabric shops, even supermarkets carry fake eggs and other Easter decorations. Children can put stickers on these eggs, which can be hidden as is, or small trinkets or other treats can be placed inside. Parents can choose to save one or two eggs their children decorate each year. You can't do that with hens' eggs!

Organize and speak. Pluck up your courage, get to know your facts, pick a video to show, and then address a class or school assembly, organize forums, and speak at club meetings, church groups, public libraries, and service groups. Hand out leaflets on factory farming and vegan food and encourage questions. Ask a local vegetarian or health food store to sponsor your effort and perhaps supply food samples and pamphlets on the issue.

Restaurants and Grocery Stores

Try new foods. Broaden your eating horizons in ethnic restaurants (Ethiopian, Indian, Szechuan, Thai, Japanese, and more) that specialize in savory animal-free dishes, and by trying new recipes in your own kitchen.

When you are in a line at the grocery store, make sure that fellow shoppers overhear your conversation about the great new video you just saw called, *Meet Your Meat.*

Compile a list of local vegetarian-friendly restaurants—give it to your family and friends, post it on the Web, and hand it out to everyone you see.

Boycott foie gras. Don't let 'em duck the issue! Ask specialty stores to take foie gras off the shelves, and politely inform restaurants and gourmet shops that sell it why you don't patronize them. Grab a stack of foie gras leaflets from PETA-Literature.com and send them to the local restaurant or store that sells foie gras to let them know that they won't be able to count on your business until they drop this cruel product.

Use frozen foods. Make sure every grocery store in your area carries frozen veggie entrées, tofu, and soy milk. Silk soy milk and Morningstar Farms' Meal Starters can be found in Wal-Marts nation-wide, so it is easy for your local store to follow suit.

Use suggestion boxes at restaurants—ask the manager to consider vegan alternatives and vegan menu items and thank him or her if they're already on the menu!

Display stickers. Ask restaurants to display PETA's WE SERVE VEGETARIAN MEALS stickers in their windows. (If they don't currently offer a vegetarian entrée or two, ask them to create vegan dishes for you, and refer them to VegCooking .com or VegAdvantage.com for fabulous recipes.) To order these stickers, please e-mail literature@PETA.org.

Make a vegetarian line. Ask your grocer to create a vegetarian line at the store checkout so you won't have to put your groceries on a conveyor belt full of blood and salmonella leaked from packages of red meat and chicken. That could get a buzz going and might make the local news!

Ask for veggie burgers. Ask major fast-food chains to introduce veggie burgers and other alternatives to meat. Suggest that they accommodate the growing number of non–meat eaters. Tell them that salad bars are great but that there are also many other tasty fast-food meatless products available. Burger King has the BK Veggie, and McDonald's had a veggie burger in select cities. If the demand is high enough, they will accommodate, so let them know you would frequent their establishment if they had veg options.

Flying

Request vegan meals. When you make your flight reservations, if a meal is to be served, always ask for special vegan meals. A few days before your departure, call the airline to make certain that your special meal request is still in the computer. There's still time (they need a day) for the airlines to reorder the meals if your initial request disappeared.

Get Your Family Involved

Share the Cooking. Take turns making a different vegan meal every night or once or twice a week for family and friends.

Grill vegan. Challenge your whole household to outdo one another with vegan dishes. Or just grill up some tofu hot dogs and veggie burgers, and provide lots of good "fixin's" on the side (Vegenaise, nutritional yeast, and grilled onions and mushrooms go great on the burgers) for your family, friends, and neighbors. Round out your menu with chips, a big salad, or a platter of raw vegetables with hummus or Tofutti's Sour Supreme Guacamole flavor, and Tofutti Cuties.

Buy grandkids, nieces, nephews, and any other kids in your life great animal-friendly books (like *Whose Goat?*) and get them free PETA comic books. Use the books as stocking stuffers, Hanukkah presents, birthday presents, etc.

Stand on a busy street corner and pass out free PETA literature on going vegan to passersby. Or, with permission
from the city or private property owner, man an information table.

Use leaflets. Literature can be left in hospital waiting rooms,
health spas, beauty salons, in "pet" shops, libraries, public
bathrooms, on subway, bus, and train seats, and on car
windshields.

Set up tables. Find out where other groups in your community
set up tables, and/or get a list of festivals and fairs from the
chamber of commerce, department of parks and recreation,
or tourist department. (To set up at certain locations, you
may need a permit from the mayor's office or police station.) Distribute literature about animal rights, the environment, health and diet, and the low cost of vegan meals.
(You can order a General Tabling Pack, which includes stickers, Vegetarian Starter Kits, leaflets, and more for twenty dollars from PETALiterature.com.)

**Put your laptop or portable mini DVD player on your litera-
ture table.** Set the DVD or CD-ROM on "repeat" so that
it will play over and over again (or you can just keep pushing PLAY). If you don't have a table and your laptop/DVD
player is small enough, you can just have an activist hold it
outward for people to watch. Visit PETACatalog.org to order *Meet Your Meat* and others or download videos from
PETATV.com.

**Rent a cheap chicken costume and some crutches and stage
a "crippled chicken" demonstration** in front of a fast-
food restaurant that serves chicken. Contact PETA to see
which restaurants need pressuring and for more tips or
assistance.

Join a parade. Find out when parades are planned and enter
a vegetarian float. Remember, your message could be seen

by millions if it's included in newspaper or television coverage.

Protest the Wienermobile. Call the Oscar Mayer hotline, 1-800-672-2754, to find out if the Wienermobile is coming to your area. Organize a demo to protest the Wienermobile's exploitation of pigs and children.

Hold a demonstration. Even a one-person demonstration can do a lot of good. Someone wrote: "One hot summer day, as I drove up a busy highway in Florida, I noticed an elderly man at the stoplight. He was seated in a cheap aluminum lawn chair with a table, lemonade, and a sign that simply said, DON'T BUY A CAR HERE. THEY SOLD ME A LEMON. One brave soul in the blazing sun, alone but bursting with conviction. I will never forget that man. More importantly, I will never buy a car from that dealer."

Liberate a lobster. You may be able to persuade stores or restaurants to give you the lobster, especially if the lobster is large (old). Since lobsters require special handling, you may want to organize the liberation through PETA.

Get visual. PETA activists drew attention to the ills of meat eating and killing animals for food at the National Maalox Pork Cook-off by clamping clothespins to their noses. Don McIntosh, eighty-four, demonstrated at a meat-processors convention by holding a sign that expressed his disgust at their cruel methods. A vegetarian for thirty years, McIntosh says that he has been repulsed by meat processing since he was a boy. Easy and inexpensive to make, a protest sign pictured in a newspaper has the potential to send an animal rights message to millions of people.

Write to your elected representatives. Ask your congresspeople to stop the obesity epidemic in children by supporting healthful, vegetable-based lunches in the National School Lunch Program. Some schools now serve nutritious lunches that are not only low calorie and all-around healthful, but are vegetarian as well. For more information on child obesity and the benefits of a vegetarian diet for children, please visit PCRM.org.

Letters should be short and simple. Ask that your letter be answered (it will be, as voters' comments are rarely ignored). Beware of misleading replies and respond to anything you disagree with.

Meet the Press

Call your radio station. Jump into radio call-in discussions with animal issue tie-ins. (For example, call in to a health show and offer information on the impact of a vegan diet on the environment.)

Get into the newspaper. Ask your local paper's Lifestyle or Cooking section to write a story on the advantages of a vegan diet, what great food is available in local stores or eateries, or the cruelties of the factory farm. Send a letter to the editor on any local veggie food or farming news.

Write about restaurants. Write to restaurant critics to suggest more vegetarian articles, reviews, and recipes.

Contact your television station. Ask your local television stations to air a story about how young people are switching to vegan foods and what's available locally.

Go to animal industry sites. Visit your local factory farm, stockyard, or slaughterhouse, if they'll let you in. Take photographs and video to record what you witness. Then publicize what you discover.

Special Actions for Young People

Decorate to liberate. Skateboard champion Mike Vallely uses his popularity to influence other young people positively. Every year thousands of skateboarding fans all over the world see the message PLEASE DON'T EAT MY FRIENDS, painted on his colorful, unique deck. You can spread the word by decorating lunch boxes, lockers, motorbikes, and other accessories.

Talk to your teachers or your children's teachers about incorporating animal issues into their curriculum. PETA can send you lesson plans and all the materials needed. (Visit TeachKind.org for more information.)

Give a speech or write a paper. Research vegetarian diets or animal rights. Danny Martinez of Huntington Beach, California, got an A+ when he chose to enlighten his classmates and teacher with an essay about what's wrong with meat consumption. After reading his essay to a school assembly, he was assailed by questions from curious students and teachers alike.

Use flyers. Copy flyers and post them on bulletin boards at your school and in your neighborhood.

Send a message with your mortarboard—attach animal rights messages to your graduation gear and start the rest of your life off on the right foot!

Make art. Enter art or poetry competitions and create a piece that speaks for animals, or create a photo collage that shows meat for what it really is.

Make a display. Create a campus or student union display about helping animals.

Talk to your teachers. Ask your English teacher to have an essay assignment called "Animals Need Our Protection."

Start a group. Start an animal rights group in your school. Visit peta2.com for all the information you'll ever want to get started and be successful.

Clean up. Really shock your parents and offer to do the dishes for a week if they substitute soy milk for cow's milk and cook vegan meals.

Vegan Tips

Dump dairy! For more information and recipe ideas, visit Veg-Cooking.com.

Try taste-alikes. If you crave the taste of chicken or sausage, explore Boca, Morningstar Farms, Amy's, and other taste-alikes made of soy and wheat gluten and available at Seventh Day Adventist food stores, many major supermarkets, and health food stores. There are fabulous Chinese restaurants, like Candle 79 in Manhattan, the Longlife Vegetarian House, in Berkeley, California, and the Harmony in Philadelphia, Pennsylvania, that specialize in mock duck and soy ham dishes that would fool the most discerning diner!

Look closely at your grocery store. Nowadays, Wal-Mart carries wonderful veg options such as Morningstar Farms Chick'n and Morningstar Steak Strips, Boca Burgers, Hormel Vegetarian Chili, Lightlife Tofu Pups and deli slices, Silk soy milk, and more. What your local grocery store doesn't carry, a health food store will. Check your local health food store for Yves Fat Free Veggie Deli Slices, Tofurky's oven roast, stuffing, gravy, deli slices, bratwurst, Italian sausages, and more. Tofutti's Better Than Cream Cheese, Sour Supreme, cheese slices, or Tofutti Cuties (vegan "ice cream" sandwiches), Follow Your Heart Vegan Gourmet cheese in various flavors, Vegenaise, Imagine Foods' Rice Dream brand rice milk and "ice cream," and the list goes on!

Veganize your recipes.

- *Eggs.* When a recipe calls for eggs, simply leave the eggs out or use an egg substitute, such as the one made by Ener-G Foods. (For the store nearest you carrying this product, visit Ener-G.com). For breakfast, scramble mashed tofu with onions, mushrooms, and a dash of mustard, turmeric, and soy sauce. Soft or extra-soft tofu makes a great binder, as do bananas.
- *Milk.* Try Silk or the other commercially available vanilla, carob, almond, and plain soy milks (rice milk or nut milk are great too) for cooking, cereal, tea, coffee, and hot chocolate. Offered in vitamin-fortified and low-fat varieties.
- *Butter.* Sauté food in water or vegetable broth, flavor veggies with lemon, "butter" toast with vegetable margarine. (For optimum health, use all fats sparingly.) Use gourmet mustards instead of butter on sandwiches.
- *Cheese.* Try soy or rice "cheese," available in many grocery stores and at health food centers. Great on pizza and sandwiches. Or cheese up your sauces and veggies with nutritional yeast flakes (also great on popcorn). Tofu can be used in vegan lasagna and cheesecake recipes.
- *Yogurt.* Try healthful fruit-and-soy yogurts, available at health food stores.
- *Ice cream.* Delicious tofu or rice "ice creams" are sweeter and healthier. Or try tangy fruit sorbets.
- *Hamburger.* Use frozen soy crumbles or dry texturized vegetable protein (TVP) in chili, meat loaf, tacos, lasagna filling, spaghetti sauces, and other recipes.

Try one of the dozens of commercial tofu, tempeh, vegetable, and grain burgers available.

- *Seafood.* Eat sea *vegetables* instead of sea *animals.* There are about ten different varieties of seaweeds commonly available in the United States, and they can be found at most health food stores. Use nori as a wrap for avocado and cucumber sushi; try wakame or kombu in soups; or toast nori as a great salty snack. MayWah, an online Asian store, sells faux meats including faux "fish" products, such as "crab" balls, "fish" filets, "fish" sticks, "salmon," "prawns," and more. Visit Vegieworld.com to view their products.

 FREQUENTLY ASKED QUESTIONS

Isn't eating plants cruel too?

Perhaps we'll learn something different later, but because plants are devoid of a central nervous system, nerve, endings, and a brain, there is currently no reason to believe that they experience pain. It is theorized that we and all animals feel pain so that we can use it for self-protection. For example, if you touch something hot and feel pain, you will learn from the pain that you should not touch that item in the future. Since plants cannot move from place to place, any knowledge they might gain from the sensation of pain would be superfluous.

If you are concerned about the impact of vegetable agriculture on the environment, however, a vegetarian diet is better for the environment than a meat-based one, since the vast majority of grains and legumes raised today are used as feed for cattle. Rather than eating animals, such as cows, who must consume three to sixteen pounds of vegetation in order to convert them into one pound of flesh, you can save many more plants (and destroy less land) by eating vegetables directly.

Most animals used for food are bred for that purpose, so what's wrong with using them?

Being bred for a certain purpose does not change an animal's biological capacity to feel pain and fear.

Have you ever been to a slaughterhouse?

Yes, and lots of other people have filmed and written about what goes on in these places and have painted a very detailed overall picture. But you do not need to experience the abuse of animals close up to be able to criticize it any more than you need to personally experience rape or child abuse to criticize those crimes. No one will ever be witness to all the suffering in the world, but that doesn't mean that we shouldn't try to stop it.

Isn't vegetarian living a personal choice?

From a legal standpoint, yes. But from a moral standpoint, actions that harm others are not really matters of personal choice. For example, child abuse and cruelty to animals are immoral acts, not matters of choice. Today our society allows meat eating and factory farming, but at one time, society also encouraged slavery, child labor, and many other practices that are now universally recognized as wrong.

Animals kill other animals for food, so why shouldn't we?

Not all animals do, and we tend to pick on the vegetarian animals, the chickens and lambs and cows, which are the most gentle ones! However, most animals who kill for food could not survive if they didn't. They kill out of need, but that is not the case for humans who kill—usually by proxy—out of greed, old habit, and laziness or for convenience. In fact, we would be far better off if we didn't eat meat. Many animals, including our closest primate relatives, are vegetarians. We should look to them, rather than to carnivores, as models of healthy eating.

The animals have to die sometime, so what's wrong with eating them?

We all have to die sometime, but that doesn't give anyone the right to cause us suffering or kill us.

Don't farmers have to treat their animals well or they'll stop producing milk and eggs?

Unfortunately, no. Animals on factory farms gain weight, lay eggs, or produce milk not because they are well cared for, comfortable, and content but because their bodies have been manipulated with medications, hormones, genetics, and management techniques. In addition, animals raised for food are slaughtered when they are extremely young, usually before disease and misery decimate them. Factory farmers raise such huge numbers of animals for food that it is less expensive for them to absorb some losses than it is for them to provide humane conditions. Take the Middle Passage slave ships: many blacks died from misery and disease, but that didn't encourage the slave ship captains to treat valuable slaves any more humanely.

What will we do with all the chickens, cows, and pigs if everyone becomes a vegetarian?

It is unrealistic to expect that everyone will stop eating animals overnight. As the demand for meat decreases, fewer animals will be raised for food. Farmers will stop breeding so many animals (billions a year in the United States alone) and will turn to other types of healthier, more environmentally and animal-friendly agriculture. When there are fewer of these animals, they will be able to live more natural lives.

If everyone became vegetarian, many animals would never even be born. Isn't that worse for them?

Life on factory farms is so miserable that it is hard to imagine that we are doing animals a favor by bringing them into that type of fearful, painful, miserable "life" and confining them, tormenting them, and slaughtering them.

If everyone only ate vegetarian foods, would there be enough to eat?

Yes. We feed so much grain to animals to fatten them for consumption that if we all became vegetarians, we could produce enough food to feed everyone on Earth. In the United States, animals raised for food are fed 70 percent of the corn, wheat, and other grains that we grow. The world's cattle consume a quantity of food equal to the caloric needs of 8.7 billion people—more than the entire human population.

Do vegetarians get enough protein?

In Western countries, our problem is that people get too much protein, not too little. We have an obesity epidemic, and it's a health emergency. Most Americans get at least twice as much protein as they need, and too much protein, especially animal protein, can increase your risk of osteoporosis and kidney disease.

You can certainly get more than enough protein from whole grains, nuts, oatmeal, beans, soy, rice, corn, peas, mushrooms, green vegetables like broccoli—almost every food contains protein. Unless your vegetarian diet consists of a great deal of junk food like french fries and candy bars, it's almost impossible to eat as many calories as you need for good health without getting enough protein.

Don't humans have to eat meat to stay healthy?

Absolutely not, in fact the opposite is true. Both the US Department of Agriculture and the American Dietetic Association have endorsed vegetarian diets. Studies have also shown that vegetarians have lower cholesterol levels than meat eaters and are far less likely to die of heart disease or cancer and live longer. The consumption of meat and dairy products is conclusively linked to diabetes, arthritis, osteoporosis, high blood pressure, clogged arteries, obesity, asthma, and impotence.

Are humans natural carnivores?

Anthropology shows us that they are not. A vegetarian diet suits the human body far better than a diet that includes meat. Carnivorous animals have claws for tearing, short digestive tracts to expel rotting carcasses, and long, curved fangs for ripping flesh. Humans have flat, flexible nails, and our so-called canine teeth are minuscule and ineffective compared to those of carnivores. Our teeth are better suited to biting into fruits than tearing through tough hides. We have flat molars and long digestive tracts that are suited to diets of vegetables, fruits, and grains. Eating meat is hazardous to our health and contributes to heart disease, cancer, and many other health problems.

Don't dairy cows need to be milked?

In order for a cow to produce milk, she must have a calf. Each "dairy cow" is impregnated—usually artificially on something farmers call a "rape rack"—every year so that she continues to produce a steady supply of milk. In nature, the mother's calf would drink her milk, that's who it's meant for. But on factory farms, calves are taken away from their mothers when they are just a day or two old so that humans can have the milk that nature intended for the calves. Female calves are slaughtered immediately or raised to be dairy cows. Male calves are confined for sixteen weeks in tiny veal crates that are so small they cannot even turn around.

Because of the high demand for "cheese on everything," cows are genetically engineered and fed growth hormones to force them to produce quantities of milk that are well beyond their natural limits. Even the few farmers who choose not to raise animals intensively must get rid of the calves, who would otherwise drink the milk, and send the mothers off to slaughter when their milk production wanes.

Can't I eat meat? I didn't kill the animal.

You may not have killed the animal yourself, but you hired the killer. Whenever you purchase meat, the killing was done for you, and you paid for it.

If you were starving on a boat out at sea, would you eat an animal?

I don't know. Humans will go to extremes to save their own lives, even if it means hurting someone innocent. People have even killed and eaten other people in such situations. This example, however, isn't relevant to our daily choices. For most of us, there is no emergency and no excuse to kill animals for food.

Chickens lay eggs naturally, so what's wrong with eating eggs?

The cruelty of egg production lies in the treatment of the "laying" hens, who are perhaps the most abused of all factory-farmed animals. Each egg from a factory farm represents about twenty-two hours of misery and came from a hen who was packed into a cage the size of a filing-cabinet drawer with as many as five other chickens. On factory farms, cages are stacked many tiers high, and feces from the top rows falls onto the chickens below. Hens become lame and develop osteoporosis because they are forced to remain immobile, balancing on a wire, and because they lose calcium when they repeatedly produce eggshells. Some birds' feet grow around the wire cage floors, and they starve to death because they are unable to reach the food trough. At just eighteen months or so, most hens are "spent" and are sent to the slaughterhouse. Egg hatcheries don't have any use for male chicks, so many are suffocated, crushed, or ground up alive for fertilizer.

Can fish really feel pain?

Yes, every study on whether or not fish feel pain shows that they can and do. According to Dr. Donald Bloom, animal welfare adviser to the British government, "Anatomically, physiologically, and biologically, the pain system in fish is virtually the same as in birds and mammals." Fish have fully developed brains and nervous systems and very sensitive mouths. Fish use their tongues and mouths the way that humans use their hands—to catch or gather food, build nests, and, in some species, to hide their offspring from danger. Fish experience fear too. An Australian study found that when fish are chased, confined, or otherwise threatened, they react with increased heart and breathing rates and a burst of adrenaline, just as humans do.

Isn't seafood healthy and low in fat?

Fish is far from a health food, and even the government warns everyone to limit fish consumption, especially if you are pregnant. That's because fish flesh contains toxins like mercury and PCBs from the water, and those toxins get passed on to people who eat fish. Fish raised on farms are given antibiotics, which are also passed on to those who eat them. According to the Centers for Disease Control and Prevention, 325,000 people in the United States get sick or die every year from eating contaminated fish and other sea animals. Even if you could be sure that the fish you eat were free of chemicals, the flesh of some sea animals, especially shrimps and scallops, contains even more cholesterol than beef! As for omega-3 oils, they are available in green leafy vegetables.

Why should animals have rights?

PETA believes that animals have an inherent worth—a value completely separate from their usefulness to humans. We believe that every living being with a will to live has a right to be spared unnecessary pain and suffering.

Doesn't milk prevent osteoporosis, especially in older women?

Although milk is promoted mainly as a source of calcium to slow bone loss, according to the Physicians Committee for Responsible Medicine, the loss of bone integrity that is particularly common among postmenopausal women probably results from a combination of genetics and diet/lifestyle factors. It seems the most important of these is animal protein, which actually leaches calcium from the bones, leading to its excretion in the urine. A medical study showed that when people switched from a typical American diet to a diet eliminating animal proteins, i.e., meat and milk, calcium losses were greatly reduced. Sodium, caffeine, tobacco, and a sedentary lifestyle also contribute to bone loss.

High milk intake does not appear to be protective against fractures. The Harvard Nurses' Study, involving 77,761 women, age thirty-four to fifty-nine, revealed that those who drank three or more glasses of milk per day had no reduction in the risk of hip or arm fractures, over a twelve year follow-up period, compared to those who drank little or no milk, even after adjustment for weight, menopausal status, smoking, and alcohol use. In fact, the fracture rates were slightly, but significantly, *higher* for those who consumed this much milk compared to those who drank little or no milk.

Green leafy vegetables and beans are good calcium sources with advantages that dairy products lack. They contain antioxidants, complex carbohydrate, fiber, and iron, and have little fat, no cholesterol, and no animal proteins. Many green vegetables have calcium absorption rates of over 50 percent, compared with about 32 percent for milk. Calcium absorption is about 52.6 percent for broccoli, 63.8 percent for Brussels sprouts, 57.8 percent for mustard greens, 51.6 percent for turnip greens, and about 40 to 59 percent for kale. Likewise, beans (e.g., pinto beans, black-eyed peas, and navy beans) and bean products, such as tofu, are rich in calcium.

SAMPLE VEGAN RECIPES

BREAKFAST

Vegan French Toast

MAKES 3 SERVINGS

1 cup soy milk

2 Tbsp. flour

1 Tbsp. nutritional yeast flakes

1 tsp. sugar or sweetener of your choice

1 tsp. vanilla

½ tsp. salt

Pinch nutmeg

6 slices whole wheat bread

- Mix all the ingredients (except the bread slices) in a shallow bowl.
- Dip the bread slices into the soy milk mixture and cook on medium-high heat on a nonstick griddle until browned on both sides or on a greased cookie sheet in a 400°F oven until golden on both sides, turning once.

Tofu Scramble

MAKES 4 SERVINGS

2–3 Tbsp. extra virgin olive oil

1 sweet onion, cut into small chunks

5 garlic cloves, minced

½ tsp. ground ginger

½ tsp. chili powder

½ yellow or green bell pepper, seeded and chopped

1 cup sliced mushrooms

4 tomatoes, chopped

1 lb. firm tofu, drained well and cut into bite-size pieces

Tamari, to taste

Freshly ground pepper, to taste

Fresh snipped chives, to taste

4 fresh corn tortillas, warmed

- Heat the olive oil over medium heat in a large skillet and sauté the onion for five minutes, until softened.
- Add the garlic and spices, stir, and cook on medium heat for 1 minute. Add the pepper and mushrooms, stir-frying until tender-crisp.
- Add the tomatoes and slices of tofu. Gently stir-fry for 3 to 4 minutes. Sprinkle with the tamari sauce and season with fresh pepper and chives. Serve on a warm plate with a warm tortilla.

LUNCH

Vegan Sloppy Joes

MAKES 4 SERVINGS

Fool the baseball fans and the barbecue set with this easy vegan classic.

1 Tbsp. olive oil

1 Tbsp. molasses

½ lb. tofu, crumbled

1 6-oz. can tomato paste

2 Tbsp. water

2 Tbsp. Dijon mustard

1 small onion, chopped

1 medium tomato, chopped

Oregano, to taste

Chili pepper, to taste

1 small jar mushrooms, sliced

2 Tbsp. ketchup

1 Tbsp. rice vinegar

Salt, to taste

Pepper, to taste

Sandwich buns, tortillas, or pita bread

- Heat the olive oil in a saucepan on medium heat and add the molasses. Add the crumbled tofu and let it brown, stirring to prevent burning.
- Add the tomato paste and mix well, add water (use more water to make it thinner and less if you would like a thick sauce). Stir in the mustard, onion, and tomato, then add the oregano and chili pepper and continue mixing.
- Stir in the mushrooms, ketchup, and vinegar, and season with the salt and pepper.
- When thoroughly heated, serve on toasted sandwich buns or in tortillas or pita shells.

Tex-Mex Tortilla Wraps

MAKES 4 SERVINGS

Brown baggers: you can turn lunchtime into a fiesta if you pack these portable Tex-Mex treats.

1 15-oz. can black beans, rinsed and drained

2 Tbsp. lime juice

2 Tbsp. orange juice

2 cloves garlic, coarsely chopped

⅛ tsp. salt

Cayenne, pepper to taste

3 scallions, finely chopped

¼ cup red or green bell pepper, finely chopped

4 flour or corn tortillas

Salsa

- Place the beans, lime juice, orange juice, garlic, salt, and cayenne pepper in a food processor and process until smooth. Spoon the mixture into a bowl and stir in the scallions and bell peppers.
- Spread one-fourth of the mixture on each tortilla. Roll the tortillas tightly and top with salsa.

DINNER

Better Than "Beef" Stroganoff

MAKES 4 SERVINGS

Short on time but looking for a hearty meal to serve that lumberjack? Then try this vegan version of the classic—it's both filling and pleasing.

1-lb. bag egg-free pasta

½ cup onion, chopped

1 Tbsp. vegetable oil

1-lb. pkg. Morningstar burger crumbles

1 10¼-oz. can Franco-American mushroom gravy

2 4½-oz. cans sliced mushrooms, drained

⅛ tsp. garlic powder

¼ tsp. pepper

⅛ tsp. salt

½ carton Tofutti "Sour Supreme"

¾ cup white cooking wine (optional)

- Cook the pasta in boiling water until the desired tenderness is reached.
- In a large skillet, brown the onion in the oil over medium heat. Add the remaining ingredients, stir, and cook over medium heat for 15 minutes.
- Drain the pasta, and serve the sauce over the noodles.

Mama's Mock Meat Loaf

MAKES 6 SERVINGS

An all-American farmhouse favorite. Serve with ketchup, mashed potatoes, and gravy.

1 medium onion, diced

½ green pepper, diced (optional)

3 Tbsp. vegetable oil

2 packages beef-flavor Gimme Lean Beef (or similar, if unavailable)

¼ cup oatmeal, dry

2 slices white bread, crumbled

3 Tbsp. ketchup

2 tsp. garlic salt

1 tsp. pepper

COATING INGREDIENTS

¼ cup ketchup

¼ cup brown sugar

½ tsp. dry mustard

½ tsp. nutmeg

- Sauté the onion and green pepper in the oil over medium heat until soft. Transfer the onion and green pepper to a bowl and add the ground beef alternative, oatmeal, bread, ketchup, garlic salt, and pepper. Thoroughly mix with a spoon or your hands.
- Press the mixture into an oiled loaf pan. Cover with foil and bake at 375°F for 30 minutes.
- Meanwhile, mix together the ingredients for the coating and set aside.
- Remove the loaf from the oven and turn it out onto a baking sheet. Spread the coating over the entire loaf. Cook, uncovered, for another 15 minutes at 375°F.

DESSERT

Apple Cobbler

MAKES 6 TO 8 SERVINGS

One bite of this scrumptious cobbler and your taste buds will be turning cartwheels.

3–4 Granny Smith apples

1 tsp. ground cinnamon

½ tsp. ground cloves

½ tsp. ground allspice

½ tsp. grated nutmeg

1 cup plus 1 tsp. sugar

½ cup (1 stick) soy margarine

1 cup unbleached all-purpose flour

- Preheat the oven to 350°F. Grease a 9-inch pan.
- Cut the apples into thin slices; layer the slices in the pan. Sprinkle the spices and 1 tsp. of the sugar over the apples.
- Melt the margarine in a medium saucepan over medium heat. Add the flour and remaining sugar to the saucepan and stir. Remove from heat and pour over the apples, making sure the apples are evenly coated.
- Bake for 20 to 30 minutes at 350°F or until the crust is lightly browned.

"Cheese"cake

MAKES 8 SERVINGS

Nondairy cream cheese is the secret to this decadent dessert that delivers zero cholesterol but big taste. Smother it with fresh fruit or melted vegan chocolate, caramel, and pecans for a heavenly treat.

    2 8-oz. containers plain nondairy cream cheese
    1 cup sugar
    Juice of one whole lemon
    2 Tbsp. cornstarch
    Dash of vanilla
    Graham cracker crust (you can usually find a vegan version at
        your local grocery store)
    Fresh raspberries or canned cherry pie filling

- Preheat the oven to 350°F.
- In a blender or food processor, thoroughly blend together the nondairy cream cheese, sugar, lemon juice, corn starch, and vanilla and pour into the graham cracker crust.

Bake at 350°F for 60 minutes or until the top is golden brown.

- Allow to cool to room temperature and then cover the top of the cheesecake with fresh fruit or pie filling and chill in the refrigerator until firm, several hours or overnight.

3

Those Incredibly Amusing Animals

On television I saw a hostage who had returned from Iraq. He was asked if he had been abused and he said, "Well, they took me from my home and family and freedom, and there is no greater abuse to anyone."

—A PETA MEMBER'S LETTER

There is an extraordinary place tucked away in the rolling hills of Tennessee. It is the Elephant Sanctuary, and almost as soon as it opened, Barbara, the sanctuary's first rescued elephant, came there to live. I will resist saying "with her packed trunk." She was a "circus elephant"—one of Ringling Bros. and Barnum & Bailey's rejects, but she was extremely knowing and a great communicator. The minute she entered this unexpected refuge, she assumed the role of teacher, bringing everyone at the sanctuary closer to understanding the true nature of elephants.

One unusual thing about Barbara was that she made her own orange juice. Though she didn't like to eat oranges, she loved the juice. The staff members would place her daily mixed produce in front of her, and she'd separate out all the oranges, leave them, and eat everything else. Then she would pull the oranges in, one by one, squish them with her foot to juice them, keep the juice in one place, toss the peel away, and then suck the juice up with her trunk!

Since the beginning of recorded time, human beings the world over have used animals and their body parts as ready sources of amusement. Elephants like Barbara are dressed up in clothes and reduced to a parody of themselves, but the view of animals as objects and sums of their parts goes back a long way.

Animals' bladders and heads were used as footballs long before their whole bodies were put to the test in the gory shows of the Roman circus. Games requiring fewer and less exotic animals were popular in Europe until quite recently; bullbaiting and tying cats' tails together "in sport" were popular wagering activities throughout Europe well into the 1800s.

Today, although cockfighting, like most animal fights, has been rendered illegal in the West, it still thrives in parts of the world like the Philippines, Puerto Rico, Afghanistan, Turkey, and Pakistan, where bears are still pitted against dogs, and international animal protection groups like the World Society for the Protection of Animals are raising a ruckus.

Animals are still dragged all over playing fields and paraded around for sport. For ceremonial purposes to mark the opening of games, doves are often trucked in, held in cages until the magic moment, and then released to fend for themselves in strange surroundings or to try to make their way home. (The Olympic Committee has now switched to bird-shaped kites following complaints that disoriented birds released at the Korean games were burned alive in the Olympic flame.) At county fairs, baby pigs may still be found racing for food, and camels race because someone is digging them in the ribs with their heels. Overweight college students still hit and kick donkeys across gym floors in donkey basketball games, although PETA has persuaded many a school to stop contracting for such tawdry amusements. Ponies—denied water so they will not make unsightly messes—turn endless circles in children's carousels, and hermit crab races and lobster crane games bring thoughtless patrons into beach bars. What a state of affairs.

In Spain, the "proud tradition" of bullfighting has suffered a setback with the revelation that the bulls' eyes are smeared with petroleum jelly to blur their vision and the animals are given laxatives to debilitate them. All that must make it a tiny bit easier for the men and, occasionally, the women, decked out in spangled outfits, to stick their daggers into the bull's shoulders without too much risk. In the barbaric grand finale, as the crowd rises to its feet, the bull's ears are severed and presented to patrons as a trophy. The picadors' horses are often gored, occasionally to death.

Thankfully, there is light at the end of the bullfighting tunnel. Spanish sports television has stopped showing the fights, many Spanish towns have banned them, and a large and ever-growing number of young people look down on such gruesome affairs as their "grandfathers' shame." It is the tourist trade that keeps the gruesome spectacle alive.

In North America, we have our own shames. When the country was being settled, cowboys in the "Wild West" made a sport out of roping, chasing, and otherwise harassing the animals they herded to slaughter. In recent years, this mortifying practice has added new variations: we now have gay rodeo, black rodeo, and other animal-abusive games created by people who, having themselves experienced the sting of prejudice, should know better.

Aside from the more oddball events, the greatest cruelties we visit upon animals in the name of entertainment are institutionalized, just as they are in meat production and experimentation. The institutions under the microscope here are the zoo, the circus, the rodeo, and the animal racing industry. The image of these once harmless-seeming places and pastimes is fast being rightfully tarnished as we gain more knowledge about animals.

In 1849, Thomas Macauley was one of more than 150,000 people who camped out for days to see the first hippopotamus ever to be exhibited on British soil. He was amazed by the sight. Said Macauley, "I have seen the hippopotamus both asleep and awake, and I can assure you that, asleep or awake, he is the ugliest of the works of God."

Today, young people in North America or Europe, whose counterparts in 1849 would have thought a trip to the zoo or circus an experience akin to taking a trip to Mars, no longer get a thrill out of watching a hippo standing virtually motionless near a fake rock in an enclosure the size of their backyards or a lion being controlled by a man in silly boots with a big whip. These children are far more entertained by taking a walk in truly natural surroundings or playing interactive video games or engaging in a myriad of other easily obtainable distractions.

Take a closer look at what's wrong with the biggest animal entertainment institutions in our nation: circuses and zoos. In the What You Can Do section at the end of the chapter, you will find information about other cruel institutions, such as rodeos and racing.

ZOOS: FINE PLACES TO WALK AROUND
AND GRAB A SNACK?

Dale Marcellini, a curator of reptiles at the National Zoo in Washington, D.C., decided to do something interesting one day. He turned his attention from zoo lizards to zoo visitors. He began studying what he calls "this huge population of animals we know nothing about."

Marcellini and his colleagues watched and listened to more than seven hundred people over the course of a few summers. "Basically, we just tracked them," Marcellini says "We'd pick them up at one of the entrances and tail them and record what they did."

The data Marcellini collected was quite surprising to zoo administrators because it exploded the myth that zoos provide an excellent way to teach people respect and understanding for animals. The study showed that zoos are little more than backdrops for people's other preoccupations.

The visitors' conversations rarely pertained to the animals. When a person did make a passing comment about an animal, it was usually to remark that someone they knew looked like that baboon or hippopotamus in the enclosure in front of them or to speculate as to how an octopus or some other animal could eat a person. The most common words used to describe animals showed no respect or newly found knowledge of the species. Rather, animals were mostly described as "dirty," "cute," "ugly," "funny-looking," and "strange."

Marcellini found that almost 60 percent of visitors' time was spent walking from place to place, almost 10 percent was spent eating, and other chunks of time were spent resting, taking bathroom breaks, and shopping. When visitors were actually milling around in exhibit areas, they spent less than eight seconds per snake and one minute with the lions. Père david's deer, expected to be extinct when the last deer dies in the zoo, received a mere twenty-seven seconds of attention per person. Marcellini concluded that people were "treating the exhibits like wallpaper."

It is not that zoos have gone downhill. They began as menageries for the well-heeled, including Kublai Khan, Alexander the Great, Henry III, and Pope Leo X, then developed into moneymaking enterprises that the public could visit, usually for a fee, to view the "weird and wonderful creatures" captured from then relatively novel expeditions to South America, Africa, and other "faraway" places.

When the Aztec ruler Montezuma's private zoo was unearthed, archaeologists found not only the bones of pumas, jaguars, and birds of prey, but also the skeletons of albino and hunchback humans, people whose deformities had made them curiosities exotic enough to put on display. In about 1904, the Bronx Zoo put a Congolese Pygmy on display. He spoke no English and no one spoke his language, but everyone had a good gawk. At about the same time, some "Eskimo boys" from northern Greenland were exhibited in a traveling show, and over the family's protestations, the skeleton of one Inuit's father ended up in the American Museum of Natural History. One can only imagine how future generations will shake their heads at today's practices and wonder how we could be so blind to the family relationships and rights of today's animals.

Early on, zoos figured out that adult gorillas, giraffes, and other animals were too strong and difficult to capture, so zoo collectors devised a simple plan; they shot all the adult animals in the family group and netted the babies. However, most of the babies didn't make it. Field zoologists and behaviorists, like Dr. Birute Galdikas, estimate that for every primate who arrived alive in the West, eight or more perished, succumbing to untreated injuries or illness, dehydration, and malnutrition at the holding stations, cruel transportation through the jungle, and the trauma of overseas shipment. It is a shameful toll.

Removed from their real mothers, baby gorillas and other great ape infants grow up bottle-fed, diapered, and spoken to in baby talk until they reach puberty. At that point, a chimpanzee is at least ten times as strong as the strongest man and can lift him off the ground, something a juvenile chimpanzee, trained to walk on a harness and leash, illustrated perfectly by running up a tall tree and pulling his handler up the trunk behind him.

At puberty, the combination of these animals' powerful hormonal drives and their phenomenal strength dooms them to sudden banishment from human company. After years of being mollycoddled and treated as precious little people, the chimpanzees suddenly find themselves booted out of the house, dumped in a barren cage, and treated like dangerous beasts.

Added to this traumatic upheaval is the often horrifying experience, for an ape raised only with human beings, of coming face-to-face for the very first time with others of his own kind. Washoe is a chimpanzee who was raised to eat at the table with her human "parents." She lived as part of a human household and went to the drive-in for ice cream. She wore diapers, played in the yard, and was taught American Sign Language. When she matured, Washoe was introduced to other chimpanzees and nearly went into cardiac arrest. Frantic, she signed to her humans something along the lines of, "Washoe want out! Let Washoe out! Big dirty black hairy dogs here!"

As for marine animals, whales, dolphins, and orcas usually come to the aquarium after being kidnapped from their pods and families at sea by "aqua cowboys," men who use speedboats to corner a whole group of sea mammals and then net the babies. Like ape infants raised in captivity, these babies have missed out on the mothering skills nature intended them to learn in the bosom of their real families. When they give birth in captivity, they can be frightened and confused by the presence of the new life-form that has suddenly appeared before them, not knowing what to do with it and not realizing they are meant to suckle and nurture the infant. The result is the sort of article in the newspaper that reads, "Zoo/Aquarium Keepers Step in to Save Baby (whale, panda, gorilla) When Mother Abandons Her."

Of course, the cycle is perpetuated if the baby animal survives. Most do not.

A ZOO BY ANY OTHER NAME . . .

Although the majority of big zoos have finally done away with such debasing and silly shenanigans as dressing chimpanzees up in human clothing and making them have tea parties or juggle, zoos have a long way to go to redeem themselves. Nor do they live up to all their public relations talk about breeding endangered species to preserve the gene pool. It is estimated that only 5 percent of the world's ten thousand or more zoos can honestly claim that they do anything whatsoever for the "conservation" of animals—assuming that there is even a mouse hole of habitat left into which to reestablish these endangered animals.

Some zoos recognize that they do not have the best reputations, but instead of doing an about-face and putting their money into habitat protection *in the animals' disappearing homelands*, or setting up programs in Africa and other countries that would provide an incentive for native peoples to stop poaching and encroaching, they simply change their names. When one New York zoo decided to call itself a "conservation park," it prompted a local radio commentator to remark that, given the zoo's wretched record of animal care, "that's like a bunch of rapists deciding to call themselves a dating service."

Existing zoos would provide a valuable service by evolving into desperately needed sanctuaries for displaced wildlife—the elderly bears dumped by a bankrupt circus, the baboons left on the New York docks by a traveling show that sailed back to Russia, the gorilla who spent twenty years in a cage in a shopping mall before activists persuaded the owner to let him go. Instead, the majority of zoos still treat animals as commodities, moving "specimens" about as if they were lifeless portraits in a traveling art exhibit, and separating lovers of many years standing, simply to provide a new mate for some other zoo's collection.

In 1996, I wrote an editorial that appeared in newspapers in several states, wondering what would happen to the gorilla baby at the Brookfield Zoo in suburban Chicago whose mother is Binti Jua.

Binti captured international headlines, and a great deal of fuss was made over her, after a three-year-old boy fell into the zoo's gorilla pit. He tumbled over the wall and landed in the dry concrete pit that divides the gorillas from the public. The boy lay there motionless while his mother watched helplessly and on-lookers screamed because several large gorillas were in the enclosure, including a male silverback who was many hundreds of pounds of sheer muscle.

Binti was not small either, and a gasp went up from the crowd as she began to head for the child. Before anyone could stop her, Binti had clambered down into the pit and picked up the human child. Very gently, she cradled him in her arms, despite the weight of her own child on her back. She headed directly for the gate through which her keepers came and went and deliberately set the boy down there, then waited for help. The child recovered.

Binti Jua was not the only gorilla to show such concern for the young of her captors' species. A few years earlier, in a zoo on an island off the coast of France, a huge male silverback named Rambo performed a similar act, using his body to shield a child who had fallen into an exhibit from younger male gorillas. Both Rambo and Binti revealed that a soft heart beats inside that King Kong chest.

I asked in my editorial whether the zoo was likely to return the favor and save Binti's child. The answer would likely be a resounding "No!" Babies in zoos do not often remain with their mothers and family, as would happen in nature. They are commodities, and that means they are usually lent, swapped, or sold to another zoo, sometimes even shipped overseas to spend their lives in confinement elsewhere. In most zoo's eyes, a baby gorilla is not an individual or part of a gorilla family unit. He or she is a marketable good to be displayed, bred, shuffled about, and used. Miraculously, perhaps because of Binti Jua's fame, her children have been allowed to stay with her.

Compassionate people might question the wholesome facade of zoos if they knew the truth: many zoos enjoy cozy and very hush-hush relationships with research departments at universities and allow experiments on animals to be conducted on zoo premises. These experiments take place in buildings that are off-limits to the public, and sometimes zoos ship animals off to labs. I remember, years ago, learning that the Detroit zoo had sent a group of crab-eating macaques to terminal research when they became "unstylish." They replaced them with an exhibit of trendier snow monkeys. Zoos often compete for public attention by entertaining and providing ever more titillating species rather than educating the public about the animals unlucky enough to be common or out of style.

Today, the Detroit zoo has taken positive steps by hiring a more knowledgeable and compassionate director. Ron Kagan caused a furor when he was among the first zoo directors to declare that keeping elephants in zoos had to stop because their behavioral needs are too complex for any zoo to meet.

Some zoos still haven't learned the basics about animals. They have gone as far as buying certain exotic reptiles and primates on the black market when trade in them is illegal, and some dispose of their "surplus" lions and other animals by sending them to cheap, run-down traveling shows in South America or even to game ranches to be shot for a fee. So much for their so-called respect for the animal kingdom.

NOT EVEN A NICE PLACE TO VISIT

The Born Free Foundation in the United Kingdom has done its homework on how animals feel about captivity. The foundation's opinion, based on studies by investigators who spent three years traveling to over one hundred zoos across Britain, Europe, India, and North America, is that the animals go mad in captivity. Deprived of their natural homelands, natural social structures, and outlets for many of the skills that have naturally evolved in their species, animals develop abnormal "stereotypic behavior," "psychosis," or "zoochosis."

This means that animals try to compensate for their great loneliness, frustration, boredom, and loss of control over their lives by making repetitive and obsessive movements. They bob their heads up and down constantly, rock back and forth, walk in circles, wearing dirt trails through their enclosures or indentations in the cement of their cage floors, suck their bars like Popsicles (factory-farmed pigs do this, too), throw up and repeatedly eat their own vomit, and mutilate themselves by picking on their arms even after they have created bloody wounds.

Dr. Phil Murphy, head of Clinical Psychology for Mental

Handicap in Norfolk, England, told reporters that such behaviors "can still be found in institutions caring for our severely mentally disturbed patients." Of course, a zoo fits just that description because its inmates are driven mad.

Sometimes zookeepers resort to medication to treat the misery zoos cause. A case in point is Gus, a famous polar bear housed in New York's Central Park Zoo. Gus came to the public's attention when he became the first "zoo animal" to be given Prozac. For over four years, this very depressed bear spent almost every waking moment swimming, back and forth in the small cement pool in his enclosure. Perhaps the viewing public enjoyed the look of the "icebergs" constructed in Gus's enclosure, but to a lonely, bored bear a long way from home they were just big meaningless pieces of fiberglass that did nothing to prevent his descent into madness. We are told that the Prozac helped. But Gus is still swimming alone—back and forth, back and forth.

In aquariums like the much-touted one in Baltimore Harbor, dolphins and other sea animals routinely die of stress, which sometimes is physically manifested as ulcers. SeaWorld has an abysmal record. They were recently quoted in the media as acknowledging eleven dolphin deaths since 1990 at the Mirage Hotel dolphin exhibit in Las Vegas. Dolphins and orcas can develop a drooping dorsal fin before noticeably losing weight or dropping dead; some marine mammals develop vision problems from the chlorine and other chemicals put in their tanks, while some develop nutritional problems from the diet they are fed. (Zoos often provide food that departs so far from the animals' natural diet that they have been criticized by even their own keepers for feeding low-quality "straw" to grazing, hoofed "stock," and feeding horse meat to naturally vegetarian gorillas.)

The stress animals in aquariums experience is likely caused

in large part by never having freedom or privacy. Enormous sea animals are kept in tanks that, compared to the hundreds of miles they may travel in their true homes, must be like living in a bathtub. They have to breathe and drink their own diluted urine and the waste of the others in the tank with them; they are unable to use their sonar, which, in captivity, simply bounces off the tank walls; they can never jump in the waves or choose a mate; and they can never escape the noise of tens of thousands of visitors, whose steps vibrate through the cement walls of their tanks all day long, every day.

Zoos and aquariums are artificial constructs that are antithetical to our contemporary understanding of our place in nature—not as its master, but as one part of a whole. They display to children mere shadows of animals, defeated beasts who are not behaving as they should, and they teach all the wrong lessons: that it is acceptable to imprison animals, to deprive them of free flight and travel, to forbid them the chance to establish their natural territory, to breed and separate them as we, not they, please; and to let them go nuts from a great loneliness of spirit.

A truly educational experience might be one in which human beings returned to the zoo as exhibits. Actors have performed this role at the Baltimore, Maryland, zoo, at a zoo in Canada, and in France. The purpose is the same: to inspire introspection about our own roles in the great web of life.

In the future, we may see robots replace the conventional zoo, like the 439-pound virtual reality gorilla developed by the Georgia Institute of Technology. To interact with him, you put on a headset, step into a computer-generated gorilla habitat, and meet up with a gorilla troop. If the "visitor" behaves properly, she or he may be rewarded with a grooming session from a motherly female.

Until those happy times arrive, every summer, during peak zoo visiting time, volunteers from PETA can often be found standing on the sidewalks outside zoos such as the National Zoo in Washington, D.C. They are there to hand out pamphlets, urging visitors to "Be a Zoochecker." The pamphlets contain a series of boxes visitors can check off whenever they see an animal whirling in circles or showing some other "zoonotic" behavior. Realizing such problems exist allows parents and their children to reevaluate their opinions about zoos and to focus on the plight of the animals.

Many will never see only zoo in quite the same light again.

RANI'S STORY AND HOW TYKE ESCAPED

Rani was the first captive elephant I ever met. Every single day for many years she stood outside the Ashoka Hotel in New Delhi, India, from sunrise to late at night, waiting to be prodded into action whenever a tourist fancied a ride. She wore a jewel-encrusted cloth mantle over her head, and her brow and pink skin were painted with an intricate pattern of paisley and dots.

When I first saw Rani I couldn't have been much taller than her knee, but she was extremely gentle with me, even when she could see that her handler, Ram, had succumbed to the midday heat and conked out under a bush. She allowed me to hang on to her legs and would gently blow air into my hair and down my neck to cool me in the blistering heat or hold my wrist in her trunk and sway slowly back and forth.

If business was slow, Ram would dig the bull hook into Rani's neck, just behind her ear, to make her kneel. Then he would hoist me into the pretty wooden howdah on her back. I would kick my legs over the edge of the little box as Rani lurched up and forward, then lumbered slowly down the hotel driveway and into the street. I remember the air was choked with the fumes of unfiltered fuel from the hundreds of little putt-putt motorcycle cabs and decorated trucks fighting it out on the street. Even high up on Rani's back, I could feel the carbon particles in my throat. I didn't think how much worse it must have been for her.

In fact, I didn't think about the quality of her life at all! Until one day when I asked Ram where Rani had come from and he explained that young elephants are taken from their families and "broken." He described how they must be chained and beaten until they learn to listen and behave. (It wasn't until many years later that I saw a *National Geographic* special on American television showing men carrying out exactly that barbaric and inhumane system. Since then, I've learned that deep in the jungles of Thailand, elephants are also chained down, flat, to the ground and beaten in preparation for circus life in Europe and North America.)

Rani died long before I had learned that elephant calves left unmolested in the wild, like orca infants, stay at their mothers' sides for a decade or longer; that elephants cradle their lost relatives' skulls in their trunks; that they use branches as flyswatters and to sweep paths, and sticks to draw pictures in the dirt and scratch themselves in inaccessible places; that they communicate in rumbles at frequencies so low humans cannot detect the sounds without sophisticated equipment.

There are up to 16,000 Asian elephants in captivity worldwide—including as many as 300 in North America—and up to 700 African elephants in captivity—including 230 in North America. Sometimes the elephants stop behaving like windup toys and crush the bones and breath out of a keeper, make a break for it, go berserk, and head for the unreachable hills. They never get there, of course, as they are gunned down, felled in a barrage of forty, fifty, or more shots.

Most simply endure. Their spirits are broken during capture and, later, God help them, when they are trained for the ring. Many are drugged to calm them down. Otherwise, they would all use their immense strength to fight back against the human hand of tyranny. They would refuse to be kept chained between performances like coats on a rack, refuse to be backed up ramps into railroad cars and into trailers like so many cars being parked out of the way.

In Queens, New York, Debbie and Frieda, two elephants from the Clyde Beatty-Cole Bros. Circus, bolted from a circus tent during a performance, triggering a panic that left a dozen people injured. It was the second incident with Debbie and Frieda in just two months. Earlier, the pair had run amok, smashing through a plate glass window in downtown Hanover, Pennsylvania. A few years later, while with another circus, Debbie rampaged again throughout a church in Charlotte, North Carolina, nearly trampling worshippers.

Three times in one summer a "circus elephant" went berserk and crushed her captors. "Flora" crushed the skull of a Moscow Circus interpreter minutes before a planned appearance on a morning television show. In Honolulu, a twenty-one-year-old elephant named Tyke deliberately stomped her trainer to death, waving his body aloft in her trunk afterward, then injured spectators as she tore out of the Circus International tent, only to die in a barrage of gunfire. It was the second elephant attack at that circus in a week. The summer before, Janet, an old elephant who had been kept on repeated doses of tranquilizers, charged out of the Great American Circus ring in Florida, carrying a box full of children on her back. She was shot forty-seven times by an off-duty police officer before she died. Police officer Blaine Doyle, the man who pulled the trigger, said, "I think these elephants are trying to tell us that circuses are not what God created them for."

Janet, the elephant shot in Florida, had appeared under several names. When an elephant starts to "act up" or "go bad," it is common to pass him or her on to another circus under a different name or to keep them and start calling them something else to deflect attention and, presumably, to escape liability. This ruse goes back many years. Hannibal, who was brought to the United States in 1824, killed at least seven people, and when he went on a rampage was stabbed repeatedly with pitchforks, a technique that couldn't have helped improve his disposition.

While pachyderms' polite protestations have sometimes turned desperate, circus proprietors remain complacent, sitting in their countinghouses counting out their money while their habit of slugging and drugging uppity elephants only worsens the problem.

Elephants have the largest brains of any mammal on the face of the earth. They are creative, altruistic, and kind. Imagine what it must be like for them to be ordered around, courtesy of a bull hook, every moment of their lives. They live over seventy years in their homelands, but their average life in captivity is reduced to fourteen years. Because of stress, traveling in boxcars, and being stabled in damp basements, many captive elephants have arthritis, gammy legs, and tuberculosis in a strain that is contagious to their keepers and to children who ride on their backs.

Left to their own devices on their own turf, elephants enjoy extended family relationships: aunties babysit, mothers teach junior life skills such as how to use different kinds of leaves and mud to ward off sunburn and insect bites, babies play together under watchful eyes, lovemaking is gentle and complex, and elephant relatives mourn their dead. In captivity, of course, elephants are deprived of all such experiences. Life under the Big Top means performing heavy manual labor, paying attention to your trainer, and feeling his "mahout stick" (a wooden rod with a cruel pointed metal circular end) bite into your flesh. It means leg chains between acts, including "martingales" (shackles that are used on males during "must"—a time of heightened sexual desire), and in cases of severe disobedience, fastening the elephant's head to his front feet. It means the loss of all comfort and warmth from your father and mother, your siblings and children. It means having no long-term friends.

Behaviorists tell us that elephants can and do cry from loss of social interaction and from physical abuse. Small wonder these magnificent beings can't always keep from going mad waiting in line night after night, eyes riveted on the man with the metal hook, then circling to the music in their beaded headdresses.

Civil rights activist Dick Gregory has long championed the plight of elephants in circuses and traveling shows. Standing outside Madison Square Garden on the opening night of a Ringling Bros. circus tour, he told passersby, "Elephants in circuses represent the domination and oppression we have fought against for so long," and urged them not to buy tickets.

Of course, other animals suffer in circuses. After all, leopards don't jump through flaming hoops because they find it enjoyable, orangutans don't skate around in a dress and roller skates because it is comfortable, and bears don't choose to spend their Decembers riding a bicycle over a barrel. The muzzle, the neck chain, the whip, the chair, the bull hook, and the electric shock prod clenched in the handler's palm make that deduction easy, as does a little basic understanding of animals' very nature. Orangutans are naturally arboreal, so their feet turn inward, and they have difficulty standing upright for very long; tigers and lions are afraid of fire and avoid it at all costs; and bears' biological clocks tell them to hibernate when cold weather comes.

Simply put, the circus business is not a gentle trade. In his book, *The Circus Kings,* Henry North Ringling wrote, "It is not usually a pretty sight to see the big cats trained. When he [the trainer] starts off they are all chained to the pedestals, and ropes are put around their necks to choke them down and make them obey. All sorts of other brutalities are used to force them to respect the trainer and learn their tricks. They work from fear."

That is exactly what PETA's investigator found at Tiger's Eye Productions, a now-defunct circus training school in Florida, when PETA responded to a whistle-blower complaint. Videotapes of training practices there showed big cats being dragged around in chains, hit with broom handles and fists, slapped and punched across the face, and having ax handles shoved down their throats. The cats were trucked in thunderstorms and left in open cages in the fierce Florida heat at gas stations and other cheap venues where the trainer was paid to perform as part of sales stunts.

In Taiwan, I once visited the compound and later met with performers from the American International Circus, a hodge-podge of circus stars from all over the world. When I sat down with the Russian woman who ran the bear act, unknown to her I had already seen her miserable, dull-coated bears in their small, barren, and rusty traveling cages, including one female bear who had become "unmanageable" and who sucked her teeth constantly, a sign of severe stress.

"Natasha" answered my questions with great charm. "Where do you get your bears?" I asked. "They are all orphans." She smiled. "I rescue them when they are found without mothers in the woods." She was so used to this speech that the words came out without hesitation. "What happens to them when they get old?" "I send them to a wonderful retirement park, just outside Moscow, so they can live out their old age," came the pat reply. "Is it difficult to train them?" "No, I raise them as my babies. They love me. To them, I am their mother. With little treats, they learn their tricks from me when they are very, very small." "Do they ever give you trouble?" "Trouble? To their mother? Never!"

Later I had coffee with the ringmaster, a burly Irishman. He had no idea I was with an animal protection group. I told him I was impressed that Natasha could manage such big bears.

"Oh, that woman's tough as nails," he said. "She has a little iron bar that never leaves her hand. When one of those bears gives her any lip, she smashes him on the nose with it. One of her assistants mouthed off at her a few weeks ago and she knocked him out cold. No one messes with her."

LIKE FAMILY, MY FOOT!

Bobby Berosini, once a star performer on the Las Vegas strip, loved "his" orangutans too. At least that's what he told everyone, referring to the apes he used onstage as his "children." "I am their dad" was one of his catchphrases.

Yet, what kind of "dad" was he? Octavio Gesmundo, a dancer in the casino act that appeared before Berosini's, had heard what he described as "awful sounds" coming from behind the curtain just before Berosini entered the spotlight. After hearing this commotion night after night, Octavio decided to set up a hidden camera backstage.

Berosini starred in two shows every night, bringing on the orangs in their little sparkly boxer shorts, making them sit on upturned tubs, wiggle their backsides, and give the finger to the audience in the smoke-filled room. What Octavio recorded, every night, twice a night, for eight nights in a row, was Berosini and his assistant secretly beating the animals with a metal bar, pinching their shoulders, pulling their hair, and punching them in the face just before the orangs were walked onstage.

Later, in court (Berosini sued Gesmundo and PETA for allowing the tapes to be shown on television!), Berosini, referring throughout the trial to the orangs as his "kids," told the judge that such behavior is acceptable because "you have to get the animals' attention." He likened the "discipline" he doled out as "nothing more" than what a parent would do to get the attention of a misbehaving child in a supermarket.

Orangutans are gentle animals, known in their homelands of Borneo and Sumatra as "people of the forest." But the Berosini orangutans spent their lives in isolation confinement, totally dominated by their handlers. Using one of the oldest tricks of circus lore, Berosini kept them stored, individually, between acts, on a bus in solid metal containers. He had air holes drilled into the boxes near the top. The orangutans' only "freedom" came when Berosini opened the doors to clean the boxes or to give the orangs food. Their only other excursion was generally the hour or so when the animals were "performing" onstage. Berosini cultivated their absolute dependency, making sure they knew that he held the key to everything in their perverted lives: he was the man who could let them stand up after being hunched over for hours on end in their boxes, who decided whether they would starve or receive nourishment, and who could ease their thirst or not.

Burning for revenge, Berosini filed a $20 million lawsuit against Gesmundo, PETA, and others, for invasion of privacy and libel. While at first he gained the upper hand with his "my children, the orangutans" line, the tide of public opinion and subsequent court rulings turned against the entertainer. His credibility eroded before his eyes as more and more people saw the tapes and heard a litany of testimony of abuse spanning more than a decade. Berosini told jurors he had only "tapped" the apes with "a little wooden bird perch." But one eyewitness described picking up the instrument Berosini used to strike the animals and recalled, "It was similar to a heavy-duty welding rod, approximately sixteen inches long." Yet another eyewitness reported watching in horror as Berosini "repeatedly punched an orangutan with both fists." Another reported hearing Berosini yelling at the orangutans and watching the bus in which they were kept rock back and forth as he heard them being beaten.

Berosini's career hit the skids, the USDA compelled him to build enclosures for the apes, the US Fish and Wildlife Service took away his license to buy and sell endangered species, and he found himself out of work and facing more than $1 million in legal fees and a judgment of more than $200,000 to PETA for court costs.

Things started to get a bit rocky for other members of this old circus family too. Berosini's niece, Brigitte, was bitten on the neck and face by a five-hundred-pound tiger during her Las Vegas act, and at almost the same time, Berosini's brother, Otto, ran into trouble. Government authorities found nine of the big cats Otto used in his own circus act living in small traveling crates on an Indian reservation about fifty miles outside Las Vegas. A leopard found in a pool of vomit and lions suffering from urine burns were taken into custody by the government. Pasha, one of the tigers, who had been lying in her own excrement, was not only too weak to stand up, but also dehydrated and suffering from abscesses and infection, died shortly afterward.

It took two decades, but in 2008, the Great Ape Trust, a

charity that rehabilitates apes, acquired custody of all the orang-utans who had been abused by Bobbi Berosini. In July of that year, the first two, Katie and her three-year-old son, born into entertainment in Hollywood, arrived at the Trust's sanctuary to start their new life. The others, including Poppi, then forty years old, joined them some months later. At PETA, the champagne corks were a-poppin' for Poppi and the whole long-suffering orangutan family!

BIG NAMES BLAST THE BIG TOP

The big circuses love movie stars to be seen at their openings, but many stars are too wise to touch such an event with a barge pole and reject lucrative offers to "see and be seen." Some stars have shown how much they object to the domination and abuse of animals by unhesitatingly condemning Berosini; *Golden Girls* star Rue McClanahan, PETA's honorary chairperson, flew to Las Vegas with *American Top Forty*'s icon Casey Kasem, comedian Kevin Nealon, and baseball great Tony La Russa, all at their own expense, to stand up for the apes.

Gérard Depardieu, Juliette Binoche, and other celebrities have signed letters to Prince Rainier of Monaco, asking him please to bar animals from appearing in the dreadful "International Circus Festival of Monte Carlo." Every year, to mark that "celebration," the beastwagons of notorious circus families roll over the mountains, bringing a sad collection of landlocked sea lions and monkeys in frilly dresses to perform for the Grimaldi family, their guests, and paying customers. Among the participants are the Chipperfields, a longtime circus family. In England, Mary Chipperfield was charged with multiple counts of cruelty to animals in 1998, the very same year in which one of her sons shot a caged tiger to death in a fit of rage while working with Ringling Bros. in the United States.

Box office stars like Alec Baldwin and Kim Basinger may not be together, but each speaks out fiercely against the exploitation of animals. They have attended hearings against the carriage-horse trade, protesting how overworked these poor worn-down animals are, toiling in the heat, their noses at tailpipe height in the traffic, unable to lie down at work's end because they are stored like boxes in tiny stalls that do not allow them to take two steps. Alec has narrated PETA's touching video of circus life, "Cheap Tricks," and Kim has appeared before the US Congress to appeal for stricter laws to protect the victims of entertainment. She wrote personally to the USDA on PETA's behalf in the case of Kenny, an elephant used by Ringling Bros.

Kenny came to Kim's attention when a whistle-blower called PETA to relate that, although just three years old, the little Indian elephant had already been separated from his mother and was traveling and performing for Ringling.

Ringling was fully aware that Kenny had become ill, yet they still forced him to perform. Even when Kenny was "wobbly" on his feet and "wailing," he was taken into the ring and made to perform in two shows. By the third show, Kenny somehow managed to make it into the ring but couldn't perform. He died later that day, and Ringling had his body hauled away.

Kim Basinger immediately asked the US secretary of agriculture to investigate the case. The agency did just that and charged Ringling with negligence under the Animal Welfare Act. Ringling settled the case, paying $20,000 under a court agreement. It would not be the first or last time Ringling was in trouble.

Alec Baldwin says it took him years to realize what circus life must be like for the animals. In an *Animal Times* article he wrote for PETA, he appealed to compassionate people not to go to animal circuses but instead to ask themselves four simple questions: (1) Where did these animals come from? (2) How are these animals kept between shows? (3) What would they rather be doing? and (4) What will become of them in the end?

It is unlikely that any of the answers would make us feel comfortable about supporting the continuation of any animal show. For example, in the case of an elephant, the answers are probably: (1) The lush Indian jungle. (2) Shackled constantly by their front and back legs (or inside a dark train boxcar traveling between towns). (3) Walking among the trees, bathing in the river, feeling the sun on their backs, being with their families. (4) They'll probably be sold to a cheap zoo and die lonely and sad.

Of course, the answer to "How are they kept?" is "beyond abysmally" in the case of many of the less attractive and endearing animals unlucky enough to end up in a circus. In *The Rose-Tinted Menagerie*, an exquisitely researched and very moving book about life for animals in the circus, the author, William Johnson, describes how crocodiles are kept for most of their lives in total darkness in minuscule tanks and boxes, the lids kept on, the animals' mouths taped shut.

How much better, then, if we are to have circuses at all, to have ones composed entirely of human performers: jugglers, tightrope walkers, fire-eaters, clowns, acrobats, and daredevils who are there of their own free will. There are umpteen animal-free circuses, but perhaps the most amazing is the Cirque du Soleil. This enormous circus, which performs all over the world, beautifully costumes its performers and choreographs its acts in ways highlighting human talents and feats, which leaves its audiences spellbound.

There is another unexpectedly refreshing aspect to an animal-free circus. It hits you immediately: the absence of the sawdust the old-fashioned circuses use to sop up animal waste! In fact, the only smell in an animal-free circus is that of fresh popcorn.

THERE'S NO UNION FOR ANIMAL ACTORS

Caring moviegoers need to be on their toes—sometimes all the way up on them and striding out of the theater—if they see anything on-screen they suspect could be animal abuse. Consumers should be aware too, for when animals are part of a commercial or print advertisement, if the animals are real, so too may be the problems that commonly accompany their use.

The most common abuses occur behind the scenes, where animals are trained and housed. Whistle-blowers from films and filmed advertisements have complained of animal "actors" collapsing from the heat of the bright arc lights, being deprived of food, being prodded and goaded, and being scared by the clapboards or gunfire. Abuse can be as subtle as forcing cats to stay awake for hours so they can fall asleep "on cue," and using a "tie-down," an invisible filament wrapped around an animal's waist and attached to an unseen anchor.

Even though the use of "trip wires," rigged to make animals fall, is prohibited in the United States, many movies are made overseas, in Spain, Portugal, and other countries where no such restrictions apply.

Other abuses include chickens being gratuitously run over in movie chase scenes, and even being killed on the set when the movie becomes a real-life "snuff film," with goldfish being vacuumed out of the water and tropical fish tanks purposely smashed in fight scenes. Cats have been drowned after being tied to a raft in a "river adventure," small animals are sometimes given no choice but to fight their natural enemies in contrived encounters, and rats have been killed after being put in liquid oxygen for underwater scenes.

Sawed-off pool cues and blackjacks have been used on film sets to keep chimpanzees and other animals in line. The orangutan who starred as the lovable "Clyde" in *Any Which Way You Can* is alleged to have been beaten by his handlers behind the scenes and later died after the filming. An autopsy showed that the gentle ape died of cerebral hemorrhage.

Unless you are watching a nature show, most apes you see on television or in the movies are babies. In the rain forests, they would not leave their mothers' sides for eight or more years. In Hollywood, they are props, involuntary "actors" who are already washed up and discarded as too strong and willful to handle when they reach puberty.

Primate behaviorist Dr. Roger Fouts recalls a conversation with movie producers who were considering adding live animals to a film they were making. "I told them that the traditional circus method of training chimpanzees has been referred to as the 'two-by-four technique,' meaning that the animal is beaten into capitulation. I also explained a common method is to keep the young chimpanzee in a small box and only take him out to act or for training."

Even the presence of a big star doesn't always guarantee compassion. The movie *Speed Racer* stars Emile Hirsch, Christina Ricci, Susan Sarandon, and Matthew Fox, but that star power didn't seem to matter. In June 2007, PETA contacted Warner Bros. regarding concerns about the use of live chimpanzees in *Speed Racer*. Back came the pat response from Warner Bros.: the company "does not tolerate the mistreatment of animals by any of its productions, and there has been no animal abuse on the set of *Speed Racer*." But was that true?

During filming, one of the chimpanzees bit a stand-in actor, and a monitor with the American Humane Association (AHA) witnessed an animal trainer "in an uncontrolled impulse, hit [a] chimpanzee." If a trainer is bold enough to strike an animal in front of an AHA monitor, you can only imagine what may take place behind the scenes when no one is watching.

There is also the matter of where the animals come from. Animals from one part of the world can find themselves shipped to the opposite ends of the earth to make a movie. For one of the early *Batman* movies, for instance, easily stressed penguins, native to Antarctica and the sub-Antarctic islands, were shipped to California and kept on the set for months and then harnessed into "missile" gear.

There are some safeguards. Filmmakers are required to ask the American Humane Association (AHA) to review the script and make recommendations or be present on the set or on location during filming. To get the AHA "seal of approval," or "end credit disclaimer," the filmmakers must meet certain reasonable standards, including not killing or injuring an animal for the sake of the production and not treating an animal inhumanely to force a performance. The AHA also requires that all hunting and fishing scenes be simulated; that animals in performing stunts be "properly trained"; and that all animals receive exercise, rest, and veterinary care if sick or injured.

AHA's influence has been a great help to the many animals used in movies, but in this age of animatronics, robotics, computer simulation, and special effects, there is never an excuse for bringing "wild" or "exotic" species into the act at all. If Robert Redford could use mechanical salmon in the fishing scenes from *A River Runs Through It*, today's filmmakers can certainly always do the same.

As for commercials, few are as offensive as a 2008 phone company ad where two pit bulls are shown chained in a junk yard, as if that is just how things should be, or a soda ad that tried to make a chump out of a "dumb" chimpanzee. On the other hand, there are the gorgeous ads by companies like Honda, that label a canine-friendly car as "Man's best friend's best friend," and those by Bridgestone, highlighting compassion toward woodland animals. These are a joy to see, for they show real-life relationships without interference.

After all, what is more beautiful than respecting animals by choosing to leave them in peace in their natural environs? It is a sign that we respect the subjects of our interest and that we realize that they too have other things to do, other places to go, families to raise, and lives to live. With current technology allowing moviemakers to create any illusion they fancy, from the realistic to the fantastic, from super animatronics to blue screen insets and more, there is no excuse for exploiting animals for the screen.

WHAT YOU CAN DO

Animals in Entertainments

Zoos

Observe respectfully. Instead of visiting zoos, put on your hiking boots and without interfering, observe animals' natural behaviors on their turf. Rainy day activists and less adventurous types can learn from *National Geographic* specials, travel videos, and zoology or nature books, as well as from visits to a local nature center or to wildlife preserves abroad or by subscribing to wildlife protection organizations' magazines.

Boycott roadside zoos. Never pay to visit a roadside zoo. Instead, write a letter to the local newspaper, the chamber of commerce, and the state's tourism department voicing your objections to such cruel exhibits. Ask for their intervention and support in getting roadside zoos improved or dismantled.

Be a zoochecker. When you visit a zoo, take a questionnaire with you and return it, completed, to PETA.

Draw public attention. Sandra Van de Werd of Amsterdam spent more than thirteen days in a cage in front of Artis Zoo, one of the most famous and cruel zoos in Holland, to protest conditions there. Heightened European awareness of the plight of animals in captivity led to the proposal for a revolutionary "zoo" without animals.

For Students

Create Alternatives. If your class ever goes to a zoo, ask for an alternative assignment, or ask your teacher to give each student a sheet of zoocheck questions so that the whole class can be zoo sleuths. Visit ZooInsiders.com for information on what to look for when at the zoo.

Write letters. Write to the zoo director and ask any questions you may have, like what happens to the baby animals when they get big, or why some animals are in small cages or where have all the animals come from.

Marine Theme Parks

Educate travel agents. When you make hotel reservations, tell your travel agent that you will not stay anyplace that features a dolphin swim program or caged birds.

Write to the government. Write to the US Fish and Wildlife Service (FWS.gov) and your congressperson to ask for a ban on any capture and confinement of marine mammals. To find your representative's address, go to: House.gov/WriteRep.

Join organizations. Join organizations like PETA (PETA.org), Earth Island Institute (EarthIsland.org), and the Sea Shepherd Conservation Society (SeaShepherd.org), who fight to protect marine life.

Watch local aquariums. Monitor your local aquarium's activities. If aquarium officials are considering an expansion or want to add (or replace) a dolphin to their "stock," protest vigorously to city officials, local legislators, and in letters to publications. Suggest a display of animal models, aquatic plants, and coral reefs instead. When friends and relatives visit, steer them away from the local fish and marine mammal prison. Instead, show them your city's museums and historical sites, or catch a movie.

Leaflet. It's exciting to see how many people are grateful for information and even turn back, or never visit again, when you hand them a leaflet. Go to PETA.org for resources.

Rodeos

Educate sponsors. Tell rodeo sponsors that you will not patronize their "entertainment," and get others to join you.

Demonstrate. Demonstrate and leaflet outside rodeo events. PETALiterature.com has great flyers you can use to educate countless people.

Read reports. Eric Mills worked hard on a fifteen-month campaign with a coalition of California activists who were victorious in getting Hayward Police Officers Association to abandon rodeos as fund-raisers. The campaign culminated with a gut-wrenching six-page report on rodeos sent to the Hayward Area Recreation District Board of Supervisors. Others fighting the rodeo blight can visit PETA.org for information on how to do it.

Join parades. In Davie, Florida, a red convertible Cadillac joined a procession including a float sponsored by the Professional Rodeo Cowboys Association. Entered in the parade by members of ARFF (Animal Rights Foundation of Florida), the convertible's original noncontroversial decorations were replaced along the route with banners reading, RODEOS: CRUELTY FOR A BUCK. The caring "cowboys" and "cowgirls" handed out antirodeo flyers and a "horse" waved to onlookers, including the mayor.

Racing

Educate. The horse and dog racing industries have a lot to answer for. Never fail to speak up if you hear a radio commentator or read a news article that fails to mention the cruelty inherent in racing. PETA has fact sheets on all forms of animal "sport" that you can find at PETA.org.

Adopt a "retired" greyhound. Contact the National Greyhound Adoption Network (800-446-8637) for help in finding local groups in your area that find good homes for greyhounds. David Cantor of Pennsylvania took Bruno, his adopted ex-racing greyhound, to a news conference to protest a bill to legalize greyhound racing in the state. While Cantor circulated literature, Bruno provided gentle, silent testimony to the cruelty of the greyhound industry. The bill did not receive even one vote; after seeing Bruno on television and in newspapers, compassionate citizens could not imagine condemning tens of thousands of dogs like him to death every year.

Horse-Drawn Carriages

Boycott carriage rides. Don't be taken for a ride. If you see horse-drawn carriages in any city, please write your objections to the local paper, the chamber of commerce, the board of trade, and the mayor. If the carriage-horse operation is affiliated with a hotel, tell the manager too. Visit PETA.org to find out more details and how you can help.

Report abuses. Instantly report any abuses—including overwork, overheating, horses you see working when it is too hot (the temperature at hoof level can be thirty degrees hotter than the ambient temperature), lameness, frothing at the mouth, beating, or overloading—to the police and humane society. Insist on enforcement: don't take no for an answer.

Educate customers. Talk politely to potential customers about how hard these animals work and ask them to reconsider taking a ride.

The Bullfight

Boycott bullfights. If you're traveling to Mexico, Spain, or the south of France or Italy, help spare the pain of the more than forty thousand bulls who are killed in the arena each year. Don't attend bullfights; encourage others not to patronize them; and avoid purchasing souvenirs that depict any aspect of bullfighting.

Distribute leaflets. Write to PETA to receive free leaflets in Spanish and English to distribute at your hotel and in the airport.

Protest bullfights. Protest so-called bloodless bullfights if they appear in your city. Write your objections to local papers and legislators.

Participate in the Protest at Pamplona. Help let Spain know that there are better, sexier, more fun alternatives to the annual running of the bulls by planning to participate in one of PETA's (and many international groups') protests.

Cockfighting and Dog Fighting

Call the police. If you see evidence of cockfighting or dog fighting, call the police or the local humane society right away. Because drugs are often involved and people may be armed, call the police before taking any direct action There is also the likelihood that the animals who lose will be left to die nearby.

Animal "Actors"

Contact companies. When you see a movie, or even an advertisement for one, that shows questionable activities involving animals, express your opinion by writing or calling the film or television companies involved. Moviegoers' opinions count.

Write to Critics. Ask your local movie critics to discuss real or perceived animal abuse in their reviews. Your efforts will initiate interest.

Take to your feet. Walk out of a movie or play if you are offended at how animals are portrayed, or see a scene containing cruelty to animals. By doing so, you alert others that what happened is ethically indefensible. Let the manager know that you would not have attended if you had known there would be animal cruelty. Ask for a refund or return pass. If the explanation is firm but polite (remember, it's not the theater's fault), most managers will oblige and may also learn something.

Thank publishers and producers for animal-friendly messages on TV and in print. Keep a stack of cards by your television set.

Animals in Advertising

Support compassionate businesses. Be vocal. Or drop a line. Let businesses know you will use your consumer dollars to support products that use compassionate advertising.

Help give "awards." Every year, international ad agencies vie for the coveted Kelly awards for excellence in advertising. But they dread PETA's Litter Box awards, given to companies that reek of a lack of compassion and respect for animals. Fortunately, for every company that chooses to exploit, degrade, and otherwise abuse animals, there are good guys who sell their products and warm consumers' hearts at the same time. When you see an advertisement that depicts animals in a manner that is anything other than respectful or compassionate, write to the advertiser and explain that such tactics discourage consumers from buying. Please send a copy of the advertisement to PETA as a Litter Box or Glitter Box (for the ads that respect animals) nomination.

Circuses and Other Animal Acts

Watch and show a video. Show a video to friends, coworkers, and members of your activity groups. Order *Training & Tragedy Circus* DVD from PETALiterature.com

Educate children. Children are the group to which animal circuses try hardest to appeal. Most children have a natural affinity for all living beings and are upset when they learn about cruelty. Take them to see shows whose entertainment value comes from amusing and unusual *human* performances.

Protest traveling animal acts. Get traveling animal acts to take a detour past your town. Take your message to the sponsors (business owners and managers and radio and television stations). Inform promoters about the problems with animal acts and urge them to withdraw their support. Many sponsors care about animal suffering but just aren't aware. Urge them not to repeat sponsorship the next time the show comes to town.

Use a video camera. Use a video camera to record any mistreatment of animals when a circus unloads or parades through your town. Take your evidence to PETA, the media, the police, and your local humane society.

Demonstrate. When you demonstrate or leaflet, dress as a clown, ride a unicycle, or wear a friendly smile. You're sure to reach more people. When the circus came to town, Jirleen Sandhu, Melba Lowe, Lisa Ferrell, and several other activists in Richmond, Virginia, were prepared with a protest on wheels! They drove around and around the arena with a "tiger" caged in the back of a pickup truck and a sign reading, NO ONE READ THIS PRISONER HIS RIGHTS.

Write letters to the editor. Write letters to the editors of your local papers telling them why you won't attend a circus that forces animals to perform tricks.

Pass legislation. Take your concerns to your city council. Encourage your local humane society to get involved. Hollywood, Florida, is among the cities that have passed legislation banning all animal acts and exhibits.

Report cruelty. The Burlington, Vermont, mayor's youth office chose not to invite back the Great American Circus after receiving several reports that a driver had beaten a baby elephant with a shovel. According to eyewitness Jennifer Blow, "He was hitting the elephant, fifteen or twenty times." This is a fine example of how much it helps to document and report cruelty whenever and wherever you see it.

Write to the Shriners. Appeal to the Shriners, a major circus sponsor, to hire only animal-free circuses like Cirque du Soleil, Cirque d'Ingénuité, Circus Smirkus, The New Pickle Family Circus, and Earth Circus. (For addresses, see Chapter 17, "People to Contact.")

Speak up. Jim Sicard of Florida sent a letter to the publishers of *American Heritage Dictionary* protesting the use of a photograph showing tigers performing in a circus to illustrate the entry *circus.* They agreed to remove the photograph from future printings of the dictionary. Linda Geant of Chicago solicited help from her local activist phone tree, animal control chief, and a sympathetic columnist to stop a bear wrestling event at Chicago's Club Land, dashing plans for a private party where twelve men would be invited to wrestle a bear. Animal control chief Pete Poholik warned: "If the event takes place, I'll either make an arrest or confiscate the bear. It's illegal and cruel to torment and tease an animal. The bear was not only declawed—he had no teeth!"

Protest to management. Take the plunge. Protest to the management of any fair where mules are diving (a traveling act in which mules are forced to climb up a ramp and jump into a pool of water from a height of thirty feet), as well as to your local humane society and department of animal control. Heather Gray and Debbi Liebergot made a splash at Tim Rivers's diving mule show when they jumped into the diving pool and refused to get out. Other determined activists across the nation leafleted fairgoers and reported the show to local authorities in an effort to convince them to shut it down for cruelty to animals.

Be creative. Karen Medicus of the Animal Rescue League of Martin County, Florida, didn't sit quietly when she heard Tim Rivers's High Diving Mule act had been booked at a local Toyota dealer. She voiced her concerns to the general manager, Mark Jacobson, who not only canceled the act (to the tune of the contractual $3,600) but also generously offered to donate $50 to the Animal Rescue League for every car sold.

 FREQUENTLY ASKED QUESTIONS

Don't zoos teach children important lessons about wildlife?

No, they undereducate and give misimpressions of who animals are and what they need and do. Small enclosures do not allow animals to display their natural behaviors, and signs typically tell visitors little more than the names of the animals, where they can be found, and what they eat.

Animals' normal behaviors are seldom discussed—much less observed—at zoos because their natural needs are not met in a zoo environment. Many animals who live in large herds or family groups in the wild are kept alone or, at most, in pairs, at zoos. Natural hunting and mating behaviors are eliminated by regulated feeding and managed breeding regimens. Animals in zoos lack privacy and have little opportunity for mental stimulation or physical exercise. These conditions cause them to exhibit abnormal, self-destructive behaviors like swaying (which elephants never, ever do in the wild) and turning in endless circles, called zoochosis.

Most zoos focus on attracting visitors rather than on the well-being of the animals. For example, a zoo might take much-needed space away from an exhibit and use it to create a children's play area or put in a train. A former director of the Atlanta Zoo once remarked that he was "too far removed from the animals; they're the last thing I worry about with all the other problems." Zoos teach people that it is acceptable to keep animals in captivity, where they are bored, cramped, lonely, far from their natural homes, and at the mercy and whim of people.

Don't zoos help preserve endangered species?

Most animals in zoos are not endangered, and almost none are being prepared for release into natural habitats. In fact, it is nearly impossible to release captive-bred animals into the wild. A report by the World Society for the Protection of Animals showed that only 1,200 out of the 10,000 zoos worldwide are registered for captive breeding and wildlife conservation, and that only 2 percent of the world's threatened or endangered species are registered in breeding programs.

Rather than nurturing animals to thrive in natural settings, zoos place unnatural restrictions on their residents. For example, polar bears in zoos are typically confined to spaces that are one-millionth the size of their minimum home range in the wild. Animals who roam across large distances in nature often exhibit dementia and stereotypical behaviors such as endlessly pacing or swimming in circles, from boredom when placed in zoo enclosures.

Ultimately, we will only save endangered species by preserving their habitats and protecting them from hunters—not by breeding a few individuals in captivity. Instead of supporting zoos, support groups such as Zoocheck, the Born Free Foundation, and other organizations that work to preserve habitats; and help nonprofit sanctuaries, like the Elephant Sanctuary and the Performing Animal Welfare Society, that rescue and care for exotic animals without selling or breeding them.

Aren't racehorses treated like royalty?

They are treated like commodities. For many equine athletes, injury and death are just a hoofbeat away. One study on racetrack injuries concluded that one horse in every twenty-two races suffered an injury that prevented him or her from finishing the race, and another study estimated that eight hundred thoroughbreds die from injuries every year in North America. Over time, selective breeding has made thoroughbreds' legs far too fragile for their bodies. Most thoroughbreds are owned by corporations that are only interested in the money that the animals can make for them, and such owners don't hesitate to sell horses to slaughterhouse "kill buyers" when they break down.

Before they are slaughtered, though, many horses are turned into junkies by their trainers and veterinarians, who provide drugs to keep them racing even when they shouldn't be on the track because of their injuries. Many are forced to run with hairline fractures, which would making even walking too painful for them without drugs. "There are trainers pumping horses full of illegal drugs every day," said a former Churchill Downs director. "With so much money on the line, people will do anything to make their horses run faster."

A *New York Times* reporter, present when Eight Belles broke both her front legs after being whipped down the front straight in the 2008 Kentucky Derby, called the horses "paper horses," as he criticized how they are run on everything from steroids to pain-masking drugs. A *New York Daily News* reporter remarked, "The thoroughbred race horse is a genetic mistake. It runs too fast, its frame is too large, and its legs are far too small. As long as mankind demands that it run at high speeds under stressful conditions, horses will die at racetracks."

Why is PETA against the use of animals in circuses?

In his book, *The Circus Kings*, Ringling Bros. founder Henry Ringling North wrote that trainers commonly break bears' noses or burn their paws to force them to stand on their hind legs and that monkeys and chimpanzees are struck with clubs.

Animals do not naturally ride bicycles, stand on their heads, balance on balls, or jump through rings of fire. To force them to perform these confusing and physically uncomfortable tricks, trainers use whips, tight collars, muzzles, electric prods, bull hooks, and other painful tools of the trade.

We applaud trapeze artists, jugglers, clowns, tightrope walkers, and acrobats, but let's leave animals in peace. Sweden, Denmark, Finland, India, Switzerland, and the UK have all banned or restricted the use of animals in entertainment—it's time for the United States to do the same.

What's wrong with rodeos?

In order to make them perform, normally docile cattle and horses are beaten, kicked, and shocked when they are in their chutes and holding pens. "Bucking broncos" are provoked with electric prods, sharp sticks, caustic ointments, and the groin-pinching "bucking" strap so that the animals are frantic by the time they are released into the arena. Calves, who are roped while they are running, have their necks snapped back by the lasso, which often results in neck and back injuries, bruises, broken bones, and internal bleeding.

After their short and painful "careers," animals in rodeos are sent to the slaughterhouse. Dr. C. G. Haber, a veterinarian who spent thirty years as a federal meat inspector, described the animals discarded from rodeos for slaughter as being "so exten-sively bruised that the only areas in which the skin was attached [to the flesh] were the head, neck, leg, and belly. I have seen an-imals with six to eight ribs broken from the spine and, at times, puncturing the lungs. I have seen as much as two to three gal-lons of free blood accumulated under the detached skin."

Every national animal protection organization opposes rodeos because of their inherent cruelty. Urge your commu-nity to buck the rodeo.

4

Blood Sports:
Hunting and Fishing

*You ask people why they have deer heads on the
wall. They always say, "Because it's such a
beautiful animal." There you go. I think my
mother's attractive, but I have photographs of her.*

—ELLEN DeGENERES, COMEDIAN

They're not "sports" at all, of course. Take this
case: one winter, a Michigan deer hunter
came upon a buck and a doe standing side by
side in the forest. When they did not run from
him, he raised his rifle and killed the buck. In
spite of the shot, the doe remained motionless.
As the law at that time did not permit anyone to
shooting a does, the hunter approached her. To
his amazement, she allowed him to walk right up
to her; it was then that he saw she was blind.

Further inspection revealed a large area of fur
worn away from the buck's left side and a similar
area on the doe's right side. By pressing his side
against hers, the buck had led her through the
forest and cared for her. When he saw the hunter,
the buck had chosen to stay beside her, although

he could have run. How marvelous if the hunter had felt even a portion of the buck's devotion.

One has to wonder what feelings of inadequacy or absence of feeling makes grown men (and some women) want to shoot and kill animals who are minding their own business. Some years ago, that thought was heavy on my mind as I sat in the stands at a park in Hegins, Pennsylvania, waiting with a group of activists for the right moment to disrupt a live pigeon shoot.

The Hegins pigeon shoot had to be seen to be believed. Tame pigeons were brought to the site in crates, kept in a shed overnight, then shoved into little boxes on a playing field. The "trapper boys" stuffed the birds into the boxes, then pulled the strings that released the birds at intervals so that paying guests could shoot at the birds, scoring points for every kill. The trapper boys' other job was to gather up fallen birds who were still alive, stuff them, wounded and dying, into a sack (they would be ground up and used for fur-farm food), or, if the boys could be bothered, wring their necks.

A fair number of the hunters, although they wore shirts proclaiming their marksmanship, couldn't hit the side of a barn. At one point, I saw a pigeon fly out of the box, land on the ground, look around in confusion, and then get shot. Although the man with the gun could not have been more than thirty feet from her, his aim was so poor that he succeeded only in shooting off her legs.

A little boy in front of the stands who had watched this poor pigeon get shot and turn end over end like a badminton shuttlecock turned away from the slaughter and hid his eyes. His father saw him shy away from the scene and, not willing to stand for such "sissiness," turned the boy around to face the shoot. The boy started to cry.

"Watch!" the man said harshly.

The boy turned again, buried his head in his father's pants, and sobbed, but it did no good. His father took his little shoulders forcefully and spun him back to face the field.

"You *will* watch!" he said.

I couldn't watch any longer, so off we went, over the fence, out onto the field to stop the shoot, at least for a while, to set as many pigeons free as we could, and to get carted away to Pottsville Prison for a couple of weeks.

Thanks to all the protests, which never let up, one day state officials came to their senses and concluded that the Hegins pigeon hunt violated the cruelty to animals laws. It is no more.

BIRTH CONTROL BY FIREARM

The main argument hunters offer in defense of their grisly hobby is that hunting helps control wildlife populations. We are supposed to believe that animals are so out of control and nature so inept that hunters have to sacrifice their weekend golf games to do the ultimate favor for deer and grouse and ducks: blow them away.

Hunters are such good wildlife exterminators that, in a single year, about 25,000 black bears bite the dust, as do ten million ducks, thirty million rabbits, and as many squirrels. Canada geese, who break formation if one of their flock is hit, with two geese going to ground to guard and protect their fallen friend, lose more than one million of their kind each year to hunters' guns. And, the humble mourning dove, who is not starving, overpopulated, known to attack small children, or engage in any other transgressions, apparently needs more "help" than most animals: this gentle bird has the dubious distinction of being the most hunted animal in the United States, with an annual death toll of more than fifty million.

Perhaps the cruelest part of hunting is that it makes widows and widowers. Geese mate for life, as do ducks.

Chief Luther Standing Bear of the Oglala Sioux once said, "Only to the white man was nature a 'wilderness' and only to him was the land 'infested' with 'wild' animals and 'savage' people. To us it was tame. Earth was bountiful and we were surrounded with the blessings of the Great Mystery." In hunting magazines, hunters describe the most benign animals as wild, terrifying, threatening, and oversize, rather than as timid beings who flee for their lives at the first hint that a human being carrying heavy artillery is coming after them. "Sport" is a misnomer, of course, given that the animals are out there with no defense other than their hooves (which they use to run away) or claws (for trying to climb out of reach), and that today's hunters are equipped with all-terrain vehicles, tree stands, walkie-talkies, high-powered weapons, high-powered scopes, binoculars, sock warmers, hip flasks, moose urine to deflect their smell, camouflage clothing, and even camouflage toilet paper. And only one-half of the players in this "sport" are in it voluntarily. As far as the "we must kill them because there are too many and they'll starve" argument goes, often the populations of deer and other "edible" species are purposely "exploited" in order to cater to hunters, sell more hunting licenses, and provide more recreation for residents and special interest visitors.

Game "management" programs are actually game propagation programs designed not to reduce or restrict the animals' numbers but to fool desirable species into overpopulating. The most obvious ploy is to shoot only males and to protect females so they can keep on bearing fawns. Another favorite trick is to plant far more tasty vegetation or browse than a region would normally support. Left to their own devices, deer "read" the available food supply and reproduce based on how much there is to sustain their herds. If it is a good year, a doe may have one fawn or twins. If faced with nutritional stress, a doe may simply not ovulate, and bucks will reduce their sperm count. If disaster strikes, a doe can reabsorb her fetus. When state wildlife departments (composed almost solely of hunters) fool the deer, the birth rate goes up.

"Game management" operates so much to the detriment of animals that, in Michigan alone, just one state game program *added* about 1.5 million whitetail deer. Rather disingenuously, when the figures were announced, hunters took to the airways to lobby for extended hunting seasons and bigger bag limits to reduce the very problems they had created: traffic accidents caused by deer browsing near highways and loss of ornamental shrubs.

OUT OF CONTROL

Edward Abbey dealt swiftly with the psychological aspects of hunting when he wrote, "I was once a sportsman. But I grew up." The inability to curb aggression and the belief that it is acceptable to kill for pleasure are a frightening phenomenon. Luckily, despite federally subsidized efforts to encourage children to take up firearms against squirrels, bears, doves, and deer, less than 6 percent of the US population hunts, and, of them, I'd guess that about .00001 percent do so because they have no other way to feed their families.

PETA columnist Carla Bennett believes she has found the answer to why some of these people hunt. She has unearthed many supporters of the theory that some hunters are trying to compensate for other problems in their lives. Ms. Bennett quotes Dr. Karl Menninger of the Menninger Clinic, who describes hunting as the product of "erotic sadistic motivation";

Dr. Joel R. Saper, a University of Michigan professor who feels hunting "may reflect a profound, yet subtle, psychosexual inadequacy"; and Washington, D.C., clinical psychologist Margaret Brooke-Williams, who theorizes that "hunters are seeking reassurance of their masculinity." Interestingly, some clinicians report that the incidence of wife-beating is at its peak the day before hunting season opens.

Reading hunting magazines, as author Joy Williams has, seems to substantiate the view that all is not well in the minds of at least some hunters. Much is made of the chase, the anticipation, and the conquest. Take this example from a popular outdoors periodical: The hunter has used a sex lure to draw a buck to within convenient shooting range. "The big buck raised its nose to the air, curled back its lips, and tested the scent of the doe's urine. I held my breath, fought back the shivers, and jerked off a shot."

Whatever lurks in the hunter's psyche, the effect of his all but irresistible habit on his victims is deadly. Hunters have rendered extinct, among others, the dodo, the great auk, the Florida black bear, Sherman's fox squirrel, the heath hen, the Eastern elk, and the passenger pigeon. Hunters also wound countless animals. In fact, hunters call crippling "a by-product of our sport." According to the Texas Wildlife Commission, bow hunters, whose weapons pack 1,500 pounds of pressure, expend an average of twenty-one arrows before shooting and keeping a deer. The bow hunters themselves report a 50 percent or higher rate of animals wounded and lost (not that all hunters look for or trail the animals they injure). This means animals stagger off to die of blood loss, starvation, thirst, and infection.

Trigger-happy hunters also "harvest" nonhunters, such as: a woman in Maine who was killed in her own backyard by a hunter who said he thought her white gardening glove was the fur on a whitetail deer's rump; pesky game wardens who object to the use of infrared night sights and off-season shooting; cows and horses grazing peacefully in fields; other hunters; and even themselves. In one notable case, a hunter committed inadvertent suicide when his weapon went off while he was bludgeoning a wounded deer to death with his rifle butt.

HUNTING IN THE WATER

Human beings generally have a very unfair way of thinking about animals. Favored animals go into one category, and less fortunate ones, like fish, go into another. There are many people who abhor hunting because it is cruel but who haven't realized that their "peaceful pastime" of fishing is nothing more than hunting in the water.

Lots of people who "love animals" also fish. I certainly did, standing in my bare feet in the crashing surf of Florida's Gulf Coast years ago and casting my line for sea trout. I hated catching the fish, not, I'm sorry to say, because I recognized what they were going through, but because they stunk when they died, because I hated having to wrestle them to remove the hooks, and because catching them disturbed my otherwise happy experience: enjoying the feel of the water, the sound of the waves, and the warmth of sweet sunshine on my skin. At some level I must have realized that my entertainment was less than pleasant for the fish, because, when I did catch them, I either threw them back in or killed them quickly. But I kept on fishing.

The English poet John Wolcot wrote,

> *Enjoy thy stream,*
> *O harmless fish;*

And when an angler for his dish,
Through gluttony's vile sin,
Attempts, a wretch, to pull thee out,
God give thee the strength,
O gentle trout,
To pull the rascal in!

In the last decade or so, we have learned that fish can tell time, that they have long memories and can solve problems, and that they have friends they like to "hang out" with and other fish they just plain dislike. We have learned too that fish converse underwater in a language that sounds so much like twittering that they almost sound like birds. People will have to kiss good-bye the convenient thought that fish are just swimming potatoes.

THE EYES HAVE IT

For hundreds of years, elephants were thought of as nothing but tusks and tasks. They hauled logs and ended up with those sturdy legs turned into umbrella stands and their ivory turned into piano keys and used for scrimshaw. Even whales were thought of as big gray blubbery masses, good only for parts— oil for lamps, and bones for corsets. Today, if you look at a whale's eye in a photograph or in one of the posters sold by the Cetacean Society or Greenpeace, you know there is *someone* inside that almost featureless body.

A friend of mine once opened a book and showed me a picture of a pair of very wise, familiar eyes, surrounded by wrinkled, wizened, sun-weathered skin. It made me think instantly of an old peasant woman I had met who gathered wood on the slopes of a mountain in the Kulu Valley. They were clearly the eyes of someone who had spent her entire life outdoors, the sun having carved deep furrows into that knowing face.

It turned out I was wrong. The eyes so full of life experiences and hard times belonged to Siri, an aging elephant then confined to a small enclosure in the Burnet Park Zoo in Syracuse, New York. The book was her story, as told by her keeper. He had found Siri drawing in the dirt with a stick and had given her some blank art paper and crayons, which the elephant liked immediately. Siri's work had been praised by the great Willem de Kooning and his wife, who found them "full of flair, decisiveness and originality" and called Siri "a damned talented" artist. The keeper had been fired from the zoo and missed seeing her and being with her. Perhaps Siri missed him too, and that was reflected in her eyes.

One evening, driving into Philadelphia, I stopped my car beside the Schuylkill to enjoy the water and relax. Two men were fishing on the riverbank, but I was glad to note they were not catching anything. Or, *anyone*, I should say, for a fish is not a thing. Then, as dusk fell, I saw one of the men wrestling with what looked to be an enormously long fish. He seemed to be having a hard time, so I walked over to see what was happening. When I got there, I realized he had caught an eel.

A five-pronged metal gaff, with separate sets of barbed hooks attached to the prongs, was embedded in the eel's throat. As the animal wriggled, the man pulled and twisted at the gaff, but succeeded only in making a bloody mess. I asked if I could hold the eel still because the procedure was not going quickly. The man agreed.

I took the towel the man had been using to clean his fish knife and wrapped it around the eel so I could hold his long body up to the light from the nearby lamppost. The eel's face was now level with mine. That allowed the man to use both hands to open the eel's mouth wide and use his pliers more effectively, but the going was still tough because there were so many hooks.

Suddenly, the man lost his patience and yanked hard on the gaff set. In a split second he had pulled the eel's throat clean out of his mouth. The eel and I made eye contact at that very moment.

There was no mistaking the look on the eel's face: shock, horror, sheer fright, and terrible pain. He could have been a dog, a child, the man fishing, or me.

My friend, who had come up behind me, seized the eel and crushed the animal's head quickly with a rock to end his suffering.

Afterward, the man and I had a chat, but he was unable to relate to the experience in the same way. To him, the encounter with the unwanted, inedible eel had simply been a waste of time and bait. He offered me a beer, and eventually we said our good-byes. As I drove out of the parking lot he was tying a piece of raw bacon to the gaff, ready to have another go.

It has been years, but I still can't shake the look in that poor animal's eyes. He was used as an object to satisfy the recreational whims of members of a species capable of playing chess with computers, devising elaborate games, doing crossword puzzles, and reading great books.

He had been hurt terribly and then killed, not by juveniles on drugs or evil sadists on a crime spree, but by a man who seemed respectable, decent, and polite. The miserable deed had been carried out, not in secret, down a dark alley, but in the open in a public place. It had happened a million times before, in much the same way, or worse, and it would happen as many times again. All for nothing.

I was not upset because I am a vegetarian. I was upset because I had witnessed a hideous cruelty. I was also upset because I knew, from talking to him, that the man, while inured to the eel's suffering and that of the fish in his bucket, would have been as upset as I was if what happened that evening had happened to a horse or a dog or another being he related to and who is not associated with his "sport."

DOWN AMONG THE FISH

Fish are so low on the totem pole that they get even shorter shrift than chickens, and that is saying something. Yet fish are communicative and sensitive animals. They certainly have a neurological system like ours and the brain capacity to experience fear and pain. While pain is a mental event that cannot be accurately measured, it only makes sense that the ability to feel pain is a prerequisite for the continued survival of any creature and is not a singularly human trait. Without the ability to feel pain, fish, like us, would perish.

Fish also have on their backs sensory hairs that register vibrations and electrical fields: they have taste buds in their throats, as well as in their lips and noses; and they use their mouths much as we use our fingers, to pick things up and feel them. In fact, their mouths are so exquisitely sensitive to stimuli that any pain they experience there is especially acute. They like to play in air bubbles, as dolphins do, and like bears, they enjoy the sensation of rubbing their backs and bodies along the edges of rocks and tree trunks.

When people who fish think about being more humane, they usually "move up" from killing fish to practicing "catch-and-release." As Ellen DeGeneres says, that's like running down pedestrians in your car and then, when they get up and limp away, saying "Off you go! That's fine. I just wanted to see if I could hit you."

Sadly, catch-and-release doesn't help at all. Fish not only

suffer injuries from hooks and even end up dying of infection from them, but two other physiological phenomena also occur: the tremendous stress of being caught causes lactic acid to build up in their bodies, which can weaken and kill them, and handling them to remove a hook destroys the protective coating on their bodies that shields them in the water. An Australian study found that when fish are chased, confined, or otherwise threatened, they react with increased heart and breathing rates and a burst of adrenaline: in other words, they have the same response humans do under stress.

AN ODD CATCH

Fishing certainly hurts fish, but it does more damage than that, as many hikers and park users have found out firsthand.

One spring, a couple walking their dogs in a Virginia park noticed a movement in the bushes around the lake. When they investigated, they found a seagull tangled up in fishing line, struggling to stay alive. He was upside down, very close to the water, and was trying to keep his head up to save himself from drowning. The line went around both his wings, over his shoulders, then crisscrossed over his back and around his legs.

The seagull also had a barbed fishing hook embedded under his wing. It took the couple nearly an hour to untangle the bird, cut off the barb, and remove the hook.

Every year, people who fish leave behind a trail of tackle victims that includes millions of birds, turtles, otters, seals, sea lions, bats, and other animals who suffer debilitating injuries or slowly starve to death after swallowing fishhooks or becoming entangled in filament line. In fact, officials with the Virginia Marine Science Museum Stranding Team say monofilament fishing line is one of the top three threats to sea animals, along with plastic trash—including discarded bait containers and lures—and propeller and boat strikes. On riverways, the toll can be even higher.

In Britain, one study found that in just two weeks, anglers discarded or lost 36,000 pieces of line totaling six kilometers *in an area just two kilometers long.* Fishing line is designed to be strong enough to defeat a struggling fish, long enough to reach far from a boat or pier, and is virtually impervious to the elements. You'll find it everywhere fishers have been—on beaches, at the edges of rivers, and drifting around in the water, waiting to ensnare a passerby. In Florida, where fishers on piers often joke about how many pelicans they've caught, 85 percent of the birds taken to the Suncoast Seabird Sanctuary are there to be treated for injuries from fishing line and hooks. Another study found that the cause of a mysterious illness in otters was the presence of indigestible plastic bait worms clogging up their intestines.

I doubt an aboriginal angler is reading this book, so I think it is safe to say that we can easily find something else to eat and some other way to pass our time.

It may be hard, at first, to care about what fish feel, but we know they do feel. If we can't justify impaling dogs on barbed hooks and dragging them into the water, how can we justify doing the same sort of thing to a fish?

 WHAT YOU CAN DO

Hunting and Fishing

Make it difficult. Deny hunters land to hunt on. Encourage your neighbors, especially those who own large tracts of land such as farms and ranches, to post NO HUNTING signs every hundred yards. Explain to them that aggressive human hunters with their powerful weapons are far more dangerous than wild animals who invariably flee, even if surprised.

Check out wildlife groups. Before you support a "wildlife" or "conservation" group, ask if it supports hunting. Such groups as the National Wildlife Federation, the National Audubon Society, the Sierra Club, the Izaak Walton League, the Wilderness Society, the World Wildlife Fund, and many others do not oppose hunting.

Apply for licenses. For hunts that issue a limited number of permits, apply for permits yourself. The permits are usually awarded through a simple lottery system. People in nursing homes love animals too. Follow activist Janet Palomis's lead by signing them up for *free* senior-citizen hunting licenses. Each license obtained by a nonhunter saves lives that a real hunter might have taken.

Get hunts canceled. Look for announcements of scheduled hunts in newspapers and magazines. Contact the sponsors or local authorities and ask that the hunt be canceled, both for human and other-than-human safety. Circulate petitions in neighboring areas and, if necessary, picket the entrance to the hunting grounds.

Pass an ordinance. Encourage your municipality to pass an ordinance that bans the use of weapons within its limits in the interest of public safety. Ask your congressional representatives to introduce bills prohibiting hunting and trapping on national wildlife refuges and all public land.

Work your community. Develop a strong antihunting sentiment in your community by writing letters to the editors of local newspapers, meeting with neighbors, and calling into talk shows. Post antihunting flyers in parks and other community areas. Let your neighbors know that federal

law recognizes that wildlife "belongs" to *all* people, most
of whom don't hunt.

Be a hunt saboteur. Chrissie Hynde of The Pretenders joined
a group of legal "hunt sabs" in the woods of Maryland.
Hunt saboteurs distract hunters with conversation, picnic
noisily, and use other carefully chosen, nonviolent methods
to stop shooters from monopolizing and terrorizing the
woods.

Put your foot down. At a party, Anita Monical showed antihunting literature to wives of men who were planning to
go bear hunting with her husband the next day. When the
women announced that they would not put bear meat in
their freezers or hang bearskins on their walls, it took just
five minutes for the men to call off the hunt.

Search for traps. Joy Roelofsz, an Army Corps of Engineers
construction inspector, heard a chain rattle in the bushes,
and when she went to investigate, found a young coyote. "I
started talking to her. She was so smart, she lay there and
let us release her foot. It had to hurt because we had to wiggle it so much."

Display stickers. Use PETA's FISHING HURTS stickers in highly
visible places.

Do something else. Don't get hooked on fishing. Go hiking,
canoeing, snorkeling, or bird-watching, or read a book in
that beach chair.

Go vegan. Never buy or eat fish. Visit VegCooking.com for
free recipes for delicious, nutritious (and cheap!) meals or
visit MayWah's Web site (Vegieworld.com) and stock up
on faux salmon and "fish" filets.

Use your feet. Collect unwanted fishing tackle from friends
and family after *you* convince them to stop fishing.

Write a letter to the editor. Many people have really just never
considered that there might be anything wrong with fish-

ing. A letter in the paper can open many eyes to the suffering of these animals. It can just be a few simple, sensible, heartfelt lines. (See PETA's Guide to Letter Writing online at PETA.org)

 FREQUENTLY ASKED QUESTIONS

Without hunting, wouldn't deer and other animals overpopulate and die of starvation?

Hunters don't hunt out of mercy, fearing animals will starve unless dispatched with a bullet or an arrow. And while starvation and disease are not pleasant, should they ever exist, they are nature's way of ensuring that the strong survive. Natural predators help keep prey species strong by killing only the sick and weak. Hunters, however, kill any animal they come across or any animal whose head they think would look good mounted above their fireplace—often these are the large, healthy animals needed to keep the population strong. And hunting creates the ideal conditions for overpopulation. After hunting season, the abrupt drop in population leads to less competition among survivors, resulting in a higher birth rate—which suits hunters and game management officials, who can sell them more licenses every year. If we were really concerned about keeping animals from starving, we would take steps to reduce the animals' fertility.

Aren't hunting fees a major source of revenue for wildlife management and habitat restoration?

Hunting fees pay for hunter programs that benefit hunters, like manipulating animal populations to increase the number of animals available to kill. The public lands that many hunters use are supported by taxpayers, and funds benefiting "nongame" species are scarce.

Isn't hunting okay as long as I eat what I kill?

Did the fact that Jeffrey Dahmer ate his victims justify his crimes? What is done with a corpse after the murder doesn't lessen the suffering.

Hunters are also harming animals other than the ones they kill and take home. Those who don't die outright often suffer disabling injuries. And the stress that hunting inflicts on animals—the noise, the fear, the loss of family members and friends, and the chase—severely restricts their ability to eat adequately and store the fat and energy that they need to survive the winter.

Hunting also disrupts migration and hibernation. And for animals like wolves and geese, who mate for life and have close-knit families, hunting can severely harm entire communities.

Isn't hunting much less cruel than factory farming?

Yes, and Jack the Ripper was less cruel than Hitler—but that didn't make what he did acceptable. It is true that killing an animal in the wild can be less cruel than the months of torture that animals endure on factory farms, although who knows, when we add up the panic, the loss of loved ones, and the constant vigilance that wild animals must sustain. Regardless, hunting disrupts families and causes pain, trauma, and grief to both the victims and the survivors. Why cause any suffering when we can easily reject it?

What about people who have to hunt to survive?

PETA's quarrel is not with true subsistence hunters who honestly have no choice but to hunt or fish in order to survive. But the fact is, in this day and age, meat, fur, and leather are not a necessary part of survival for the majority of us. It is dishonest for "sport" hunters to borrow from aboriginal traditions and manipulate it into a justification for killing animals for mere recreation or profit.

Isn't eating fish good for your health?

Fish absorb all the contamination from the water they live in, so fish flesh is laced with toxins such as mercury, lead, arsenic, PCBs, pesticides, and even industrial-strength fire retardant. Just two servings of fish per week can elevate your blood mercury levels by 700 percent, and study after study has linked fish consumption to fatigue, memory loss, and decreased mental function. Fish flesh can be toxic (the breast milk of some Inuit tribes is so concentrated with poisons from their fish diet that it meets the Environmental Protection Agency's standards for toxic waste).

But don't I need omega-3 from fish?

There are small amounts of omega-3 fatty acids in fish. But you can get plenty of omega-3 fatty acids in nuts and leafy green vegetables.

What's wrong with catch-and-release fishing?

"Catch-and-release" fishing sounds good, but it causes no less harm to fish than catching and keeping. Fish who are caught and then returned to the water suffer such severe physiological stress that they often die of shock, or their injuries may make them easy targets for predators.

Fish often swallow a hook so deeply that to remove it, the fishers shove their fingers or pliers down the fish's throat and, along with the hook, rip out some of the fish's throat and guts. A hook through the mouth causes a serious and extremely painful injury that can often be fatal without treatment. But anglers just toss injured fish back into the water—often without realizing what they've done.

In addition to the wounds that are caused by the hook, fish released after being caught can suffer from loss of their protective scale coating, dangerous buildup of lactic acid in their muscles, oxygen depletion, and damage to their delicate fins and mouths. Upon being returned to the water, these fish are easy targets for predators. Researchers at the Oklahoma Department of Wildlife Conservation found that as many as 43 percent of fish released after being caught died within six days. Catching fish is cruel and unnecessary, whether they are killed on the spot or thrown back into the water, injured and exhausted.

We can appreciate nature and bond with friends and family without hurting animals. Find out more at FishingHurts.com.

Didn't Jesus eat fish?

It's an interesting question, and some biblical scholars think that *fish* is a mistranslation of the word *fishweed*, which was plentiful in the Galilee, but whether or not that is correct, biblical scholars can agree that the appropriate question for Christians is: "What should *we* be eating now?" The Bible clearly says that our bodies are temples and that we should take care of them. Yet it's a fact that all fish flesh today is contaminated with heavy metals and other toxins. In fact, fish flesh is just about the most polluted thing that humans put into their bodies. On that basis alone, Christians should not be eating it.

Today's fishing practices are also horribly cruel. Christians believe that God cares for all his creatures, and the Bible counsels compassion for all beings. It is contrary to the concept of Christian mercy to torture and kill (or pay others to torture and kill) any animal, including fish. Although they may not be able to scream out in pain, fish have the same capacity for suffering and the same right to compassion as all living beings.

5

Cute "Pet" or Complex
Individual and Friend for Life?

an's best friend *isn't*, in many parts of the world. In Korea, the Philippines, Vietnam, and China, among other places, dogs are kept in the burning sun in small cages behind restaurants, tin cans shoved over their muzzles, their forelegs often broken and tied behind their backs. They are "tenderized" by being beaten while alive, strangled to death, and skinned for their meat. In some of these countries, dog soup, like rhino horn and tiger penis, is considered an aphrodisiac. In Thailand, dog-hide factory trucks trawl the streets, offering to trade plastic buckets for live dogs to be slaughtered and made into bags, drum skins, and golf club covers.

Although dogs are not eaten in India, where I grew up, mange-covered and starving stray animals are so common and so pathetic there, they can't help but capture your attention. Even when I was supposed to be admiring the jeweled walls of the Taj Mahal or concentrating on where to place my feet on the icy paths of the "Everlasting Snows," the helpless wandering dogs could not be ignored. The animals I didn't see fared worse. In the pounds, death was courtesy of a crude electrocution machine that seared the skin and set the dog's hair on fire, or via blows from men with billy clubs. In light of our treatment of them, it is particularly humbling to read a Press Trust of India report about how stray dogs on the streets of Calcutta kept a night-long vigil protecting an abandoned baby from harm and then waited outside the police station she was taken to, apparently concerned over her fate.

In Taiwan, a rich country with a large Buddhist population, one would think animals would fare much better. The truth is quite the opposite. Death for dogs in the pounds can come from live burial (digging a pit and throwing the dogs into it), electrocution of their metal cage with the dogs inside it, poison-laced food, starvation, or drowning. In Keelung, in April 1998, I rescued eleven dogs from the drowning tank and extracted a promise from the minister of the environment to immediately stop all drowning in that area. The city administrators have kept their word, but, all these years later, in other pounds like those in Sanchung and Tu Chung, the cages are still filthy and overcrowded, food is scarce if available at all, and the attitude of the workers toward the old, dying, and diseased dogs they "care for" is repulsive. Pressure is still desperately needed to bring about reforms.

I used to harbor the illusion that in Europe and North America, at least, animals were all well treated. But we have plenty of room for improvement here too, to say the least.

In Baltimore, Maryland, there is an organization called Alley Animals. They have seen it all, right here in America: animals with festering wounds from slingshots and bottles, animals made lame and terrified of human beings, cats with elastic bands embedded into their necks, kittens blinded and used as bait in pit bull fights, dogs with nails so long they have grown back into the pads of their feet, abandoned Easter rabbits, a rooster wearing a broken ankle leash, even a green iguana, now "the *most* common exotic throwaway pet," according to news reports.

The group operates simply and on a shoestring. When dusk comes, its volunteers drive into the most run-down parts of that sprawling old city. Their job is to find the animal waifs and strays who creep from their hiding places when the city gets quieter and know they are less visible to juveniles armed with free time and a rock or a firecracker. The animals are searching for that little morsel of food or the puddle of rain-water that can keep them going for yet another day.

In many alleys, the volunteers are known, and so from the boarded-up buildings and storm drains come animals, mostly cats, who are grateful to receive something nourishing to eat.

One evening, volunteer Alice Arnold and her partner for that night's trip, Eric, were just pulling out of an alley where they had put out food when Eric said, "Did you see that puppy?"

Eric pointed, amid the trash, to an overturned reclining chair. Alice squinted and saw what he was talking about. A tiny head was sticking out ever so slightly, her reddish brown fur almost blending in with the color of the old chair in the alley's black shadows. The stuffing had come out of the chair and the puppy had gone in, claiming the interior as her shelter from a world that had rejected her.

The puppy had very quietly watched as Alice and Eric arrived at the alley and then backed up to leave. No doubt she was fearful of the noise the car made and worried that people were so near her safe place. She didn't realize that the car offered hope. Alice cringed at the thought that she had almost driven away, oblivious to the little life needing help hidden in the discarded furniture.

Within a week of little Stuffing's rescue, it was obvious that she was very intelligent and lovable. After a few weeks, she had gained weight, become paper-trained, and was doing wonderfully, snuggling up in bed every night with her new human being. Alice says that, to look at her now, no one would ever guess that this happy little girl spent the first months of her life eating from trash cans, sleeping inside an overturned chair in the middle of an alley.

Most people don't think the problems of strays and chained backyard dogs have anything to do with them. But they do. The biggest nightmares plaguing domesticated animals in our society do not involve wanton acts of violence toward them. Their greatest dangers are the acts of thoughtlessness by otherwise intelligent and caring people who simply do not understand what or who, exactly, a dog or cat is and what they need.

It is easy to pick five major contributors to the mastiff-size headaches facing dogs and cats the world over. They are casual acquisition; overpopulation; ignorance of animals' needs and underestimation of the depth of their feelings; carelessness; and improper placement when an animal is given away. Alley Animals and similar groups can't round them all up, but they can make a dent in the suffering, a dent that matters to each individual they save. If you would like to be a Community Animal Project volunteer, call PETA or go to HelpingAnimals .com for more information. Your personal efforts do not have to be on the scale of those of Alley Animals or of PETA (which builds doghouses and provides straw, spay surgeries, vaccinations, and even food to needy animals in low-income areas), but in every community there are homeless and neglected animals who would give their eyeteeth to have a friend like you.

POUND PUPS DIE WHEN YOU BUY

Pet shops that sell animals, rather than just supplies, are part of the problem, not the solution. They contribute to the high mortality rate of birds, reptiles (the decline in the population of the North American box turtle is directly linked to the pet trade), and small rodents. They, like breeders, also compete directly with pounds and shelters and are busy creating more animals at a time when overpopulation of dogs and cats is at a crisis level, with far too few good homes available. As we say at PETA, "When you buy, a pound puppy will die," or "Breeders kill . . . pound pups' chances."

Pet shop sales contribute to abandonment, whether on the street or at the shelters. Since anyone can plunk down a credit card in any pet store in virtually any shopping mall and walk off with a "pet," that cute little puppy in the window often goes home with someone who has given the proposition only fifteen minutes' thought, if that. An animal should be a lifetime commitment, not an impulse purchase.

The idea that overpopulation is someone else's problem is naive and false. Sadly, lots of people who keep a young animal into adulthood do not get the dog or cat "fixed" because they don't act quickly enough or because they think it acceptable to have at least one litter. After all, they surmise, they can place the offspring. However, for every home they find for those new puppies and kittens, they create one fewer adopter who might go to the local pound or shelter and rescue an equally precious animal waiting on death row. Of course, that's not counting the following generations of puppies and kittens who will be born to the females of that litter, for sexual maturity arrives in a matter of only a few months for dogs and cats. And no one has to wait for a dog or cat to be "all grown up" before having them sterilized. That operation can be carried out safely when your little angel is just eight weeks old and weighing more than two pounds, helping make sure there are no "accidental" pregnancies later on. Such sterilizations cost less than the price of dinner and a movie but are far more valuable!

A PUPPY OR KITTEN IS A LIFETIME COMMITMENT!

Buying an animal is akin to adopting a baby. Animals make noise, make messes, require food and water, and have a score of vital needs that can interfere with a person's own interests. If that is boring, tiring, or doesn't fit into the purchaser's schedule, out the animal goes, confused at suddenly losing his or her home and newly accepted family and probably psychologically traumatized for having been yelled at for doing what comes natural to a baby animal.

When I worked at the Washington Humane Society/SPCA, a little dog was turned in because she ripped things up when the family went to work. Tracing her back through three failed homes, we discovered to our horror that she had been locked in an apartment during a fire in the building and had suffered from smoke inhalation before being rescued. While her last family had been furious at her unexplained behavior and unwilling to try to correct it, the little dog had been desperately trying to communicate the fact that she was terrified of being left alone in the house for good reason, based on her past experience. The lesson is that all animals, human or not, do things for a reason, sometimes deep-seated in their psyche. It is up to us to be patient and understanding.

GETTING RESPECT

It is not just "pocket pets" or "exotics," like lizards, snakes, and prairie dogs (who need everything from a daily misting, to ultraviolet light, to room to unwind and move about or dirt to dig in), or birds (pity the poor macaws and lovebirds who are kept in cages and denied their most basic desires to fly and be part of a flock) who are misunderstood. Cats and dogs are often treated as if they are not individuals in their own right, but accoutrements to a human lifestyle, who must fit in or be modified. For example, cats are commonly declawed to preserve the furniture, although declawing (a misnomer if ever there was one—it means removing not just the claw, but also the first section of each toe bone, ligament and all) is a painful surgery with the potential for creating subtle lifetime problems. Cats who are declawed often have spinal problems from imbalance, insecurities from knowing they have lost their natural defenses, and may start urinating and defecating out of the box, as covering their own waste can be painful and confusing to them when they lose their claws.

Dogs and cats are always expected to fit *our* plans. Dogs are yelled at not to tug on their leashes. They are pulled by the neck or told sharply to "come along" when they might rather look around or stop and smell something. How many people take the dog out for a walk only when it is absolutely necessary, rather than think when *the dog* would like to go, just for his or her pleasure? How many times do you see people hurrying their dogs on their walks, resenting the few minutes it takes for them to move their bowels or urinate, even if it is the only excursion they will get all day?

When two dogs meet in the park, some owners never consider allowing them to sniff and socialize, even for a moment. Even while they themselves are yakking their hearts out with friends on their cell phones, they pull their lonely dog away from that cherished little contact with others of their own kind.

Think of this too: people talk and laugh together all the time, but if dogs dare to bark in fun or to warn their people that a stranger is approaching, they are told, sometimes in a quite irritated tone of voice, to "be quiet!"

Imagine the discomfort a dog feels when people are eating from a dish of snacks at dog nose level, and the only person not allowed to try this tantalizing appetizer is the dog whose nose may be smacked away when he or she tries to join in.

Could the man who tells you confidently that his dog is "perfectly fine" not relieving herself for the ten hours he is at work and traveling there and back, be able to comfortably withhold those functions himself every day? And whatever gave anyone the idea that the way to toilet train any living being is to rub her nose in her own mess?

WHAT'S WRONG WITH CRATING?

A sign on the PETA dog park bulletin board reads:

> No, he doesn't "love" his crate.
> He loves YOU. And he will do anything to please you, including sitting behind bars, waiting patiently for you to free him.

> No, a crate is not a "cozy den."
> A real den doesn't come with a locked door.
> No, a crate is not like a playpen.

A crate is an extremely cramped and impoverished environment. Sure, it keeps dogs safe.

It also keeps them from living.

How would YOU like being locked inside a small see-through box?

Gating off a puppy-proofed room, using an exercise pen, making arrangements with a dog walker during the day, putting in a doggie door, deciding that your couch isn't more important than your relationship with your dog, going home at lunchtime and not working late, and tethering your puppy to you are better options than a crate. But mostly, puppies and dogs need consistent, attentive, knowledgeable training and care—not warehousing in a crate.

No more denial! No animal on the planet "loves" being locked inside a cage, including your dog.

OFF YOU GO! GOOD LUCK!

Cats and dogs are often sent out unattended. Sometimes they don't ever come home. Not that they have decided to go live somewhere else. Some are abducted, others are found dead or injured. In a world of tractor trailers, psychopaths, intolerant neighbors, juveniles out for a lark, strange animals, rabies (in some states a six-month quarantine is required if a dog or cat returns home with a scratch or bite from an unknown animal), steel traps set for other animals, and storm drains that flood suddenly, an animal's disappearance still seems to come as a surprise to many people who "love" their animals.

"But he wants to go outside," "But we live on a very quiet street," "But it's cruel to keep her in" are the silly justifications that could never be used by someone dispatching their toddler into the street.

The way we learn not to let the dog or cat out unaccompanied is usually by way of disaster. In Pompano, Florida, lost dogs and cats were found in a storage warehouse used by a pit bull training school. In Washington, D.C., a cat let out for her daily stroll returned covered in hot cooking grease. In California, a woman searching for her two cats found both with arrows shot through them. Before I knew better, my cat went missing for three days and finally crawled home to die on the step of my back door, her lung collapsed and her ribs broken. Prince Charles's favorite terrier disappeared into a rabbit warren and was never found, despite a massive search and the inevitable fanfare that would have greeted the dog's rescuer.

MOVING OR MOVING ON

Millions of wonderful dogs and cats every year are dumped—what other word is there for it?—at US shelters, which, if well run, are certainly much better options than casually passing a dog or cat on to the first person who answers an ad or says they'll take the animal. No one can explain to these once-secure dogs that their people are moving, divorcing, or being transferred abroad. And how could anyone explain that, unlike a child or human loved one, this "member of the family" isn't important enough to accommodate?

Elsie and Bob Anderson of California found out the hard way that not all prospective adopters of unwanted animals are what they are cracked up to be. The Andersons had rescued countless animals from the nearby desert, pulled the cactus needles and porcupine quills out of their skin, built them back up to health, and placed ads for permanent homes.

An impressive, lonely old lady took two of their dogs but turned out to be the mother of a licensed dog dealer who sold them, and at least fourteen other dogs from the "free to a good home" ads, to a laboratory. A few of the dogs were still alive when they were traced, but many of their teeth had been mysteriously knocked out, and they were debilitated and scared to death. The others had been experimented on and killed. What must the ordeal have done to the survivors? How could they rest, or trust that they would be safe ever again?

Barry Herbeck is a Wisconsin man who was arrested after answering "free to good home" ads in his local newspaper. But he was not caught soon enough. People say Herbeck always seemed a model placement because he brought his two young children with him to their homes, and the children fell in love with the animals. That helped Herbeck obtain numerous dogs and cats. Animal bodies were later found in the Dumpster behind Herbeck's workplace, and a dead sodomized cat was found inside Herbeck's home. Herbeck's arrest arose from the torture killing of a dog he punished for making a mess by taping her mouth shut and sealing her inside a plastic trash can. She reportedly whimpered for over a week before she died.

NO KILL OR NO CLUE?

Let no one take comfort in the "no kill shelter" movement. While it may sound good, it does not address the very heart of the problem, and funds channeled into placement are funds that do not go to "fix" the dogs and cats who are churning out ever more offspring.

In most "no kill" shelters, animals are simply warehoused. Others are not shelters at all but animal storage units run by "hoarders," people who have a psychological need to collect cats, dogs, or any animals. Being doomed to a cage or small run for life makes animals crazy and withdrawn, inspiring them to be aggressive or unpredictable, certainly miserable. As any law enforcement officer who has "busted" a "no kill" shelter where animals were discovered stacked in crates in back rooms, living in their own waste (even places with "break your heart" names like Life for God's Little Animals), sometimes there can indeed be fates worse than death.

Open admission shelters, ones who never slam their doors in the face of any old, sick, abused, or unwanted animal, do most of the dirty work yet get short shrift when "no kill" shelters, who turn many animals away, damn them for having to euthanize. A closer look, however, shows that "no kill" may be a successful public relations gimmick that pulls at the heartstrings, but it is definitely not the way to help the largest numbers of animals.

JUST OUT OF REACH

There are other forms of torture that are simply accepted in our society. I'm sure readers of this book would never chain up a dog as if he or she were no more than a bicycle. But in every town there are dogs who spend their whole lives on chains, watching forlornly from a distance as the family comes and goes and life passes them by. They are scared to death out there in thunderstorms or blizzards. They are hot in summer, cold in winter, and thirsty when their water bowl, if they have one, overturns or freezes. Their sicknesses go undetected because no one pays them any real attention, and their unfulfilled longing to be part of a "pack," a family of dogs or humans, makes them lonely indeed.

Dogs like this need a friend like Linda Tyrrell, who in addition to her own full-time responsibilities at PETA, worked with her staff to build waterproof doghouses, buy straw, and make neglected dogs comfortable. These dogs need their own neighborhood watch: they need someone who asks permission to walk them, makes sure they are all right, even looks out for them in case of a flood or fire, for, hideous thought that it is, people evacuate during emergencies, leaving their animals behind without even bothering to expend the one minute it would take to unclip the chain or open the pen door and give their animal a fighting chance. Dogs drown, swimming to their deaths in the rising waters, in every single flood, just as surely as caged birds are left to succumb to pneumonia and hamsters are abandoned in their cages.

THEY TOOK THE SCISSORS TO HIS WINGS

When his wing is bruised and his bosom sore—
When he beats his bars and he would be free;
It is not a carol of joy or glee,
But a prayer that he sends from his heart's deep core,
But a plea, that upward to heaven he flings—
I know why the caged bird sings!

That poem, by Paul Laurence Dunbar, the son of two runaway slaves, is a reminder of how impervious people can be to the desires of others. Without much of a thought, they take a blade and cut the wings of beings who were born to fly, to soar, to float on currents and feel the sun and wind on their bodies. They are then put alone into a see-through box, never allowed to be part of a flock, to be able to preen their brothers and sisters, murmur to their mothers, or touch the beaks of their lovers.

Millions of birds, all precious individuals, are taken from their tropical homes every year and shipped to pet shops. The baby birds are usually snatched from their mothers (whole trees are hacked down in some forests to get to the fledgling macaws in their high nests), glue is spread on branches to trap birds, or mist nets are used to trap flocks of birds as they commute home from the fields to their nests at sunset. Many are fatally injured then and there. Others do not survive the trip from South America or Asia to the pet store.

The singer James Taylor once rescued a cockatoo named Cory from a New York health spa. Cory had annoyed his keepers and been put into solitary confinement for five years. He had torn out all his feathers.

James Taylor placed Cory with another rescue case, a lesser sulphur-crested cockatoo named Charlie. Charlie once lived free in Australia until trappers caught him and made him into a "lure bird" by hacking off portions of his wings and staking him to the ground. Charlie's pitiful cries brought other birds to the trappers' nets. His wings were badly damaged, and he will never be able to fly properly because of his ordeal. Charlie was sold through the pet trade to an owner who quickly tired of him and let him go to a PETA-endorsed sanctuary.

Francisco Serrano, when he was director of national parks in El Salvador, estimated that more than 60 percent of baby parrots and 80 percent of baby parakeets die during capture or soon after from stress, suffocation (some are shipped in hair curlers with their beaks taped shut), and rough handling.

Typical survivors end up on a perch in a pet store, wings clipped, traumatized, and bewildered, having lost all friends and family. And of course they are unable to escape. Some, like a macaw named Bucky, cannot stop themselves from screeching with fear or rage whenever they see a human being. They end up locked in dark closets or have things thrown at them and are constantly yelled at to "shut up."

Birds bred in captivity, the ones you often see in small cages in hotel lobbies or stuck on a gilt perch somewhere like a living decoration, come from bird factories. In those places, breeders warehouse hundreds or thousands of birds to produce offspring for the trade. Most of the breeding females never leave their nest boxes, never choose their own mates, and are denied lifetime bonding. (In the wild, males and females share all parenting, and most widows or widowers will not take a new partner if the first dies or disappears.)

Hand-raised birds, like those caught in the wild, often become neurotic, pulling out their feathers and self-mutilating. Graham Sam was such a bird. He spent ten years in a cage so small he couldn't spread his wings and from the stress had torn his own flesh, leaving it bloody. He too is one of the few lucky ones who found their way to a PETA-approved sanctuary.

CLEVER MINDS AND BIG HEARTS

Dr. Theodore Barber, author of *The Human Nature of Birds*, has studied how intelligent and innovative birds can be, even in captivity. He recounts how jays, ravens, and other birds have made useful tools by carefully selecting their materials. They have used strips of newspaper or sticks to make a rake for pulling in grain from outside a cage, placed solid objects in drinking bowls to raise the level of water in them, and inserted something of the right size to plug up a hole in a leaking dish. They can crack walnuts by placing each nut carefully between two cross branches, using one foot to keep the nut steady, and lining it up so that its seam splits when a few sharp blows are delivered with the beak. In Scandinavia, crows catch fish by using the lines that fishers leave suspended through holes in the ice of frozen lakes. The bird seizes the line in his or her beak, walks off with it away from the hole, then walks on top of the line back to the hole (thus preventing it from slipping), and repeats the process carefully until the fish is brought up.

Dr. Barber tells many beautiful stories about bird behavior in his book, but I particularly remember one tale of a young injured jay who was found on the ground and brought to a wildlife clinic run by Robert Leslie, a naturalist. Leslie and his wife nursed the injured little bird and got him back on his feet again. They called him Lorenzo, and he lived freely in the household for nearly three years, then he left to start a new life nearby with a mate.

Lorenzo communicated to the Leslies everything that appeared to matter to him, using special sounds and body language, which included movements of each part of his body supplemented by changing eye expressions. According to Leslie, Lorenzo impressed visitors with the intensity and exactness of his ability to communicate curiosity, enthusiasm, likes and dislikes, resentment, restless boredom, and once in a while, downright anger.

Lorenzo always kept careful track of the roughly two dozen toys he owned. He checked daily to see that each toy was where he had placed it, and if one was missing he complained immediately by wailing and pecking on Mrs. Leslie's hand until he got it back.

He understood the idea of trading and would tug at a visitor's ring or other jewelry, leave to quickly bring one of his toys to the visitor, then tug again at the object he wanted.

Lorenzo was not above using sleight of hand to procure the bauble if a swap was not forthcoming. His technique was to distract and then swipe. In one case, he tweaked the earlobe of his victim, in another he messed up the victim's hair, and in a third, he placed an after-dinner mint down the victim's shirt. When each person was distracted, he swooped down and yanked hard on the desired object. Lorenzo was generous and understood sharing and helping. He was seen giving his own food to a mother squirrel with a hungry brood of young, and he once led Mr. Leslie to a baby bird who had fallen from a nest. He accomplished this by making agitated "hollering" sounds and pulling on Mr. Leslie's chest hair while skillfully leading him to the right tree. Lorenzo shared his food, his sleeping cage, and his toys for two months with this recuperating representative of a different bird species.

BIRDS OF A FEATHER

Humans did not invent love or friendship. But how quick we are to deny these bonds to animals. Avian couples—from parakeets to hornbills—caress, cuddle, kiss (often intertwining their tongues in each other's mouths), sing to each other, and carry out other loving interactions that may or may not be followed by mating. Birds who love each other murmur and talk to each other in complicated ways we cannot hope to understand and take enormous comfort in grooming each other and simply being together. They will even attempt to lift injured mates to safety if they cannot fly and will carry food in their beaks to help ailing loved ones when they are dying.

Of all the cruelties of thoughtlessness, including the loss of flight and liberty, depriving them of companionship may be the most heartless.

There is no such animal as a "cage bird." All caged birds were either captured or captive-bred. No bird was born to be in a cage. In the wild, these beautiful beings are never alone, and if separated for even a moment, they call wildly to their flock mates. They preen one another, fly together, play, and share egg-incubation duties. Many bird species mate for life and share parenting tasks.

Unfortunately, the brilliant colors, speech capabilities, and intelligence of these animals has made them the third most popular animal companion in the United States, with an estimated forty million birds confined to cages in homes across the country. As a result, many birds do not get the mental stimulation or companionship that they need, and normal bird behaviors, such as flock calling, biting, chewing, and throwing food, are often unwelcome to unprepared human guardians. The result may be abandoned or isolated birds who, as reported in the *Washington Post*, "lose their minds." Bird sanctuaries report that they cannot take in even a small fraction of the birds no one wants.

BREEDING FOR PROFIT

In the late twentieth century, the popularity of keeping birds as companions resulted in a smuggling business based in Central America. It proved devastating to wild bird populations, and many birds who were caught died during transport or soon after. The Wild Bird Conservation Act stemmed the flow of birds into the United States (although it is still a problem in other countries), but breeding operations have not only perpetuated the myth that baby birds will grow up to become great companions but have also allowed consumer demand to continue. Just as there are puppy mills, there are bird factories, where breeders warehouse hundreds or thousands of nondomesticated birds for their offspring.

To a "breeder," a bird is a commodity to be placed with a "mate" to reproduce and is seldom—if ever—allowed out of the nest box. Birds who are returned to breeders because of behavioral problems are often kept as "breeding stock," thus perpetuating the problem behaviors in future generations, as birds are bred for color, not for temperament. Birds do not have to be kept in healthy, hygienic conditions or fed high-quality food to produce eggs. Typically, eggs are removed and hatched in incubators, and babies are hand-fed special formulas. Egg removal signals the female to produce another egg, and another, and another . . . eventually ruining her health by depleting her body of much-needed calcium and increasing her risk of becoming egg-bound, a condition in which the egg will not drop, but remains inside the bird, and that is nearly always fatal.

Even in low-profit enterprises, most birds live in small cages, surrounded by the frightening sounds of many unfamiliar birds. A bird who cannot choose his or her own mate may become depressed, especially if separated from a previous partner. Birds forced to cohabitate in small quarters with a "mate" who is not of their choosing may also become aggressive. The frustration and confusion that they experience after being thrust into a cramped environment with a "stranger" is often displayed as "mate aggression," in which the male mutilates or even kills his female companion.

ENSLAVED AND STRESSED

Unlike dogs and cats, captive-bred birds are only a few generations from their wild ancestors, so many of their natural behaviors do not mesh well with human companionship. Birds are meant to fly and be with others of their own kind. Considering that some parrots fly thirty miles per day in the wild, it's no wonder that confinement can cause birds to have temper tantrums and mood swings. Birds can also be mischievous and highly destructive. In the wild, they typically play in the tree-tops and chew on branches or leaves. In captivity, birds display this behavior by chewing on walls, door moldings, electrical or telephone wires, furniture, or any other material that they can get to. "Screaming" is really a bird's way of calling out to flock mates who, in the wild, might be half a mile away. Punishing birds only increases their frustration and makes them more unruly, as they do not understand that their natural behaviors are not welcome in a human home environment. One researcher who spent time in Australia and Indonesia observing wild lorikeets stated, "Parrots are the primates of the bird world. They are not content to sit on a perch and sing. They actively want to go and manipulate objects all the time."

Birds imported from the wild are often frightened and high-strung, and both hand-raised and wild-caught birds often become neurotic, pulling out feathers and mutilating themselves, sometimes to the point of death. When ready to breed, many species naturally pluck some feathers to prepare for nest building and egg sitting, but when humans interfere with their natural behaviors and disrupt biological and instinctual cycles by imprisoning birds, plucking becomes a destructive compulsion. Plucking can also be caused by physical problems, such as malnutrition or allergies.

Hand-raised birds crave affection and companionship, human or nonhuman, and sometimes they do not like to let their human companions out of their sight. They don't understand the separation that occurs when their humans go to work or, worse, on vacation. Birds interpret the disappearance of a mate or companion as trouble and may think that they are vulnerable to predators. These fears can compromise birds' immune systems, and they may succumb to sickness or death.

ASK NOT WHAT YOUR ANIMAL
CAN DO FOR YOU . . .

When you start wondering, "How can I enrich my animal companion's life?" a new and healthier relationship begins: one based on respect, humility, and understanding, instead of on domination, impatience, and human convenience.

When that animal dies, you will not have to look back with regret and ask yourself, "Why was I always yelling at him?" "Why didn't I take her to the park more often?" "Shouldn't I have known not to fly her in the hold of a plane?" "Did I make him as comfortable as possible in his old age?" or "How could I have waited to take her to the vet when there was blood in her urine?" You will have diligently learned all you could about him and his nature and needs, his desires and peculiarities; you will have sacrificed some things you wanted to do, often, and truly have done your best to love him with all your heart. That love will have been returned a thousandfold.

Thomas D. Murray of Franklin, Ohio, penned a beautiful essay called "What George Taught Us" when his beloved spaniel died. He wrote:

> I'd tried to teach him with a rolled-up newspaper to stop barking and dancing through the house every time the doorbell rang or he heard a car in the driveway. I think he was trying to make me understand that a friend at the door, or even a stranger or the mailman, can be a nice little diversion on a humdrum day, and something to celebrate with a little excitement.
>
> I thought he should be more patient as we fixed his food instead of prancing around the kitchen, standing on his rear legs and then gulping down the full bowl almost before it

was set in front of him on the floor. But he never stopped his kitchen parade, likely to remind me of the pure joy of wanting and waiting for something and, by always wagging his tail the entire time he was eating, demonstrating that gratefulness is a priceless part of good manners and doesn't cost a thing.

Early on I had tried to teach him to quickly finish his business in the yard so we could come inside. In time, he taught me the joy of a much longer sunrise walk to see the new day, even in winter, and another after dinner to help put the day's work and worries in perspective.

We thought maybe a big red ribbon on his collar and some special treats might make him sense some of the season's spirit at Christmastime. But on all the days that weren't Christmas, he tried to teach us to erase the boundaries and limits we drew around the holidays by showing us they didn't start for him when the tree came into the house or the holly went up, but when the family came in on any day or night of the year. I think he was trying to show us how to simplify the spirit of Christmas and spread it out over the other eleven months, and perhaps point out that the only presents that meant much of anything to him were those waiting for him, not just on Christmas, but every morning of the year—his family, his friends, his food, his freedom, and not too many baths.

No one in our family will ever forget George. But, of all the memories, the only one I'm a little ashamed of is that right up until the end, I was still trying to teach him things.

If we open our eyes and our hearts, there are a million ways to thank the animals who, whole and complete as they are, find themselves at our mercy.

WHAT YOU CAN DO

Companion Animals

Spay and neuter. "Every Litter Hurts!" Spaying or neutering not only helps fight the tragic cat, dog, and rabbit overpopulation problem, but it also eliminates diseases of the ovaries, uterus, and testicles and drastically reduces the risk of prostate and mammary cancers, both common in older animals. Many municipalities and humane societies have low-cost spay/neuter programs, or try calling SPAY USA at 1-800-248-SPAY. Even paying top dollar for this once-in-a-lifetime surgery beats the tragedy of bringing unwanted litters into the world.

Sponsor a spay/neuter surgery or provide a doghouse for a dog left outside in the cold. See PETA.org for details.

Support your local "open admission" animal shelter. Never patronize pet shops and breeders—they contribute to the dog and cat overpopulation crisis. The animals at your local open admission (where the doors are open to all) shelter have personality, affection, charm, and looks. You could be their lifeline.

Liberate your language! An animal is "he" or "she"—not "it." Avoid using animal-derogatory terms such as "sly as a fox" or "that man who assaulted someone is an animal."

Clean up your pound. Volunteers can transform grim, neglected pounds into nice places to visit, and comfortable places for animals. Volunteers walk and groom dogs, assist with calls, and collect blankets and newspapers.

Support pet-supply only stores. Buy leashes, toys, and other supplies for companion animals only at stores that don't sell animals.

Educate others. If you attend a fair, flea market, or other event at which animals are being given away, educate those responsible. If people are offering a litter of kittens or puppies, explain the risks of giving animals to unknown passersby: some people sell dogs and cats to laboratories or dealers, and others abuse, neglect, or abandon them. Ask PETA for flyers on spaying and neutering and share copies of the brochure "Finding the Right Home for Your Companion Animal."

Give gifts carefully. Don't give anyone an animal as a gift unless you have discussed the matter with the person beforehand to make sure he or she is fully prepared to care for a companion animal for *life*.

Be considerate! Think of your companion animal's needs for exercise, companionship, and stimulation. Don't leave him or her alone for long periods of time. Set aside some time each day for interacting with him or her. Provide a second companion of the same species to help alleviate loneliness and boredom.

Give them a door. Provide a dog or cat door (into a fenced yard, of course). No one expects human beings to keep their legs crossed for eight to ten hours a day! Because cats and cars don't mix, if cats can go outside, be sure to add a forty-five-degree interior angle to the top of your fence.

Help build doghouses for chained backyard dogs in your community. Be sure to include dry straw for them to use as bedding. See HelpingAnimals.com for design details.

Call people who place "free to a good home" ads in your local paper, warning them that "bunchers" are known to scan such ads for animals they can sell to laboratories. Order

PETA's free "free to a good home" pack, which is available at HelpingAnimals.com.

Make their food. Avoid off-the-shelf commercial food, which, no matter how fancy sounding or highly priced, is made from rejected, chemical-laden, slaughterhouse meat. Instead, buy a vegetarian pet food or make food for your companion animals yourself. (Even cats can have a vegetarian diet now, thanks to a supplement called Vegecat.) Visit IamsCruelty.com for a list of vegan cat food companies.

Bake for your dog or cat. Try these recipes:

Vegan Dog Biscuits

9 cups whole wheat flour

1 cup nutritional yeast

1 Tbsp. salt

1 Tbsp. garlic powder

- Mix dry ingredients. Add approximately 3 cups water. Knead into a pliable dough.
- Roll out until ⅛ inch thick. Cut into shapes.
- Bake for 10 to 15 minutes at 350°F. After turning off oven, leave biscuits in oven overnight or equivalent so they become hard and crunchy.

Garbanzo Cat Chow

¾ cup sprouted or cooked garbanzo beans

1½ Tbsp. nutritional yeast powder

1 Tbsp. chopped or grated vegetables

1 Tbsp. oil

½ tsp. Vegecat (see Chapter 14, "Products, Services, Restaurants" for address)

⅓ tsp. soy sauce

• Mix all ingredients together. Refrigerate any unused portions.

Get information. Learn about your friend's needs, instincts, and natural behaviors by reading up on that species or breed. You may be surprised at the motivation behind some behaviors.

Buy cruelty-free toys. Buy only safe, cruelty-free toys and products for your companion animals. Don't buy rawhide, which is a slaughterhouse by-product.

Make a bed. Provide a foam pad for your companion animal to rest and sleep on. This will keep dogs and cats out of drafts and provide relief from arthritis and protection for joints, especially for older ones.

Pay attention. Never ignore stray animals on the street, where they can become victims of disease, starvation, cars, and the cruelty of humans—as well as being left to reproduce and add to the overpopulation problem.

Create a network. Swap information on good and bad experiences with boarding facilities, veterinarians, groomers, "pet sitters," and even dog-door suppliers. Keep a card file for neighbors' reference.

Help them get home. When you find lost animals, your principal aim is to reunite them with their families, without alerting unscrupulous people to their plight. Most newspapers will place a free ad if you find an animal—but make your description less than thorough; the person looking for a lost companion should be able to describe the animal *in detail.*

Apply your business skills. Gwendolyn May uses proceeds from her thrift shop to pay for veterinary care and food for companion animals of needy elderly people. She also runs a twenty-four-hour advice-about-animals hotline.

Be persistent! Call the humane society as often as needed to report cruelty and get action. (You can request anonymity.)

Alert schools. If a school is keeping animals—either as "pets" or as teaching "tools"—protest to the teacher, the administrator, and if necessary, the school board. Ask school boards to forbid the use of animals in classrooms.

Protecting Dogs

Fence your yard. A pen is not good enough. If dogs must ever be left outside, they would like nothing better than to be able to explore every nook and cranny of their yard. A six-foot privacy fence is safest—it's harder for them to escape and harder for people to hurt your pup. If a fence is out of your budget, attach a swivel hook to a running line that enables the dog to run back and forth without getting tangled. Never leave a choke collar on an unsupervised dog—they can be strangled if the collar becomes snagged, or they can hang themselves.

Never crate your dog unless you are transporting them. No one likes to be in a cage. Rather than using a crate, section off a portion of your house for your dog to stay in while you're out.

Use a harness. Swap that collar for a harness. Pressure on a dog's neck can be stressful and lead to injuries, and who wants to be dragged around and tugged by the neck, anyway?

Let your dog be a dog! For example, don't flat out prohibit barking or digging—give dogs their very own special places to dig. Never turn your dog over to a trainer but teach them to use their "sandbox" by burying favorite toys in it.

Take a class. Enroll your dog in a humane training class that you attend too. If your dog is outdoors because of behavior problems, confinement and isolation only make the problems worse. Humane training teaches you to communicate with your dog, who is eager to please but isn't always clear on what you expect.

Be gentle. Avoid giving your dog orders except when essential for the dog's safety. Try to make suggestions and ask questions too. Learning the meanings of words and phrases like "Cookies," "Outside?" "Water?" "All done," and "Wanna go for a *walk*?" can make your dog's life happier.

Bring your dog inside. Don't kid yourself that dogs "get used to" living outside. Unless you or other dogs are out there to share it with them, the dull, unchanging scenery of the backyard quickly loses its charm. If their constant barking (really cries for attention) has finally stopped, it's not because they're content but because they've given up hope of rescue.

Look out for "hot dogs." Dogs can't perspire, so in hot weather they should never be left in a car. Even with car windows cracked, a dog can quickly suffer brain damage or death. Check that pavements are not burning their pads on a hot day.

Get exercise. Provide your dog with lots of exercise. Dogs crave running, sniffing, and exploring. Go for long walks daily, if possible, and use a retractable leash that allows your dog to run ahead and check out interesting fire hydrants.

Watch out for lamppost dogs. Jim Yeargin waits with dogs tied outside stores to apprise their guardians that the dogs could be stolen and sold to the vivisection industry. If he can't wait, he ties a tag reading: "I could have stolen this dog to sell to a laboratory" to the animals' collars.

Provide information. Develop and distribute seasonal alerts (for example, "Remember not to leave cloth bedding in doghouses in winter—it freezes when wet") and general tips (for example, how to secure a water bucket and how to make homemade biscuits for the health-conscious dog).

Be a friend. Offer to take "forgotten" dogs for walks and visit them regularly. Fix a running line and/or attach a swivel (available at hardware stores). Make sure the dog can't get tangled up and that his or her water is accessible and in a container that can't be knocked over. Your kindness means the world to these animals.

Reject electric fences and shock collars. Horror stories abound. Not only have fast-moving dogs found themselves on the wrong side of the electric fence, unable to return, but faulty shock collars have shocked dogs at the "wrong" time, although I'm not sure when it is the "right" time to receive a nasty bolt from out of the blue, are you?

Offer tips. Whether you talk to them in person, send an anonymous letter, or contact the humane society, let owners of neglected dogs know exactly what needs to be done. Although it may seem unlikely that simply pointing out the neglect will be enough to remedy it, sometimes that's all it takes.

Cats

Trim your cat's claws. Don't declaw. To prevent furniture damage, those hooks simply need to be snipped off. Have your veterinarian trim the nails, or invest in a decent pair of nail clippers (available from your veterinarian and from pet supply catalogs and stores). Press the paw between your fingers and thumb to unsheathe the claws. Trim just enough to blunt claws but not enough to cut into the quick. Only do kitty's front paws. Hind paws pose no threat except during cat ninja kicking contests and will help kitty climb trees to safety if he or she accidentally slips outside. Visit HelpingAnimals.com for more information.

Buy or make a scratching post. Vertical scratching posts should be sturdy and tall enough for a cat to stretch out fully (a wobbly post will frighten cats away). Posts should be covered in sisal or carpet turned inside out. Cardboard posts need to be changed when worn out or your cat will lose interest.

Use a harness. Train your cat to walk on a harness; just be sure to use an ultralightweight leash attached to a harness (not a collar). Start by getting your cat used to the harness and leash for short periods of time indoors; then bring along some favorite treats and pick an open area (away from trees and fences) to walk.

Wear a collar. Use a quick-release collar with a tag for every cat. Even cats who never set a paw outdoors can slip out accidentally. One PETA member outfits her cats with tags that simply say, I'M LOST, with the phone number printed below.

Watch their diet. Cats' special dietary needs are more critical than dogs'; for example, cats can suffer loss of eyesight and die if they are deprived of taurine, which until recently was virtually impossible to find in a nonanimal form (now available as Vegecat, a derivative of an organic, renewable, nonanimal source). While most cats appear to do well on a vegetarian diet, some have not adapted so well. Monitor your companion *closely* when you switch her or him to a nonmeat diet. The cat food company Harbingers of a New Age's Web site (vegepet.com) can answer any questions you might have.

Give digestible treats. Many adult cats have trouble digesting the milk sugar lactose. Instead, give treats like corn (maize), peas, squash, sweet potatoes, and melon.

Give cats a room with a view. Windows are cat "TV"—a bird feeder placed near a window beats the most gripping soap opera!

Look out for ferals. A colony of feral cats (domestic cats gone wild) exists (and multiplies!) in almost every community. Feeding them from time to time is helpful but not enough. These animals or their recent ancestors probably once lived in homes and are lost or were abandoned. They are subject to disease, starvation, injury, and accident; and they need help. Borrow a humane box trap from your local animal shelter, or have neighbors chip in to purchase one from a hardware store. Take the cats to the vet or the local shelter to have them examined, given the appropriate shots, and spayed or neutered—or euthanized if ill or if adoption efforts fail in your neighborhood and beyond. Preventing feral cats from continuing to reproduce is the best and kindest assistance you can give them.

Fish

Keep company. Don't buy fish, but if you already have done so remember that most fish enjoy companionship. If you have a single fish, check with friends and neighbors to find another loner whom you may be able to adopt. (But don't support the fish trade by going to a dealer.)

Clean the fish tank. Clean the tank regularly, about two to three times a week. The natural waste of fish emits ammonia, which can accumulate to toxic levels. Also be sure to clean the glass well with a pad or brush so algae doesn't form.

Give your fish plants. Plants provide oxygen, shelter, and hiding places, and fish enjoy snacking on them as well. Provide live plants, not plastic ones.

Make it fun. Create places for your fish to hide and explore. Ceramic, natural rock, and driftwood all work well. Make sure objects are thoroughly cleaned and disinfected (with an approved cleaner) before putting them in the tank. Do not use metal objects, as they will rust.

Birds

Boycott cruel hotels. Refuse to stay at resort hotels that keep birds caged as "decorations." Let your travel agent and the hotel managers know that you will not support this cruelty.

Don't buy birds. Never buy or cage a bird (except for the bird's safety). Birds were born to fly and, being flock animals, live with others of their species. Wild birds make sad, lonely, and sometimes dangerous "pets." Captive-bred birds are more docile, but breeders must constantly introduce new genes from wild-caught birds, so even buying only captive-bred birds supports the wild-caught bird trade.

Work your town. Discourage pet shops from carrying birds. Work to get your city or town to pass an ordinance banning the sale of birds.

Care for a bird by providing: *A private place,* like a screen to go behind, in their room or flight enclosure. *"Special time"* with you every day. *Baths or mistings* when the birds desire them. Provide shallow containers or a birdbath with lukewarm water. Some birds like to be misted with water from a spray bottle. One person built a perch in her shower; the birds sit on the shower curtain rod, and when the (lukewarm) shower is turned on they can descend to the perch if they so choose. *Between eight and twelve hours of sleep a night,* preferably from dusk on, in a draped flight enclosure or a covered cage. *Regular nail and beak trims* to avoid difficulty in eating. If birds are allowed to chew hard toys, beak trims may not be necessary. *Bird-safe toys*, including wood, on a rotating basis for chewing and playing. Make sure the wood is not poisonous. Apple tree branches are good if they haven't been sprayed. Companion-animal supply companies sell suitable wooden bird toys. It may take months before interest in a toy is stimulated. *Classical music*, especially Mozart, during the day.

Never buy a bird from a pet store or buy companion-animal supplies or food from stores that sell birds. If you or people you know already have birds and are unable to provide them with companionship and space to fly, please consider taking one of the following actions:

- Find out if there is a bird sanctuary or large indoor/outdoor aviary (or an outdoor one in a very warm climate) where you can release the bird. Ideally, you should place birds with members of their own species. Check the climate, opportunities for mating and privacy, and other key factors.
- If you cannot find a reputable sanctuary, consider placing the bird with someone who has other birds of the same species, allows them to live in a free-flight situation, and will never separate them once they have bonded. Also, make sure that they don't breed birds and have learned to collect eggs to avoid hatching. Confirm that they frequent a board-certified avian veterinarian.

If you wish to keep the bird, find a companion bird of the same or similar species. A list of avian rescue organizations can be found at AvianProtectors.Homestead.com or AvianWelfare.org. Check shelters, humane societies, animal rights groups, newspapers, and nursing homes—some birds can live for more than a hundred years, often outliving their human companions.

Many people do not want to get another bird because they are afraid that the first bird won't pay enough attention to them anymore. If the bird does pay less attention to his or her human friends, it just proves how starved for same-species attention he or she was. Two birds can actually be easier to care for than one—with the companionship of another bird, they may be less disruptive and destructive. When the birds have become friends, you can be comforted by the fact that when you are not home, they have each other's company.

The following tips will help keep birds healthy, calm, and contented:

- Before introducing a new bird, take him or her to an avian veterinarian for a checkup. If the newcomer is in good health and free of diseases, put his or her cage inside the larger flight enclosure so that the birds can see each other. Watch to see how they get along. If they seem friendly, open the door of the small cage after a week. The newcomer will come out when he or she feels comfortable enough. Leave this cage in place, door open, for as many days as the newcomer may want to use it as a safe place—until he or she totally abandons it. Until you're absolutely sure that the birds have bonded, don't leave them alone or in a situation where one cannot get away from the other. Do not assume that these two birds will definitely become friends. Be prepared to house the birds separately if they do not bond.
- Let the birds fly free for long periods of time every day—spending as much time out of the cage as pos-

sible. Convert your balcony or porch into an aviary or build a good-weather aviary in your backyard if possible. Otherwise, provide a "bird-proof" room or rooms, with no ceiling fans or other bird hazards. Include a bird "gym" or nonpoisonous tree branches (such as dogwood, apple, or elm) for exercise.

- Eliminate hazards like ceiling fans, pots of water, open toilet bowls, electrical wires, large glass windows and mirrors, places where birds could become stuck, etc., and be extra-cautious to keep birds safely away from dogs and cats, especially when you leave the home.

- The fumes emitted by overheated nonstick cookware and self-cleaning ovens are deadly to birds—never use them in a home with birds. Use ecologically safe products—no strong cleaners, aerosols, artificial air fresheners, or insecticides. If your apartment complex demands that you make your apartment available to an exterminator, you can legally refuse for "health reasons."

- Keep food and water containers above perches, high enough so that they do not get soiled with droppings. Containers that have become soiled should be cleaned immediately. Some birds dunk food in their water, and those water containers should be cleaned at least twice a day to prevent bacterial growth. Vitamins should never be administered through the water unless the containers can be thoroughly cleaned every couple of hours, as this encourages bacterial growth.

- Birds don't live on seeds alone, so you shouldn't condemn your companion bird to such a bland and nutritionally inadequate diet. Offer a variety of fruits and vegetables along with grains, nuts, cooked beans, and seeds. Birds have tremendously fast metabolisms and cannot be without food for long. Different species have different nutritional needs, so it's imperative that you read up on your bird or consult with a veterinarian. Malnutrition accounts for more than 90 percent of the health problems and deaths of companion birds. Birds need the proper combination of vitamins, minerals, and amino acids to remain healthy. A good supplement can help, although a variety of proper foods should meet any bird's needs. Visit PassionTree-House.com for information on birds' natural diets and how you can mimic them.

- Never provide grit for your birds. This supplement is marketed as an aid to digestion and contains calcium. Grit is not found in the wild and has no place in a bird's diet, as it can mineralize in the gizzard and cause crop impactions. Fresh organic vegetables such as broccoli and spinach should be offered instead.

- Make sure that your plants are not poisonous to birds. Common plants that are toxic if birds ingest them include: English ivy, philodendron, azaleas, and holly. A good avian veterinarian can provide you with an extensive list.

- Provide shallow containers or a birdbath filled with water. Some birds like to be misted with water from a spray bottle. After your birds bathe, keep them away from drafts until their feathers dry.

- Nail trims may be necessary but can often be avoided by providing cement swings and perches. Beak trims should not be needed unless there is an underlying health problem. Chewing on toys is necessary and good for birds—an overgrown beak requires a trip to a good avian veterinarian.

- Provide numerous bird-safe toys for chewing and playing, including clean, nonpoisonous wood. Companion-animal supply companies sell suitable wooden bird toys.

For more information on keeping birds as companions, please visit the Avian Welfare Coalition's Web site at Avianwelfare.org.

Rabbits

Hug your bunny. Rabbits need lots of love and attention. Tame rabbits are social beings who are happiest living indoors with you. Isolated rabbits become bored, withdrawn, and depressed. They can make friends with other rabbits, cats, and some dogs.

Groom your bunny. Groom at least twice a week with a small, fine soft wire brush or soft-bristled cat brush. Grooming shows affection and lets you examine the rabbit for signs of illness.

Exotic Animals

Don't keep exotics as pets. Regardless of their size, exotic animals should never be kept in captivity. If you want to share your home with an animal companion, please visit your local shelter—millions of unwanted animals are literally dying to be someone's friend.

Travel Tips

Flying your animal. Never fly an animal in the hold of an aircraft, no matter what the airline says. Many animals arrive injured, dead, or disappear, and the experience is horrify-ingly frightening. If you absolutely must, use only a direct, nonstop flight, making sure to fly at night in summer, dur-ing the day in winter, and never during temperature ex-tremes (animals can freeze to death, suffocate, or die of heat prostration in cargo holds—especially if there is a de-lay). Be sure you or someone very reliable sees the animal safely aboard, meets the arriving flight, and knows how to raise Cain if the animal doesn't arrive on time. If your companion animal is high-strung, your veterinarian may give him or her a tranquilizer. Sturdy, roomy, well-ventilated carriers and clear identification are essential, and accustom the animal to the carrier at home long before the departure date. Recommended carriers must be USDA approved and can be purchased from most airlines.

Take your friend on board. If your animal friend is small (can fit into a carry-on kennel that goes under your seat), choose an airline that allows him or her to fly in the pas-senger compartment with you. Avoid heavy traffic days, such as holidays and weekends. Reserve space for your ani-mal well in advance, as airlines limit the number of "pet" spaces per flight. Don't feed your companion animal solid food for at least three hours before flight time, but a little water and a peppy "walk" are a must before boarding.

Provide reassurance. If you go away on vacation, remember your animal companions love you and will miss you, so greet and leave them with this foremost in your mind. Al-ways remember to say good-bye. Use a kind "stay," look di-rectly into your friend's eyes, and say, very reassuringly and firmly, "I'll be back." Leave a worn piece of your clothing with them to reassure them that you'll return. The idea that your absence will not be forever is reinforced in this simple way.

Keep them at home. Keep your dogs or cats safely at home, rather than boarding them out with strangers. There's a lot to be said for familiar surroundings; they are generally the safest and least stressful. Try to find a responsible (adult) friend or relative to stay at your home or to come by *at least* three times a day to keep an eye on the animals and tend to their needs, such as allowing them to relieve themselves. Even if there are ample provisions, accidents happen, and someone should make safety checks often. If you can't find someone you know and trust, explore a "pet sitting" service that has *several* verifiable and reliable references—from a humane society, veterinarians, and bona fide clients. Make sure the chosen caretaker has all the important information posted near the telephone, including emergency numbers (veterinary night service and numbers where you can be reached).

Thoroughly investigate boarders. If you *must* board your animal, veterinary hospitals are not recommended because animals can be exposed to illnesses and can often sense the pain of others around them and fear that they are about to get a shot or their nails cut, at the very least. Be very careful when choosing a boarding facility—smiling people can run little shops of horrors. Humane officers have frightening stories to tell, such as animals stacked in crates during peak boarding seasons, and families returning home to find that their animal friends had "escaped." Ask friends for references, and check with your local chamber of commerce and department of consumer affairs for possible complaints against the facility. Make sure that you inspect the *entire* premises. If you are told that this is inconvenient or that insurance regulations prevent your inspection, head out the front door, pronto.

Animal Theft

Plant a microchip. Cat and dog tags and collars can fall off or be removed. Microchips, on the other hand, are permanent, which means that your dog or cat will enjoy increased protection in the case of theft or in the event that she becomes lost.

The microchip (about the size of a grain of rice) is inserted under an animal's skin between the shoulder blades, and the process takes no longer than administering a vaccination. Fortunately, it won't hurt your pocketbook, either. On average, having a microchip implanted costs around $30, in addition to a $12 to $15 registration fee to put your animal's I.D. into the national registry.

And add a tattoo. Tattoo your animal companion too. Sometimes people don't check for the microchip, and tags can be lost or removed, rendering the animal conveniently anonymous. Veterinarians, shelters, pounds, and laboratories often do check for tattoos, and many animals have been happily reunited with their families because they were "wearing" tattooed identification on their inner thigh.

Organizations that can help:

AVID Microchip. AVID stands for American Veterinary Identification Device.

National Dog Registry (NDR). To report a lost dog with a Social Security number tattoo, visit Nationaldogregistry.com.

Tattoo-A-Pet (TAP). Tattoo-a-pet.com

Safeguard against theft. Never leave dogs unsupervised in a yard or chained or tied up alone. They can be whisked away in seconds by someone armed with a tasty treat. Cats should be allowed out only with you. Animals left unattended in cars are also a favorite target for thieves.

Run an ad. Place an ad in the classified section of your newspaper that says: "PET THEFT ALERT: Don't let your companion animal end up in a research experiment. Don't leave animals alone outdoors. Check out new homes thoroughly before you give an animal away. Call _____ (your phone number or PETA's) for more information."

Read a book. Read *Stolen for Profit* by Judith Reitman.

In Case of Emergency

Be prepared. Carry an animal rescue kit (nonperishable food, a cardboard cat carrier, a leash, a cloth bandage for a muzzle, and emergency phone numbers of vets and shelters) in your car.

Get help. In case of a medical emergency, seek veterinary help right away. Describe symptoms or injuries clearly, and take careful note of instructions. Generally, keep the victim quiet and still; in the case of traffic accidents, move victims carefully and gently out of danger, and then follow these procedures: when waiting for a veterinarian, the general principle is to stem any bleeding (without cutting off circulation) and keep air passages clear of obstructions while disturbing the animal as little as possible. If you need to carry an injured dog, make a stretcher out of a blanket, board, coat, or sack; put it on the ground and gradually slide it under the animal. Keep the stretcher taut. Stem bleeding with a clean handkerchief, piece of sheet, or any cloth by making a pad and securing it to the wound, then elevate the injured body part.

An injured animal, however familiar, may snap or bite out of fear and pain. A bandage or belt can be used as a makeshift muzzle, looped around the snout a couple of times and then tied behind the head. Make sure the animal can breathe easily (watch out for heaving sides, a sign of breathing difficulty) and isn't vomiting, or she or he may choke. Release the muzzle as soon as you can. Shock can often occur with any form of trauma, so keep animals as quiet and warm as possible. If possible, put one person strictly in charge of monitoring the animal.

Heads up! Take the following symptoms seriously. Get help immediately! Bleeding from any orifice: nose, mouth, ears, rectum, sex organs; any problems with eyes: watering or half-closed, third eyelid exposed; straining to urinate or repeated trips to the litter box; bloating or collapse after eating, exercise, or rapid intake of water; unusually lethargic or agitated behavior; drinking lots of water; fur standing on end; loss of appetite; continuous vomiting; dragging or holding limbs; sudden weight loss, diarrhea, coughing, lumps.

Use care with antifreeze. Be careful not to spill antifreeze, which is highly toxic to animals, who like its sweet taste. Better, shop for Sierra antifreeze, a nontoxic and biodegradable alternative.

 FREQUENTLY ASKED QUESTIONS

Does PETA believe that people shouldn't have pets?

There will always be animal guardians, but we dislike the word *pet*, and we are opposed to breeding animals and treating them as if they were toys or surrogate children rather than the whole, interesting, and culturally different beings they are.

The earliest fossils that resemble the bones of modern dogs are about twelve thousand years old, so we know that humans' fascination with domesticated wolves began at least that long ago. About five thousand years ago, Egyptians became the first to tame cats, whom they used to control the rodent population. Since then, the breeding and care of cats and dogs has exploded into a love affair, a sport, and a booming business. This international pastime has created an overpopulation crisis, and as a result, every year millions of unwanted animals suffer at the hands of abusers, languish in shelters, and are euthanized. Adopting a cat or dog from a shelter—preferably two, so that they can keep each other company—and providing a loving, respectful home full of patience and understanding is a small but powerful way to prevent some of this suffering. The most important thing to do is to spay or neuter the animals in our care and never buy animals from breeders or pet stores, which contribute to the overpopulation crisis.

If I can find homes for all the kittens or puppies, why shouldn't I let my cat or dog have a litter?

While your intentions may be good, every kitten or puppy you bring into the world is going to take up a home that could have been filled by an existing homeless animal who will be destroyed for the lack of that home. There's also no way to know what will happen to the offspring of all the animals born from the litter you allow, once they have been adopted. Every single year, millions of healthy, wonderful animals will go through the front doors of shelters—and go out the back doors in body bags. Many more will be abandoned on the streets. All this misery and death could be prevented through spaying and neutering (surgical sterilization). Every stray cat and neglected dog came from an animal who had not been spayed or neutered.

*Don't puppies in pet stores need homes just as much as
puppies in shelters? Besides, how else can I choose
the breed?*

Most dogs sold in pet shops come from hideously cruel puppy
mills, as Oprah Winfrey has warned on her show. In puppy
mills, female dogs are kept in small outdoor wire cages without
adequate protection from rain, sweltering heat, bitter cold, or
biting winds. They are denied companionship and comfort
and treated like breeding machines. Their puppies are taken
from them, packed into crates, and shipped to dealers, often
arriving in poor condition. The adult dogs go mad and whirl
like dervishes in their cages from lack of movement and social
interaction. Poor breeding practices lead to numerous health
problems for the pups, including distemper, parvovirus, respiratory conditions, physical deformities, deafness, eye diseases,
psychological problems, and a host of other ailments.

Once puppies arrive at pet stores, life in cramped cages adds
more strain to their already stressed systems, increasing their sus-
ceptibility to disease. Some stores have been caught killing un-
sold dogs on the premises. While breeders churn out millions of
shiny new puppies each year to sell, millions of wonderful animals have to be "put down" in shelters for want of a good home.
Animal shelters are able to find loving homes for only a fraction
of the animals they receive. Because of the overpopulation crisis,
there is no such thing as "responsible" breeding, not one litter.

If you have the time, energy, space, and money to care for
a dog (or two), please visit your local animal shelter and adopt.
Mixed-breed dogs are typically healthier and more even tem-
pered than purebred dogs, but if you're determined, you can
usually find purebred dogs at shelters or through "breed rescue" clubs.

Rather than euthanizing dogs and cats,
couldn't we just build more animal shelters?

Building more and more holding areas to contain more and more animals is not a solution to the problem of companion-animal homelessness because it does not solve the root problem—continued breeding. Dogs and cats need more than food, water, and shelter from the elements. They need loving care, regular human companionship, respect for their individuality, and the opportunity to play and run. As difficult as it may be for us to accept, euthanasia (carried out without pain or trauma by veterinarians or trained shelter professionals via intravenous injection of sodium pentobarbital) is often the most compassionate and dignified way for unwanted animals to leave this uncaring world.

Isn't it better to declaw a cat than to give
him or her away if she's ruining my furniture?

Do you really value and love your furniture more than you value and love your cat?

If you asked your cats if it would be okay to put them through ten separate, painful amputations that can weaken their legs, shoulders, and back muscles, they would probably say no—and they wouldn't be alone. Many veterinarians in the United States and abroad refuse to declaw cats. In fact, in Germany and some other parts of Europe, declawing is illegal. Cats who have been declawed experience extreme pain when they awake after surgery and have difficulty walking until their paws heal. Some never use the litter box again, associating it with pain when they scratched in it after the operation. Without their claws, cats are virtually defenseless, and this can lead to neuroses, changes in behavior, and even back, skin, and bladder problems.

The part of the claw that pulls threads from drapes and sofas is the hook. It is fairly easy to learn how to clip the hook, blunting the nail to prevent such damage. And, with the aid of a scratching post or two, cats can be taught where to do natural stretching and scratching.

What does PETA think about trapping, altering, and releasing feral cats?

Our experiences with trap-alter-and-release programs and even "managed" feral cat colonies have led us to believe that in most circumstances these programs are not in the cats' best interests. We have witnessed far too many incidents in which feral cats have suffered and died horrible deaths at the hands of cruel people, in traffic, from poisoning, freezing, accidents, and from untreated disease.

It is precisely because we would never encourage anyone to let their own cats outdoors to roam that we do not encourage the same for feral cats. In fact, the act of releasing a feral cat is, in the eyes of the law, criminal abandonment.

Altering feral cats prevents the suffering of future generations but does little to improve the quality of life for those already fending for themselves outdoors. Allowing feral cats to continue their daily struggle for survival in a hostile environment is not usually humane.

In exceptional circumstances, PETA believes it is sometimes acceptable to trap, vaccinate, alter, and release feral cats if the cats are truly isolated from roads, people, and other animals who could harm them; are regularly attended to by people who not only feed them, but also provide them with veterinary care; and are situated in an area where they do not have access to wildlife and where the weather is temperate.

What's wrong with chaining dogs outside? Isn't that better than having them run loose outside?

A dog is not a bicycle to be kept chained up. Condemning a dog to solitary confinement on a chain is so cruel that it is illegal in a growing number of cities. Chained dogs are often exposed to searing heat, bitter cold, rain, and wind, putting them at risk for heat prostration, frostbite, and exposure-related health problems. Chains can wrap around trees or other objects, water bowls can easily tip over, and food can quickly spoil in summer or freeze in winter.

Chained dogs often become fearful of intruders and overly protective of their tiny patches of ground. They are easy targets for cruel people who taunt and tease them, and as a result, many chained dogs become defensive and untrusting. Not surprisingly, dogs who spend much of their lives outside on chains often can become dangerous, while dogs who are well socialized and supervised rarely bite.

Perhaps worst of all, chained dogs are terribly lonely. After all, dogs are pack animals who long to love, live with, and be loved by others. Denying a dog companionship is so cruel that some dogs are driven crazy by their loneliness. It's best for everyone when dogs are treated as treasured family members.

Why shouldn't cats be allowed outdoors to explore and exercise?

Cats can travel far and get into all sorts of trouble, even fatal trouble. They should be allowed outdoors for walks on a harness and leash, just as dogs are, and to explore securely fenced yards. A product called Cat Fence-In, a flexible mesh barrier that can be placed on the tops of privacy fences to prevent cats from climbing out, can help you keep a cat safely in your yard.

Like dogs or small children, cats who are let outdoors without supervision are vulnerable to the dangers of cars, other animals, cruel people, and disease. Feline leukemia, feline AIDS (FIV), feline infectious peritonitis (FIP), toxoplasmosis, and rabies can be difficult to detect and, in the case of FIP, impossible to test for. Most of these ailments are highly contagious and can easily be passed on to other animals in the home.

Some people consider free-roaming cats to be pests. They do not want cats to urinate, defecate, dig, eat plants, or kill birds on their property. Free-roaming cats have been shot, poisoned, trapped, and drowned or abandoned in the woods, and stolen by angry neighbors.

Fortunately, cats can live happy lives indoors. Learn how to make your indoor cat forget all about the great outdoors. Look at the petamall.org for my book *250 Ways to Make Your Cat Adore You.*

What's wrong with keeping birds in cages?

All caged birds have either been captured from the wild or bred in captivity. In the wild, these beautiful beings are never alone, and if they are separated from their often enormous flocks, even for a moment, they call wildly to their flock mates. These highly intelligent, highly social animals preen one another, talk to one another, fly together, play together, and share egg-incubation duties. Many species of birds mate for life, becoming grief stricken over the loss of a loved one. In the wild, most birds will not take a second mate.

Every squawk is a cry for attention that often goes unanswered, or birds are told to "be quiet!" Life in captivity is often a living death sentence for birds, who may suffer from malnutrition, loneliness, and the stress of confinement in improper environments. Being cooped up causes birds to have temper tantrums and mood swings born of severe frustration and of having to deny their natural behaviors. The *Los Angeles Times* reported that parrots "quickly become frustrated 'perch potatoes' in captivity. . . . Many end up obese and with serious behavioral problems such as screaming, biting and self-mutilation by plucking out their feathers." James Serpell, director of the Center for the Interaction of Animals and Society at the University of Pennsylvania says, "Parrots are the primates of the bird world. They are not content to sit on a perch and sing."

Birds are smuggled into the United States more frequently than any other animal. Before being shipped, many birds are force-fed, their wings are clipped, their beaks are taped shut, and they are crammed into everything from spare tires to luggage to hide them. It's not unusual for 80 percent of the birds in a shipment to die. The rest are emotionally scarred for life.

Birds taken from the wild can pose a health threat to both humans and domesticated animals. Parrots have transferred potentially deadly psittacosis to humans. Exotic Newcastle disease (END), which devastated whole flocks of chickens and turkeys in the 1970s, was believed to have been brought to the United States by South American parrots who were smuggled in for the pet trade. More recently, Mexican parrots who were smuggled into California were suspected to have caused an outbreak of END, leading to the government-sponsored slaughter of more than three million chickens and turkeys. "We're not trained to detect diseases," said a US Fish and Wildlife inspection officer.

Captive-bred birds don't fare much better. Birds who are older than eight to ten weeks don't sell well at pet shops, so many are kept for breeding and condemned to small cages for the rest of their lives.

If you love birds, contact a bird-rescue group in your area to learn how you can foster or adopt an abused or neglected bird, better yet adopt several, who can keep one another company.

6

What's Really Going on in Laboratories

I have always been moved by this poem, sent in by a PETA member years ago. It seems to sum up our naïveté and our blind trust, in "science":

> *Look Mommy, isn't he cute?*
> *Can he really fly?*
> *Of course, my dear, watch him.*
> *How do they teach him, Mommy?*
> *See those little wires*
> *coming from his head.*
> *Yes, what are they for?*
> *Every time he makes a mistake*
> *he gets an electric shock.*
> *Doesn't it hurt him, then?*

No, of course not. . . . Or they
wouldn't do it.

—PAUL HAGGARD

Some months after PETA was founded, we led the police into a laboratory called the Institute for Behavioral Research (IBR), in Silver Spring, Maryland. Once inside, police officers served a search and seizure warrant, seizing seventeen macaque monkeys, survivors from a group originally twice that size.

The monkeys were in bad shape. Many had open, festering wounds, and much of their once lustrous hair was missing. Their normally bushy tails were bare because of malnutrition, and they had pulled out whole clumps of fur on their arms and legs from boredom, frustration, anger, and misery. Although once vigorous and even fierce defenders of their jungle homes, after years of confinement in feces-encrusted cages barely larger than their own bodies, they were now frail and vulnerable. They stared up anxiously at the crowds of uniformed officers and media, almost blinded by the sunlight they had not seen since being snatched many years before from their families in the Philippines.

As the state's veterinary witnesses would later testify in court, many of the monkeys had been operated on in a crude experiment, their backs cut open and their nerves severed, making movement of their arms difficult or impossible.

One timid little monkey named Billy had not only lost the use of both his arms, but both were also broken. He had been forced to push himself on his elbows across the cage grating and to eat his food by bending over and grasping it between his teeth, although his teeth were painfully infected.

The monkeys would accidentally injure their deadened

limbs, sometimes catching and then tearing off their fingers on the jagged, broken, and rusted wires that protruded from their cages. (Police documented thirty-nine of the fingers on the monkeys' hands were severely deformed or missing.) The experimenters forced the monkeys into a dark, blood-spattered refrigerator and a jury-rigged restraint chair, tying them down with duct tape and burning them with a cigarette lighter, squeezing their flesh, including their testicles, with surgical pliers, and administering electric shocks to them to "test" the feeling in monkeys' limbs.

Sadly, the Silver Spring case was not an isolated incident. Millions of animals are used in experiments every year. More often than not, they are acquired without much thought, housed abysmally, and denied anything remotely similar to a natural or comfortable life. In addition to suffering through the experiments, they are under constant stress from fear, loss of control, and the denial of all that is natural and meaningful and pleasant to them, such as enjoying freedom and the company of others of their own kind.

All species of animals, from chimpanzees to cats, are used for everything from forced aggression and induced fear experiments to tests on new football helmets and septic tank cleaner. Baboons are violated via AIDS-infected rectal swabs, great apes are purposely driven mad to make them crush their infants' skulls in child abuse studies, and researchers are changing pigs' genes so they can no longer walk and genetically engineering chickens so that they can no longer fly.

As if that isn't more than enough, animals are also burned alive in the cockpits of planes, exploded in weapons tests, and forced to inhale pollutants until they choke to death. They are starved and shot; they have hallucinogenics and electrical shocks administered to them; they are force-fed poisons and used to demonstrate already well established surgical procedures. They are treated as if they were nothing more than "test tubes with whiskers."

The list of wasteful and ludicrous experiments PETA and others have uncovered would fill a library of books. This rubbish research comes at a time when many Americans cannot afford basic health insurance, alcohol and drug treatment clinics have closed due to the loss of federal and state funds, the elderly and disabled go without new eyeglasses or dental care, disabled people are left without state-of-the-art wheelchairs and home aids that would allow them to participate more fully in society.

WOULD *YOU* FUND THESE STUDIES?

At the Yerkes Primate Research Center in Atlanta, Georgia, experimenters fed high-fat foods to monkeys to see if they would eat more when stressed. Elsewhere, rats were killed by being fed huge doses of Louisiana hot sauce (the human equivalent of half a cup per ten pounds of body weight). At Georgia State University, researchers spent a great deal of taxpayers' money to see if chimpanzees value items more if they own them (obviously the chimpanzees did and you would too); pregnant and nursing monkeys and their children were forced into a chamber pumped full of smoke for six hours a day, five days a week to "prove" that smoking is bad for children; monkeys were kept in a cage without food or water to see if they would "pay" with food to look at female monkeys' rumps and at other high-ranking monkeys; and the list goes on.

Forgetting the just plain daft experiments, there are tens of thousands of experiments that cause enormous pain and panic to animals every day in the name of basic medical research. For example, at the University of North Carolina, mice have been given arsenic-laced water; behavioral tests on mice and rats include "aversive stimulus response tests"—such as hot plate tests, which involve dropping the animals onto a heated surface, and injecting painful burning capsaicin in rats' tails. At Wake Forest University, researchers have removed infant monkeys from their permanently caged mothers to study the effect on right- and left-handedness; traumatized babies taken from their mothers are also studied for their tendency to turn to alcohol—a completely unnatural behavior for monkeys; and monkeys taken from their jungle homes and families in Indonesia have been confined to metal isolation cages and used to study the effects of chronic alcohol consumption on their heart rate.

Pigs, mice, and other animals are intentionally burned and scalded in experiments, swum to the death, forced to balance on planks in water-filled tanks, and strapped into "smoking machines" and addicted to nicotine. In some cases the animals suffer from burns and wounds that are intentionally infected so that the effects of extreme physical trauma can be measured.

Healthy animals are mutilated and injured—for example, they have their spinal cords or nerves severed or weights are dropped onto their backs to cause paralysis; they have electrodes implanted into their heads and metal coils threaded into their eye sockets.

As if that weren't enough, hundreds of household product and cosmetics companies and big pharmaceutical houses, many marketing the fortieth version of basically the same old antidepressant or headache remedy, still contract with laboratories that conduct the "standard four" tests. These crude tests, first hurriedly devised between 1920 and 1930, when large quantities of new pills and lotions were flooding the market, are carried out on large groups of animals every day.

Behold the unsophisticated nature of these tests: a researcher takes a substance—say, an acne medication or a nail polish remover—and (1) drips it into restrained rabbits' eyes; (2) thrusts massive quantities of it down dogs' or monkeys' throats; (3) forces rats to inhale it through a mask or by spraying it into their sealed cages, and/or (4) smears it on the raw, shaved backs of guinea pigs. Then the researcher sits back, and he or she records the damage.

Obviously, if you force-fed a pint of drain cleaner to a monkey, the monkey's internal organs would be eaten away, along with the lining of his throat, and the monkey would probably go into convulsions and die. His pain will not soothe or save the person who tries to commit suicide by swallowing drain cleaner, nor will it help the person who, somehow or other, inadvertently gets drain cleaner in her eye. We already know the likely result and the proper treatment, and these tests are not designed to determine how to treat the injury.

HOW DOES IT FEEL TO BE A GUINEA PIG?

Ask experimenters why they experiment on animals, and the answer is: "Because the animals are like us." Ask experimenters why it is morally okay to experiment on animals, and the answer is: "Because the animals are not like us." Animal experimentation rests on a logical contradiction.

—PROFESSOR CHARLES R. MAGEL,
MOORHEAD STATE UNIVERSITY

Rabbits, guinea pigs, and other small animals suffer silently because they are "prey" animals who do not wish to draw attention to their vulnerability. If they howl, nature tells them that a predator (like the man in the white coat with the syringe) could come kill them. So they try hard to tough it out, their convulsions violently wracking their bodies As for the dogs, they will have been "debarked," their vocal cords severed to cut down on the "annoying" (in the words of one laboratory chief) noise.

It's hard to get into a laboratory without an invitation or a search warrant. But some years ago, an animal rights activist did manage to get a job inside the British headquarters of Huntingdon Life Sciences, a laboratory that tests for some of the top companies in the industry worldwide, including in the United States. He caught on videotape, workers punching dogs in the face, screaming at the animals, and even simulating sex with one another while trying to inject a frightened beagle. In the United States, Huntingdon moved quickly in court to prevent PETA from showing exactly what its own investigator had videotaped when she worked in their New Jersey facility that same year. The truth about how the animals were treated was about to be revealed.

Luckily, the PETA investigator's tapes were aired on television in Cincinnati, Ohio (home of Procter & Gamble), and Norfolk, Virginia (home of PETA), before the gag order took effect. The tapes showed monkeys who were scared out of their wits being taped to an operating table; their fear was almost palpable. The animals were supposed to be kept calm and quiet to facilitate accurate readings from an electrocardiograph, yet joking staff played loud rock music, yelled in the faces of the restrained monkeys, yee-hawed at the top of their lungs like drunken cowboys, and stuck lotion bottles into the helpless animals' mouths. Following these high jinks, workers body-slammed the primates back into their steel cages.

After this exposé, came another, this one inside the world's largest animal testing laboratory, Covance. In PETA's undercover tapes, workers are shown slamming the monkeys against the cage walls, shoving them into Plexiglas tubes, and yelling into the faces of monkeys who struggle to escape, their teeth chattering in fear at the men holding them down.

In this case too Covance moved into court quickly to try to stop the public from seeing PETA's tapes. They did not succeed.

Should you harbor the illusion that most researchers would immediately denounce such cruelty, dream on. They will defend almost anything, as indeed the top US research lobbying groups did, openly applauding Huntingdon for trying to bar PETA from allowing the public to see the photos and tapes and judge for itself. In fact, Huntingdon's injunction went so far as to specifically prohibit PETA from answering the federal government's questions about the lab or giving the tapes to members of Congress. However, Huntingdon was too late: PETA had already turned over its eight months of investigation notes, hundreds of photographs, and hours of videotapes and had filed a thirty-seven-page formal complaint with the US Department of Agriculture (USDA).

Federal authorities found Huntingdon in violation of the Animal Welfare Act (AWA), the only federal law that offers any protection whatsoever to animals in laboratories. Not that this finding has put them out of business.

Covance too is still in business, and numerous companies you have heard of, top personal-care product makers, use them to test their goods.

Perhaps some researchers defend abhorrent practices because they are inured to the suffering of those around them. Perhaps, just as some people can stare at a Picasso for hours without "getting it," they can't understand for the life of them what all the fuss over animals is about. Or perhaps they see that in any way acknowledging that there are problems would be a chink in the armor that could one day crack the whole suit.

There are certainly some truly arrogant experimenters, like Robert White, the Cincinnati man who performs horrific head transplant experiments on monkeys and watches the anguished eyes of their disembodied but live heads follow him about the room. One morning in Cincinnati, White told me it is "never acceptable" to put limits on science. Later, when he and I addressed a group of high school students, White railed to them, "Who are *you* to question a scientist?"

The Silver Spring prosecutor, Roger Galvin, learned how researchers unite to protect their own kind, like a mob defending itself against the authorities. When given every opportunity to distance themselves from the disgusting cruelty, filth, suffering, and unscientific conduct in that case, what did the research community do? Did it condemn a facility in which police found dead monkeys floating in barrels of formaldehyde, their infected limbs and rotted bandages weighed down with auto parts? Hardly. Its distinguished members flocked to the courthouse to testify *in support of* the accused, Dr. Edward Taub, a researcher many of them had never met or spoken to. Taub was convicted twice of cruelty to animals, but his convictions were ultimately overturned, in part on the grounds that federally funded animal experimenters are not subject to state law.

George Bernard Shaw may have hit the nail on the head when he said, "He who would not hesitate to vivisect, would not hesitate to lie about it." After each glowing endorsement, Mr. Galvin would ask the witness for the defense whether he or she had bothered to visit this laboratory. "No." "Did you ask to see the police photographs?" "No." "Did you bother to speak to the state attorney's office about the charges?" "No." The defense witnesses mocked concerns for the animals, describing the monkeys as "nothing more than defecating machines" and a cockroach infestation as an "ambient source of protein" for the primates. They described Taub as a "modern-day Galileo," an apt comparison perhaps, given that, in his time, Galileo's opinions allowed experimenters, like the evil René Descartes, to nail live animals to a board, eviscerate them, and disregard their screams as nothing more important than the sound of squeaking wheels.

As with everything, there are exceptions. One is Donald Barnes. Once an experimenter for the US Air Force, Barnes used to torture rhesus monkeys. His job was to irradiate them, then strap them to treadmills to run, vomiting, to their deaths. Over time, a light came on in his head. He realized that the experiments had yielded nothing of use and were simply a line item on the base budget that his superiors would never sacrifice.

Barnes also came to see that what he was doing was unethical. In his own words, he decided one day to "call in well," and never went back. Mr. Barnes testified for the prosecution in the Silver Spring monkeys case.

Dr. Roger Ulrich is another example. Dr. Ulrich received many professional awards and honors for his rather nasty research, using monkeys to study the relationship between pain and aggression. One day, he wrote this to the American Psychological Association:

> When I was asked why I conducted these experiments, I used to say it was because I wanted to help society solve its problems of mental illness, crime, retardation, drug abuse, child abuse, unemployment, marital unhappiness, alcoholism, over-smoking, over-eating . . . even war! Although, after I got into this line of work, I discovered that the results of my work did not seem to justify its continuance. I began to wonder if perhaps financial rewards, professional prestige, the opportunity to travel, etc., were the maintaining factors and if we of the scientific community, supported

by our bureaucratic and legislative systems, were actually part of the whole problem.

One spring I was asked by a colleague, "Dr. Ulrich, what is the most innovative thing that you've done professionally over the past year?" I replied, "Dear Dave, I've finally stopped torturing animals."

MS. BEA AND OTHER BEINGS

When I ran the District of Columbia animal shelter, my dog, Ms. Bea, came to work with me every day. She was a mixed German shepherd who looked and acted a little like the imposing grande dame in the old Marx Brothers movies.

She had several functions. At the front desk, she greeted frightened dogs being turned in. When they saw her moving toward them with self-assurance, obviously at home and happy, they stopped shaking so much and got involved in a sniff-fest with her, tails wagging.

She was also in charge of preliminary interviews for dog adoptions. Ms. Bea would turn that corner, no small dog she, and if the potential puppy adopter shrank into the corner, screaming "Does *it* bite?" they were in trouble.

Ms. Bea worked long hours, as we did, but she loved it. She ate what we ate—Indian takeout was her favorite—and she rode the truck into the "best" and the most troubled neighborhoods, looking out of the window at them all. We loved her very much.

She only fell down on the job once, but I couldn't blame her, because by that time she was very old, had lost her hearing, and was inclined to nap a lot. One very late winter night, when she was with me on a call, some men tried to jump me as I was getting back into my van. It was only because I saw them coming, one with a tire iron in his hand, and because I used to run the heater for Ms. Bea and already had my extra key in the ignition, that I managed to escape. Oblivious to the commotion, Ms. Bea slept through it. I never told her about the incident. It would have been a terrible blow for such a responsible girl.

Ms. Bea was seventeen years old when she died. She had lived a full life and brought much joy to the world. I think of Ms. Bea constantly. When people ask me how anyone can justify breaking into labs and "stealing" the animals, all I know is that if anyone had Ms. Bea on the operating table, I'd be through that door in a minute, lock me up if you will.

Ms. Bea is my litmus test of how we treat animals. Ms. Bea was not a "thing." She had gender, individuality, life, love, and understanding inside her. No one could ever convince me that it would have been all right to burn her or sink electrodes into her head and shock her. Not to save me, my child, or my other dog, if that were the case, and I believe it is never the case. It wouldn't have been right.

They are *all* Ms. Bea, in their own way. Even the smallest of them, the ugliest or weirdest of them. I remember thinking exactly that one day when I toured the National Institutes of Health's (NIH) Poolesville Primate Laboratory.

Entering a barren room in a seemingly endless corridor of sterile, whitewashed rooms, I found a baboon. I actually *heard* him first because he was banging his head so loudly against the solid steel sides of his cage.

In this totally dull, windowless environment, this huge hamadryas baboon, the size of a small man, was so alive and so gaudy, almost surreal. He had a long dog snout that looked as if he had painted it with crazy red and pink and white and gray stripes. His long multicolored hair stood out from his body like a big colorful cloak. You could imagine him on his way to a costume party.

How must he have felt when aliens snatched him from his jungle and transported him to this cold lonely world to die in a steel cage? Most primates avoid making eye contact, yet this baboon stared straight at me. His eyes were filled not with despair, as one might expect, but with deep loathing.

I made inquiries, and my questions became embarrassing for NIH. It transpired that the baboon and several others in his "group" had been forgotten. Originally shipped to the United States from Russia, they had been used for eight years in a cancer study, but the study had been casually abandoned when the principal investigator had taken a job in another state. They would have been hosed down and fed "monkey biscuits" until the day they died. I pushed for a resolution. Eventually NIH told me it had killed them. I hoped it was true, for the baboons' sake.

THE GOLDEN RULE

If "might does not make right," as we tell our children, then we cannot possibly justify using others *against* their own best interests *just because we aim to get something out of it.* We cannot suddenly suspend our belief in such a fundamental tenet simply because we find it inconvenient to relate to some victims.

Because might does not make right, we have condemned experimenters for using slaves and poor Irish women to practice gynecological surgeries in the not too distant past; for giving LSD to enlisted men without their knowledge; for secretly exposing Asian women to chemical warfare agents; and for feeding retarded schoolboys cereal laced with radioactive isotopes. Because might does not make right, we recoil in horror at the tuberculin experiments using human orphans, the infamous Tuskegee experiments in which black men were deliberately allowed to go untreated for syphilis, and the tests in which prisoners of war were submerged in freezing water.

The white rat is a prime example of our superiority complex. Although these rats are mammals who feel hunger, thirst, pleasure, and pain as any other, they are laboratory favorites (in part because they are not the objects of wide public sympathy). Researchers do not use these tiny animals for scientific reasons. When it comes to feelings, a rat *is* a dog *is* a pig *is* a boy, but not when it comes to physiology. Rodents are not little humans: their blood-clotting factors and pulse rates are vastly different from ours. They manufacture their own vitamin C (we do not); their protein needs are ten times those of a human being; and, unlike us, they are nose breathers. Researchers use them because they are cheap, readily available, easy to handle, and easy to overlook when it comes to concerns about pain, stress, or suffering.

Should rats' feelings be so easily dismissed? Not according to Dr. Neal Barnard, president of the Physicians Committee for Responsible Medicine (PCRM). The introductory course in psychology at his college—as is the case at many colleges—used rats who were deprived of water for three days and then put in a "Skinner box" (a cage developed by B. F. Skinner that delivers a few drops of water when a bar is pressed by the thirsty animal inside). The point of the lab was to show how learning occurs. For example, if an animal is rewarded (reinforced) for an action such as pressing a bar, the animal will probably repeat the action. At the end of the course, the rats were put together in a trash can, chloroform poured over them, and the lid closed.

Students could sign up to implant electrodes into a rat's skull to show that electrical stimulation of the brain can affect behavior. During the implantation procedure, a stereotaxic device held the rat's head still, its metal bars thrust into both ear canals, breaking the eardrums. Dr. Barnard says, "My professor's response to my concern about the effects of this procedure on the rats was a joke: 'Well, I guess he won't be able to listen to his stereo in the morning.' But while I was struck by the callousness of his remark, I was sufficiently desensitized to proceed with the experiment."

One day, Dr. Barnard took a rat home from the lab. "Ratsky" lived for some months in a cage in his bedroom. And, in her cage, she behaved the way he assumed rats behave. But when he started leaving the cage door open so she could walk around, he began to observe things he hadn't anticipated. After several days of cautious sniffing about at the cage door, she began to investigate the world outside. As she explored the apartment, under Dr. Barnard's watchful eye, she took an interest in him and his friends. He wrote in *Animal Times*:

> She gradually became more and more friendly. If I was lying on my back reading, she would come and stand on my chest. She would wait to be petted and if I didn't pay her enough attention, she would lightly nip my nose and run away. I knew that her sharp teeth could have gone right through my skin, but she was always playfully careful. I realized that rats can be as outgoing and gentle as any person. Given food, water, and warmth, most rats are friendly, fun, and meticulously clean. If not forced to live in an unclean cage, their skin has a distinct perfume-like scent. If I left a glass of ice water on the floor for her, she would painstakingly take out each ice cube and carry it inch by inch in her teeth away from the glass until all the ice had been cleaned out. One day she labored for hours to pull all my dirty clothes out of a laundry bag. Like a cat, she spent hours carefully grooming herself.

One day, Dr. Barnard noticed a lump in Ratsky's skin. With time, it grew, and it was all but impossible to find a veterinarian who would treat her, since she was not a dog, cat, or "farm animal." One said Ratsky was a male and the lump was his scrotum (Ratsky was a female). Others called it a fat pad. Finally Dr. Barnard convinced a vet who specialized in "laboratory animals" to take the lump out. It was a tumor.

The vet put Ratsky in a heavy cast and said the operation was successful.

Because rats are meticulous about their bodies and work tirelessly to rid themselves of any dirt, they have to be put in body casts after surgery to prevent them from removing their sutures. When Dr. Barnard cut her out of the cast, Ratsky painfully tottered a few steps, trembling. He discovered that the vet had removed not only the tumor, but had also inadvertently removed her urethra, the tube that leads to the bladder, so that urine spilled from her bladder into the abdominal cavity and precipitated a caustic irritation under her skin.

The vet tried to correct his mistake in a second operation, but he was uncertain as to whether it would succeed. While friends could understand caring for larger animals, Dr. Barnard found that few people could understand why he cared so much about the suffering of this little mammal. "Her suffering was very apparent. At night I slept with her in the palm of my hand so I would wake up if she tried to chew out her sutures. . . . Before long it became clear that Ratsky's condition was worsening. The reconstructed urethra closed off, causing her great distress. Finally she was euthanized."

Dr. Barnard says he carried with him the vivid image of this tiny animal tottering painfully out from her body cast, of her in the palm of his hand trying to pull out the sutures that were a constant irritation to her. In the months that followed, he began to think about all the other animals whose suffering he had taken so dispassionately, and he realized that each one was an individual who can suffer as acutely as the little rat whom he had held in his hand. And that suffering was just as real as that of a dog, a dolphin, a cat, or a mouse, whether the animal was "bred for the purpose" or chained up in someone's backyard. As a practicing physician, he continues to be puzzled about the resistance to compassion that he sees so commonly in others and that he too experienced for so long. Cruelty to animals is diagnosed as a psychiatric symptom predictive of antisocial personality, yet we fail to recognize the cruelties we perpetuate so casually in our own lives.

"Not too long ago," Dr. Barnard said, "my alma mater sent me a survey asking, among other things, who had been my most effective teacher. I'm not sure they understood my reply."

It is because of prejudice alone that millions of rat bodies hit the biological waste containers annually, each one having lived a brief life as a little, once-inquisitive being like Dr. Barnard's Ratsky—each one snuffed out casually and not always quickly or cleanly.

A RAT IS NOT A LITTLE MAN

If animal experiments were as marvelous as some have claimed, we would surely have eternal life by now or at least a cure for the common cold. After all, the unfettered use of animals has been going on, with vigor, for hundreds of years. The "war on cancer," declared with much fanfare in 1950 and then again by President Nixon twenty years later, has been deemed a qualified failure, with cancer rates remaining so high that one in every three Americans is eventually diagnosed with some form of the disease. Small wonder when, in a study of cancer in mice and rats, 30 percent of chemicals found to cause cancer in one species were safe in the other. We have no cures for AIDS, spina bifida, diabetes (one slogan of the American Diabetes Society is "Insulin Is Not a Cure"), or virtually any serious disease you can name. Not surprisingly, everything important we have learned about diabetes has come from human studies. The link between pancreatic disease or dysfunction and diabetes was discovered in human autopsies, and it was J. B. Collip's work in test tubes that laid the groundwork for today's standard treatment. A fifteen-year study of Pima Indians revealed how we can tell who is most likely to get Type II diabetes, and autopsies on teenagers led to the discovery of viral diabetes. The most exciting work involved a ten-year study of human beings in clinical settings. In fact, although for more than a hundred years, experimenters have tried to reproduce diabetes in millions of dogs, mice, rats, and other animals, little has changed and no cure is in sight.

AN ANGRY DIABETIC

Despite a history of failures, animal experiments continue, a fact that particularly galls Mary Beth Sweetland, a diabetic. At NIH, one vivisector removed beagles' eyeballs to study vision problems in diabetics. The beagles did not receive painkillers after the surgery, even though veterinarians say they need them.

Mary Beth had to start taking daily doses of insulin when she turned twenty-five. Before she realized what was wrong, her weight had fallen to just over ninety-five pounds, her eyesight was blurry, if she cut herself it didn't heal, and she was always hungry, thirsty, and very tired. But when she began injecting herself with pork and beef insulin, she quickly lost muscle mass in her thighs and stomach, and her blood sugar level was a mess.

Mary Beth credits three things with changing all that and saving her life. Today she checks her glucose level five or six times a day with a monitor and takes up to four to six low doses of Humulin, a synthetic, nonanimal insulin that has restored her muscle mass. She has also cut her insulin dosage from 50 units a day to only 15 a day.

Mary Beth discovered the hard way that the key to being a healthy diabetic is to eat a vegan diet, avoid all fat, and walk briskly or do exercises for at least thirty minutes a day.

Mary Beth says, "The best part is that I can now look my fabulous Beagle Boys (her rescued beagles) in the eye with a clean conscience."

BARKING UP THE WRONG TREE

Judging side effects in animal tests is often impossible. Even our fellow primates cannot tell us if they have a crushing headache, ringing in the ears, double vision, or nausea. More importantly, different species react very differently to what goes into them. Parsley is poisonous to some birds, penicillin kills guinea pigs, and chloroform is so toxic to dogs that doctors searching for anesthetics in years past avoided using it for human patients.

It is common knowledge that you can't bathe a cat in a flea shampoo meant for a dog, yet drug companies marketed DES, or diethylstilbestrol, on the strength of animal tests. Over one million women taking DES came down with uterine cancer. Intrauterine devices also passed animal tests with flying colors, as did silicone breast implants. Formaldehyde, dioxin, asbestos, and other chemicals toxic to humans were extensively tested on animals. Drugs are often only removed from the marketplace when the insurance claims for side effects reach a level that challenges the profitability of the company that markets them.

Perhaps even more important were the drugs we missed because animal tests did not point to them as being useful. Amazingly, even aspirin was initially rejected because it causes deformities in infant rhesus monkeys.

Grave new worries are now coming to light. All animals harbor viruses. Experimenting on animals or animal tissues, or using animal organs in transplant experiments, carries a serious risk of disease transmission. The AIDS epidemic, for example, may have been caused when a virus from a green vervet monkey jumped the "species barrier" to Africans whose immune system had already been weakened by inoculation against smallpox.

HTLV, a virus that causes leukemia, has crossed the species barrier too, causing deadly Marburg disease and Lassa fever. "Foamy viruses" are common in baboons, and another monkey virus, named SV40, is implicated in cases of human brain cancer after lying dormant for decades. It is believed to have infected people who were injected with a polio vaccine administered worldwide in the 1950s.

Back in 1997, scientists first discovered that pig genes harbor viruses called PERV-A and PERV-B. While harmless in pigs, these viruses can be fatal in humans. In 1998, strains of avian flu crossed from chickens into children and poultry workers in Pennsylvania and Hong Kong. The same year, Britain and Switzerland outlawed xenografts (animal-to-human transplants), calling the procedure "too risky" and, in the United States, Harvard University's Dr. Fritz Bach joined other xeno-transplantation scientists in calling for a moratorium, citing the risk from the operations of unleashing a new AIDS-like epidemic.

There is something very primitive and ignorant in blindly trusting the use of animals to cure our ills. It is worth remembering that just 150 years or so ago, medical "experts" were able to persuade people to impale live snails on thorns to cure themselves of warts and to bury a live rooster to end epileptic fits. Physicians severed the left ear of cats and mixed blood from the wound into a potion to abate measles. Minced mouse was a common prescription for bladder trouble. Laypeople dutifully took this advice and footed the bill. Today, we are just as trusting.

MODERN NONANIMAL METHODS ARE SUPERIOR TO ANIMAL USE

Experimentation and training in human and veterinary medical practice can be done without the pitter-patter of little feet. In this day of far more technologically advanced research methods, there are in vitro tests in which human cells can be bombarded with diseases and show results in a matter of hours, the use of virtual organs, whole *human* DNA, and computer assaying, among other options. We have mass spectrometry, microscopy which allows us to detect minute, precancerous tumors, and detailed analysis of the human genome itself. Gone are the days when a rabbit was killed to determine whether or not a woman was pregnant.

When Dr. Nedim Buyukmihci, a veterinary ophthalmologist at the University of California at Davis, decided to change the old way of teaching veterinary students how to operate on dogs' eyes, he caused a huge stir. Traditionally, the university had purchased dogs from a breeder, deliberately damaged their eyes, and then allowed the students to practice corrective surgeries on the dogs. The dogs were then killed.

"Dr. Ned" believed there had to be a better way. He decided to find dogs belonging to the elderly and others on fixed incomes and have his students perform a real service, under his expert tutelage, by correcting the dogs' vision problems free of charge. These were dogs whose owners could never have afforded such operations.

The university administration went wild. When they couldn't "reason" with Dr. Buyukmihci, they suspended him from teaching and denied him tenure. Luckily for his students and the animals, Dr. Buyukmihci is a man of principle, and he fought back, suing the university. Today his teaching methods have replaced the old ways.

Dr. Peter Henricksen, a veterinary scientist, recounts his own experience at veterinary school. He remembers a dog the students called Rodney, a tall, gangly shepherd mix. Dr. Henricksen was in his third year when Rodney was delivered from the local dog pound. For the next quarter, four students would practice surgery techniques on him—the first of their small animal surgery training. Rodney was always happy to see them—tail thumping wildly against the walls of his small steel cage. "From the looks of him," Dr. Henricksen wrote in a story for *Animal Times*, "Rodney hadn't much of a life, so a pat and a little walk around the college complex made his day."

Dr. Henricksen remembers:

> The first thing we did was neuter him, a seemingly benign project, except it took us an hour to complete the usual twenty-minute procedure, and an anesthetic overdose kept him out for thirty-six hours. Afterward he recovered his strength quickly and felt good. Two weeks later we did an abdominal exploratory, opening his abdomen, checking his organ inventory, and closing him again. This was the first major surgery for any of us, and with inadequate supervision we did not close him properly. By the next morning, his incision had opened and he was sitting on his small intestine. Hastily, we sewed him up again, and he survived.

But it was a week or more before he could resume the walks he had come to eagerly anticipate. He would still wag his tail when we arrived and greet us with as much enthusiasm as he could muster.

The following week—again when he was under anesthesia—we broke his leg and repaired it with a steel pin. After this Rodney seemed in almost constant pain, his temperature rose, and he didn't rebound as he had in the past. His resiliency gone, despite antibiotic treatment, he never recovered completely. He could no longer manage his walks, and our visits generated only a weak thump of his tail. The shine was gone from his brown eyes. His operated leg remained stiff and swollen. The quarter was ending, and Rodney's days were numbered. One afternoon we put him to sleep. As the life drained from his body and his eyes lost their focus, my attitude toward animal research began to change.

A Harvard student named Rachel Freelund helped modernize teaching methods for young doctors at that august institution. Rachel went to medical school because she wanted to study medicine and save lives. When she was accepted to Harvard, she never dreamed she would be asked to *take* a life.

Like all first-year medical students then, Rachel was supposed to participate in the "dog lab" to witness firsthand how certain drugs affect the body. The students were to anesthetize a dog, slice open his chest, and watch the reaction of his beating heart as various drugs were injected into him.

At the end of the "exercise," the healthy dog would be killed.

Horrified, and believing there had to be a better way, Rachel went to her instructor, who told her she would not be forced to do the lab if she thought it unethical. That started Rachel thinking: if she could meet the course requirements without the lab, why couldn't all the students? "I didn't want anybody to do the dog lab," she says.

Thanks to Rachel's initiative, Harvard medical students can now choose to visit Boston hospitals to observe heart by-pass surgeries on human patients instead of participating in the death of a dog. Dr. Michael O'Ambra, the cardiac anesthesiologist who directs Harvard's operating room program, says that this helps students understand the human physiology they need to know. "The *only* thing a student can do in a dog lab that we don't cover in the operating room is kill the animal," he says.

Happily, the vast majority of medical schools in North America have rapidly done away with live animal labs, and in England they are illegal.

OUT WITH THE OLD, IN WITH THE NEW

Before he died, Dr. Carl Sagan once lamented the use of chimpanzees in AIDS experiments. "What crime have they committed," he asked, "that they are imprisoned for life? It is time to let them out." They have not been let out, despite the fact that HIV was isolated in human blood, not in that of other animals; how AIDS spreads was determined through human studies; and how the virus mutated was determined by looking at human cells. The "AIDS cocktail," a potent combination of drugs that keeps people with HIV alive and going strong for many years, was developed by computer analysis of the likely effects of various individual drugs and drug combinations on humans, not on mice or monkeys.

Despite the deliberate infliction of these diseases on animals, it was not medical research that stamped out tuberculosis, diphtheria, pneumonia, and puerperal sepsis; the primary credit for those monumental accomplishments must go to public health, sanitation, and the general improvement in the standard of living brought about by industrialization.

Despite decades of feeding high-fat diets to every animal under the sun, it was not those studies, but the Framingham heart study, a continuing study of people who live in and around Framingham, Massachusetts, that identified the risk factors for heart disease and how to prevent it, including the fact that heart attacks virtually do not occur in people with a cholesterol level of 150 or less.

The most impressive studies of hardening of the arteries have occurred not in baboons or dogs, despite their use, but in human autopsy studies. Similarly, the connection between lung cancer and smoking was shown to be unequivocal because of human studies: decades of research on every kind of animal under the sun rendered findings so inconclusive that they worked very much in the tobacco industry's interest.

A SLICE OF THE PIE

We should rejoice that there are alternatives to animal-based vaccines. The old ones used to be made of monkey tissue, duck embryos, and other animal bits and pieces that caused allergic reactions such as anaphylactic shock and even death. Today, vaccines can be fashioned from human diploid cells and synthetics. Beef and pork insulin have been replaced by nonallergic *human* insulin.

When PETA first started campaigning, the cosmetics industry insisted animal tests were indispensable. Today there are some seven hundred companies that won't touch animal tests. When Gillette made the switch, after an intensive PETA campaign that spanned ten years and included every tactic from crashing board meetings to, dressed as rabbits, climbing the flagpole outside Gillette's corporate headquarters, one Gillette executive said, "It's so much nicer to sit down with you now instead of seeing you dangling from a rope outside our building! But we needed the push."

Yes, there is an alternative to every cruel deed. In fact, if we direct our resources and energy away from animal tests, we stand to gain tremendous benefits as human beings.

Look back to the case of Baby Fae, the infant who made national news when Dr. Leonard Bailey of Loma Linda University put a baboon's heart into the child's tiny, ailing body. If anyone remembers this case at all, they remember a photograph of a baby in a crib and a doctor holding a giant phone up to her so she could hear her mother's voice. Sadly, her mother was alone, not very well educated, and much too trusting.

There was no happy ending for Baby Fae. She died in just three weeks, leaving in her wake freezers packed full of the bodies of more than three hundred animals who had provided the trial runs for her failed surgery. The university's news releases, the media stampede, the public appeal of a "heroic" operation all combined to squash the sensible questions that needed to be asked and which might have actually have saved the baby's life.

Only when the dust cleared after the baby's body had rejected the organ, and the baby was no more, did we discover how bleak the prospect for her had been with a baboon heart. It turned out that none of the animals Dr. Bailey had experimented on had lived for more than six months; there were two reparative procedures that the baby could have had instead, and which would have offered her a 45 percent chance of living (as opposed to the zero known chance of surviving a baboon heart transplant); and no effort had been made to search for a matching *human* heart. When animal rights activists entered

Dr. Bailey's Loma Linda University laboratory uninvited, they found baby baboons lying in the freezer there. Their hearts had been cut out, and as a joke, someone had pinned little homemade buttons on them, reading WE ALREADY GAVE AT THE OFFICE.

Money spent on animal experiments should go into far superior research methods: studies on cloned human skin for burn victims, instead of using a blowtorch on pigs, for example. It should also go into prevention, which, now more than ever, is worth a pound of cure. How much better to fund dietary education programs that would spare people heart attacks, cancer, high blood pressure, and strokes instead of causing these miseries in animals.

It's not the animals who need their heads examined. Animal experimenters spent $240 million on an artificial heart that did not buy us good health; killing three hundred baboons did not save one baby's life; decades of alcohol and heroin experiments on macaques and rats have not kept people from the bottle or needle; and forcing decades of beagles to run on treadmills has not reduced air pollution. British studies show that for every dollar spent treating heroin addiction, there is a three-dollar reduction in the amount spent fighting crime.

We could use the money from animal experiments to provide prenatal and infant care in low-income areas. As it stands, the United States spends more on animal experiments than the next top four countries combined, yet has an infant mortality rate ranging between the nineteenth and twenty-second in the world. That means, in any given year, a baby born in eighteen other far poorer countries has a better chance of surviving than one born here. That is truly shameful.

Sometimes the alternative to doing something cruel and ugly to animals is to not do anything at all, as in the case of giving liquor to quail, pigs, and crayfish and recording their impairment. And someone needs to tap all the "Joe Six-Pack scientists" on the shoulder and say, "Excuse me. You haven't discovered anything from your years of animal experiments other than how to get paid. We're going to redirect your energies, retrain you, and make you into productive citizens of society."

The only obstacle standing between the end of cruel animal experimentation and the beginning of sensible and humane health programs is that too many people still accept the unacceptable. We must expose the myths and demand a change.

WHAT YOU CAN DO

Help Get Animals Out of Laboratories

Change Your Life

Clean house. Rid your household of animal-tested and animal-ingredient products. Over seven hundred companies now test their products in sophisticated ways without the use of animals. Get a free list of which companies do test and which ones don't test on animals by visiting CaringConsumer.com. You can also request PETA's "Cruelty-Free Shopping Guide." This wallet-size reference guide is easy to carry with you when shopping. When friends visit, make sure you prominently display the products in your bathroom or on your kitchen counter, and offer them samples and literature.

Buy cruelty-free supplies for your office such as soap, air freshener, and cleaning supplies.

Join a society. Join an animal rights professional society if you are a veterinarian, physician, scientist, or psychologist.

Take care of yourself. Reduce your risk of disease and increase your energy and longevity by becoming a vegan. Don't let vivisectors use you as an excuse for torturing animals in needless experiments.

Use cruelty-free and natural cleaners. They don't pollute rivers or poison the earth. They are available in health food stores and many grocery stores.

Show your hairdresser some of the many great beauty products that weren't tested on animals.

Write to companies that conduct experiments on animals. Tell them that you won't buy their products until they go cruelty-free. If you live in the United States, log on to CaringConsumer.com for a list of cruel companies. If you live in the UK, visit PETA.org.uk.

Save receipts. Save your receipts from purchases of cruelty-free cosmetics and hair care products, then send them to any of the companies still *testing on animals*, with a note saying, "See what you're missing. If you'd stop testing on animals, my business could be yours."

Be a donor. If you are at least eighteen years old, fill out a human research donor card from the United Network for Organ Sharing (UNOS.org) and keep it with your driver's license or ID card.

Boycott cruel companies' office supplies. Ask your office's orders manager to talk to suppliers about replacing any foods, paper products, or any materials from companies that do not appear on PETA's "do not test" list.

Purchase only cruelty-free school supplies —check out PETA-Mall.com for ideas.

Use company Web sites. Web sites are usually listed on the back of a product, or you can Google the company to find their Web site. Use their contact page to voice your opinion and let them know that you will not purchase their products until they stop using animals.

Organize. Mobilize your community to encourage a company to go cruelty-free. Circulate a petition among your friends, family, neighbors, and school. Collect products manufactured by the company and send them in, asking for a refund.

Don't cooperate with cruelty. Chris Aldous returned his bachelor of education degree from Lancaster University to protest the animal experiments in the university's psychology department. His action received widespread media coverage. Aldous said, "Things aren't going to change overnight, but hopefully my protest will be added to those of many others protesting in equally valid ways."

Don't deliver. Joel Carr runs J. R. Crickets restaurant in Decatur, Georgia. When he learned of experiments conducted at nearby Yerkes Regional Primate Research Center, he and restaurant employees refused to deliver carryout food to the institution.

Quit your job. Susan Buettner and Regina Palmer quit their jobs because they were disgusted to learn that the companies they worked for and believed in still used animals instead of modern testing techniques.

Don't sell out. Radley Hirsch, owner of San Francisco Audio, refused to sell loudspeakers to the University of California San Francisco (UCSF) to blast squirrel monkeys with high-frequency-range sounds (louder than jet engines) to study the hearing loss suffered by people attending rock concerts. Radley contacted PETA, who then brought the matter to the attention of Paul McCartney and The Pretenders' Chrissie Hynde, who joined the protest.

Form a team. Join PETA's A-Team by visiting PETA.org and help team up with others.

Fill out cards. Pick up consumer request cards at your supermarket or drugstore and have friends join you in requesting brand-name, cruelty-free products. You can also go to your grocery store's Web site and e-mail the local or district manager.

Paint a bus. One British group bought an old bus, decorated it, and visited forty towns with antivivisection materials. Thousands of people visited the vehicle, signed ballot papers, and gave an overwhelming thumbs-down to cosmetics tests on animals.

Demonstrate Your Feelings

Haunt a house. When Dr. John Draize, inventor of the hideous Draize "rabbit-blinding test," retired to "get on with [his] gardening," he never expressed any regret at the suffering this test has caused animals since its introduction. Activists, dressed as the spirits of animals killed in product tests, then "haunted" his Maryland home. Draize failed ever even to advocate using anesthesia for the rabbits' eyes used to test bleach and drain cleaners, and he also invented a test in which harsh chemicals were repeatedly applied to live animals' penises.

Grab a friend or two and spend a few hours in a cage in a public place to draw attention to how animals are treated in laboratories.

Blow the Whistle

Investigate. On a field trip to Aurora University in Illinois, a gifted fifteen-year-old student from Downers Grove, Illinois, found herself in a room "filled with animals." The hosting adults at first evaded the student's questions but finally admitted that the animals were used in experiments. She wrote to PETA for help, and we discovered that Aurora University *was not registered* with the US Department of Agriculture (USDA) as required by law!

Get a job. Take a job in your local lab or, if you're already inside, blow the whistle. Call PETA at 757-962-TELL or e-mail us at whistleblower@peta.org. One lab employee had this to say about his experience: "Every few months I am allowed to take home another Norwegian rat or a rabbit. But my presence here and people knowing how I feel also stops any spontaneous sadistic things that can happen. Before I came, there were many weekends when these animals didn't even have water."

Join a campaign. When a whistle-blower called PETA in desperation about six monkeys at New York's Lehman College who were slated for retirement at a sanctuary but were instead sold to New York University for invasive brain experiments, we immediately contacted both Lehman and NYU and launched an online advocacy campaign. Within days, the colleges had heard from thousands of compassionate people. Two weeks later, Wanda, Holly, Jada, Sophie, Samantha, and Lilly arrived at their new sanctuary home, where they are happily living together in a group.

Get in touch. In another case, a call from a member of a film crew making a training film at Washington's Children's Hospital saved the life of a dog now called Guinness. For demonstration purposes, Guinness, originally from a pound in Virginia, had a tube inserted into his chest. After the film, he was to be killed. PETA contacted the hospital staff, who agreed to save him. Guinness is now safe in a loving home.

Make a call. A student at National Taiwan University College of Medicine called PETA about extremely cruel tests on animals that students were required to perform. In one, students were forced to inject strychnine into mice, watch the animals convulse as the poison painfully killed them, and then record the time of death. Students also performed invasive brain surgeries on frogs. PETA jumped in and sent the university information on sophisticated nonanimal teaching methods that are used at more than one hundred medical schools in the United States and Canada. The university quickly canceled the mice experiment, ended invasive brain surgeries on frogs, and agreed to work with PETA to consider completely replacing their current methods with nonanimal teaching methods.

Use your voice. Rick Smith, a law student at a private university in Ada, Ohio, walked in on a "Drug Awareness Demonstration" conducted by the school's pharmacology department. He was too late to keep one rat from being injected with alcohol and another with phenobarbital, but, as the third animal was prepared to receive an injection of a controlled dangerous substance, Rick said, "I won't allow you to do that," and put a protective hand over the cage opening. Rick, who placed his law school career on the line and opened himself up to peer criticism, received much support from people who admire his courage—one of them being his law professor.

Brighten their day. Cheryl Mcauliffe collected donations of toys and treats from area pet stores to give on Valentine's Day to animals imprisoned in Emory University laboratories. When she and DeKalb Coalition activists, along with TV film crews, arrived at the university to deliver their gifts, the experimenters refused to accept them. That evening the networks broadcast the experimenters' denial, displaying their cruelty to the public.

Educate yourself. See Chapter 12, "Readings and Visuals" for books that reveal the staggering range of experiments on animals and why vivisection is scientific fraud.

Educate others. Send your friends to PETATV.com and have them watch footage of actual experiments and/or labs, shot from inside by PETA undercover investigators, whistle-blowers, or the vivisectors themselves. It is the most persuasive evidence we know of about this cruelty.

Give a talk. Schedule yourself to give a ten-minute talk (with handouts) at civic association meetings, to church groups, classes, or humane societies. Set up a display in a library, school, or community center.

Use PETA's credit card or PETA's Message! checks. Each purchase you make with your card or each check you write will be seen by merchants, clerks, tellers, and others. Every time you order a supply of checks from Message! Products (1-800-243-2565) or make a purchase with your card, PETA is given about a dollar to use in the fight against animal experiments.

Make a display. Display literature and posters at your local veterinarian's office, humane society, health food store, dry cleaner, library, and at any other place that will allow you to. Brenda Crawford puts out animal rights books, magazines, and literature at her beauty salon for customers to read, She also uses and promotes cruelty-free John Paul Mitchell products.

Hang a poster. With permission, hang PETA's posters on your lunchroom and office bulletin boards and in grocery and other store windows.

Display stickers. Use PETA's LIBERATE LABORATORY ANIMALS bumper stickers, put PETA's STOP ANIMAL TESTS stickers on all your mail, and include a PETA animal experimentation brochure with your next batch of bill payments,

Send a message. Record an animal rights message on your answering machine; for example: "Three animals die every second in US labs—for more information, call 757-622-PETA."

Invest Responsibly. If you own stock in companies that test on animals, either cash it in, or use it as leverage to change corporate practices. Join PETA's Corporate Responsibility Project, or draft your own resolution. For example, lend your name to an animal protection shareholder proposal: if you have owned several thousand dollars' worth of stock in a company for one year or longer, you are eligible to sign on to existing shareholder proposals. Typical proposals ask companies to disclose detailed and closely guarded information to shareholders regarding their use of animals. Other proposals ask for an outright ban on animal tests.

Support ethical companies. Buy and give stock that supports ethical practices, choosing companies such as Clinique and Aveda.

Save the Premarin Horses and Foals

Make a switch. Switch from Premarin or Prempak-C to synthetic and plant-based estrogen drugs to manage menopause symptoms naturally. After Doris Thompson learned that mares are confined for their urine and their foals are slaughtered, she stopped taking Premarin and alerted the local newspaper. It ran a full-page story, and both Doris and the newspaper were flooded with calls from interested women.

Visit a Web site. Visit Wyeth's Web site, maker of Premarin, at Wyeth.com. Let the company know exactly what you think of its treatment of horses and foals.

Write a letter, educate others. Go to PETA.org for information on effective, nonanimal hormone-replacement therapies and pass that on to friends, newspapers, doctors' offices, and horse clubs, as well as in a letter to your local papers and in blog chat.

Dress down. Volunteer to dress as Lady Godiva in a demonstration to spread the message that Premarin is cruel to mares and foals. Visit PETA.org for more information.

Make a display. Set up a "Say Neigh to Premarin" exhibit, booth, or table at area horse shows and competitions.

Stop Vivisection in Schools

Educate students. Schedule a cruelty-free makeover demonstration during a personal hygiene lecture in a health class. Encourage junior and senior high school students to set up information tables outside the school cafeteria. For example, Brandeis Students for the Ethical Treatment of Animals educated hundreds of their fellow students about product testing with a "Dorm Inform Campaign." Going door to door in all campus dorms, SETA handed out PETA's wallet-size "Cruelty-Free Shopping Guide," explained the many nonanimal tests, and collected products tested on animals for a campus display. After the fair, all the cruel products were sent back to the companies with a request for refunds on the grounds of dissatisfaction because of animal tests!

Lobby administrators. Urge school principals to replace animal programs with ones that use plants instead. (4-H has programs on soil and plant science, weather, trees, and a bicycle program that includes a bike rodeo.) Make the same request of your school district and state board of education. If your school is raising money for a cruel charity, *insist that your dollars go to a cruelty-free one.* Check out CaringConsumer.com for a list of cruelty-free charities.

Report violations. Contact PETA if you know of any experiments in your area schools.

 ## FREQUENTLY ASKED QUESTIONS

Isn't animal testing responsible for major medical advances?

It's the least impressive method of gaining information and has, in fact, led us in completely the wrong direction on many occasions, wasting time and causing the loss of lives.

Medical historians have shown that improved nutrition and sanitation standards and other behavioral and environmental factors are overwhelmingly responsible for the ever-decreasing number of deaths from common infectious diseases since 1900. The most important advances in the field of health care come from human studies, which have led to major medical breakthroughs, such as the development of anesthesia, the stethoscope, morphine, radium, penicillin, artificial respiration, X-rays, antiseptics, and CAT, MRI, and PET scans; the study of bacteriology and germ theory; the discovery of the link between cholesterol and heart disease and the link between smoking and cancer; and the isolation of the virus that causes AIDS. Animal testing played no role in these or many other important medical developments.

But weren't animals used to develop important treatments, such as the polio vaccine?

In fact, two separate bodies of work were done on polio: the in vitro (nonanimal) work, which was awarded the Nobel Prize, and the animal tests, in which a staggering number of animals were killed. Nobel Laureate Arthur Kornberg noted that, for forty years, experiments on monkeys infected with polio generated "limited progress." The breakthrough came when scientists learned how to grow the virus from human cells.

While it can be argued, and is, whether or not some medical developments were the result of cruel animal tests, that certainly does not mean that the developments would not have been possible by using nonanimal tests or that the primitive techniques used in, say, the 1800s are still valid today. Throughout medical history very few resources have been devoted to nonanimal research methods. If they had known then what we know now, we would probably be much further ahead.

Which is Best: Experimentation or Education?

Educating people and encouraging them to avoid fat and cholesterol, quit smoking, reduce alcohol and other drug consumption, exercise regularly, and clean up the environment will save more human lives and prevent more human suffering than all the animal tests in the world. Animal tests are primitive, and modern technology and human clinical tests are much more effective and reliable.

Even if we had no alternative to using animals, which is not the case, animal testing would still be ethically unacceptable. As George Bernard Shaw once said, "You do not settle whether an experiment is justified or not by merely showing that it is of some use. The distinction is not between useful and useless experiments, but between barbarous and civilized behaviour." After all, there are probably some medical problems that can only be cured by testing on unwilling humans, but we don't conduct such tests because we recognize that it would be wrong to do so.

Don't new drugs have to be tested on animals first?

The choice isn't between animals and humans; humans are always "guinea pigs" the first time they take a drug, no matter how much it has been tested on other species with different physiologies than ours. There is no guarantee that animal-tested drugs are safe, because we cannot accurately extrapolate the results in mice or baboons or pigs to humans. Some drugs that have been approved through animal tests cause serious and unexpected side effects for humans. A report in the *Journal of the American Medical Association* found that in the last twenty-five years, more than fifty FDA-approved drugs had to be taken off the market or relabeled because they caused "adverse reactions." In one year alone, the prescription drugs removed from the market were the popular heartburn drug Propulsid (removed because it caused "fatal heart rhythm abnormalities"), the diabetes drug Rezulin ("removed after causing liver failure"), and the irritable-bowel-syndrome treatment Lotronex ("removed for causing fatal constipation and colitis"). According to the study's lead author, "Millions of patients are exposed to potentially unsafe drugs each year," and yet all these drugs passed animal tests.

If the pharmaceutical industry switched from animal experiments to quantum pharmacology and in vitro tests, we would be better protected from harmful drugs, not less protected.

If we didn't test on animals, what would we do instead?

Human clinical and human epidemiological studies, studies on cadavers, and high speed computer simulations are faster, more reliable, less expensive than animal tests and, of course, cruelty-free. Ingenious scientists have used human brain cells to develop a model "microbrain" that can be used to study tumors and have come up with artificial skin and bone marrow. Instead of killing animals, we can now test irritancy on egg membranes, produce vaccines from cell cultures, and perform pregnancy tests using human blood samples. As Gordon Baxter, cofounder of Pharmagene Laboratories—a company that uses only human tissue and computers to develop and test its drugs—says, "If you have information on human genes, what's the point of going back to animals?"

Doesn't animal experimentation help animals by advancing veterinary science?

The point is not whether animal experimentation can be useful to animals or humans; the point is that we do not have the moral right to inflict unnecessary suffering on those who are at our mercy. Saying that it's acceptable to experiment on animals to advance veterinary science is like saying that it's acceptable to experiment on poor children to benefit rich ones. We can develop promising veterinary procedures and drugs by using them on animals whose lives will be lost if nothing is tried to save them.

Don't medical students have to dissect animals?

No, they don't. In fact, nowadays almost all medical students are learning not by hurting and killing animals but instead by assisting experienced surgeons and using sophisticated simulators that breathe, vomit, and even go into cardiac arrest. In Great Britain, it is against the law for any medical student to practice surgery on animals, and British physicians are just as competent as those who were educated elsewhere. Leading US medical schools, including Harvard, Yale, and Stanford, use innovative, clinical teaching methods instead of cruel animal laboratories. Harvard, for instance, offers a cardiac-anesthesia practicum in which students observe human heart bypass operations instead of performing terminal surgery on dogs.

Should we throw out all the drugs that were developed and tested on animals? Would you refuse to take them?

Regrettably, a lot of things in our society came about through the exploitation of others. For instance, many of the roads that we drive on were built by slaves. We can't change the past; those who have already suffered and died are lost. But what we can do is change the future by using nonanimal research methods from now on.

Doesn't the law protect animals from cruelty?

There is no law in the United States that prohibits any animal experiment, no matter how frivolous or painful. The one federal law designed to help animals in laboratories, the Animal Welfare Act (AWA), is very weak and poorly enforced, and it does not protect rats and mice (the most common victims of animal experiments), reptiles, birds, or farmed animals. It is basically a housekeeping act. Under the AWA, animals can be starved, electrically shocked, driven insane, or burned with a blowtorch—as long as it's done in a clean laboratory.

Don't scientists care about the animals they experiment on?

Investigations at even the most prestigious institutions show that it would be very hard to care about animals and do what is done to them. There is a recognized syndrome that allows those who commit atrocities to become oblivious to suffering. In laboratories, most animals are treated like unfeeling, unthinking, disposable tools, and even their basic needs and interests are ignored.

Don't oversight committees prevent cruelty at institutions?

No, because many of these committees are composed mainly or completely of people who have vested interests in animal experiments and may perform them themselves. PETA has found innumerable examples of committees simply taking the experimenters' word for the necessity of animal use where nonanimal research methods were readily available. These committees often have never even set foot in the laboratory they are supposed to oversee.

Cats and dogs are killed in pounds anyway, so why not let them be used in experiments to save lives?

A painless death at an animal shelter is better than a life of severe pain and privation and an agonizing, slow, and frightening death in a laboratory.

What about experiments in which animals are observed and not harmed?

If there really is no harm, we don't object. But "no harm" means that animals aren't isolated in barren, cold steel cages. Such confinement causes stress and fear, as shown by the differences in blood pressure and adrenaline levels between caged and free animals. Caged animals also suffer greatly because they are prevented from performing their normal behaviors and social interactions.

If you were in a fire and could save either your child or your dog, who would you choose?

I would save my child, but that's just instinct. A dog would save her pup. Regardless, my choice proves nothing about the moral legitimacy of animal experiments. I might save my own child instead of my neighbor's, but that hardly proves that experimentation on my neighbor's child is acceptable.

Animals are not as intelligent or as advanced as humans, so why can't we use them?

Possessing superior intelligence does not entitle one human to abuse another human, so why should it entitle humans to abuse nonhumans? But there are animals who are unquestionably more intelligent, creative, aware, communicative, and able to use language than some humans, as is the case when a chimpanzee is compared to a human infant. Should the more intelligent animals have rights and the less intelligent humans be denied rights? Should Harvard graduates be able to experiment on dirt farmers?

7

Fur, Feathers, Baubles, Bits, and Bones . . .

I stood there, trying to stop my knees from shaking, knowing that if the men holding the raccoon by the back legs spotted my hidden camera, I would never be able to show anyone what is happening to animals in the world's biggest fur-producing nation, China.

—JASON BAKER, DIRECTOR PETA ASIA-PACIFIC

As Martha Stewart found out when she watched the footage PETA obtained from a Chinese fur farm—and made the decision, then and there, to stop wearing fur—most fur sold anywhere in the world, including in the United States, originates in China, where there are *no laws at all* to protect the animals used.

But fur is also obtained right here at home. And while you may know that Chinese fur includes dog fur—although it is carefully mislabeled for export as some other species, even dogs in the United States get caught up in the fur trade. Let the story of two dogs, Aurora and Cindy, paint the picture.

Aurora was a stray dog who, one winter, stumbled into a steel-jaw leghold trap set for a coyote. In a haze of pain, she limped along, taking one slow agonizing step after step, the trap clamped like a vice to her swollen leg. After three long weeks, the infection in her leg was making her woozy. She had lost a lot of weight because she had been unable to find enough food to sustain herself.

Exhausted and worn out, Aurora saw an unused camper shell in someone's backyard and crawled under it to lie down to die, still dragging the deadly trap with her. Miraculously, along came a local dog named Ranger, who discovered Aurora's hiding place and set out to rescue her! Ranger was very bright, and he figured out how to bring mouthfuls of snow to her, to try to abate her thirst. He also snuggled up to her, covering her body with his own to keep her warm as fever swept through her. Sensing the urgency of Aurora's condition, Ranger stood beside the camper and howled incessantly, refusing to budge when called.

Not sure what to do, a woman in the neighborhood put a plastic cup filled with food next to Ranger. While she stood and watched, Ranger carefully picked up the cup and carried it under the camper shell to his friend. Although reluctant, Ranger let Aurora be carried out and taken to the veterinarian. Her mangled leg was amputated, and Aurora pulled through.

Beautiful Aurora—a priceless treasure, whose photographs show her jumping with joy in the snow with her new family— is what fur trappers call a "trash animal." Trash animals by the thousands are crippled or killed "by mistake" in traps set for other animals like foxes. Aurora was lucky. She escaped with her life. Another "trash catch," Cindy, did not fare as well.

Cindy was a hound with floppy ears and a long, sweet face. She had been let out to play in the woods and had not come home. Although the family searched the area and called her name, it was days before her cries were finally heard and Cindy was found. The poor dog had steel leghold traps clamped on both back paws and one on her front leg.

Animal control officer Joy Bannister said of Cindy, "When I came up to her it was clear that she had been trying to chew off her own paw to break free and was crying in pain."

Cindy was taken out of the traps, but it was too late. Her injuries were so severe that the veterinarian had to euthanize her. I wish I could show you the last picture ever taken of her, looking so brave, her little white hound face gazing hopefully up at the photographer, three bloody stumps of sinews and bone where her feet should have been.

"Target" animals—foxes, lynxes, minks, raccoons, and coyotes among them—die badly in the traps or when, like Cindy, they try to chew their own paws off to escape. Some are driven to such desperate measures because they know they must return to their young in the den who depend on them for food. If a foot or paw comes off, gangrene and infection sets in, and that, or the loss of blood from the wound, is usually enough to kill them.

If they stay in the trap, after a day or two, perhaps even longer, the trapper will arrive, causing the animals' hearts to pound in their chests like steel drums. The trapper will beat them to death with a club or baseball bat, shoot them in the head (although shooting is not favored, because it can damage the value of the pelt), or stand on their chests and jump up and down to squash their ribs and puncture their hearts.

It is a bloody and painful business, and the amount of blood shed is far from minor—not counting the "trash catch," it can take more than forty raccoons or one hundred squirrels to make a coat.

Not that fur farms are any more humane than trapping. The animals in them are not coddled, and they do not die in their sleep on fluffy pillows. PETA investigators who went to a chinchilla ranch in Michigan to learn firsthand how the animals were killed, found it was by genital electrocution. The animals were given an electrically induced heart attack while fully conscious. It's cheap and doesn't harm the pelts.

The electrocution was carried out cheaply, a metal "alligator clip" attached to the chinchilla's ear, another to her labia, then into the socket on the wall goes the lead end, a switch is flipped, and a jolt of electricity passes through the animal's skin and down the length of her body.

According to biologist and wildlife specialist Leslie Gerstenfeld-Press the current causes unbearable muscle pain, and death can come slowly, yet the chinchilla is paralyzed, unable to scream or run away.

"Nope, still beating," one fur rancher told PETA's investigator, feeling for the heart, then shocked the chinchilla again. Another rancher admitted that he had come back into the room after electrocuting a chinchilla, only to find the animal had revived and had to be electrocuted again.

Before the First World War, it was considered impossible to farm chinchillas. No one could get these little animals, who live in altitudes of eleven thousand feet or more above sea level, to survive a move to lower ground. Then, sadly, an American trapper embarked on a six-year project to slowly move the animals "down mountain," resting for a full year every few thousand feet, then taking them by sea to Los Angeles. Chinchilla ranches boomed.

Fur farmers, like experimenters, do not like anyone to see what goes on inside their operations. But they have not always succeeded in keeping animal-friendly people out. As a result, farmers have been caught using anal electrocution; leaving animals out in open pens in blizzard conditions (in nature, the animals would burrow or dig into the ground or keep moving to stay warm); throwing live chickens, feet first, into a grinder to create ground meat for the caged fur bearers; and killing animals by injecting weed killer into their chests.

On one fur ranch in Illinois, where anal electrocution was carried out in full view of other foxes who were next in line, a PETA investigator made a deeply disturbing video showing raccoons and foxes whirling like dervishes in their filthy, tiny cages and tearing at the mesh until their feet were bloody. Sir Paul McCartney's daughter the designer Stella McCartney said she felt sick when she watched it and was determined to help. She went into the studio, stuck a pair of headphones on, and narrated the video, then popped it in the mail to every design house. "Please stop using fur," she wrote.

There are millions of reasons not to wear fur garments, counting the millions of beautiful ocelots, beavers, nutria, and other wonderful beings who get their necks broken and worse to make the garments. When people didn't care, the late Fund for Animals founder, Cleveland Amory, asked them to consider that wearing a fur coat makes a person look "fat and uninformed." Environmentalists remind dishonest furriers who tout fur as "a natural" that it can only be "natural" while it is on its original owner's back. When the coat is treated with mortants (a horrid but descriptive word) and other cancer-causing chemicals, as is always done, it will break down about as fast as a piece of heavy plastic, that is, perhaps never. It also smells when it gets wet.

As for the energy conscious, it may matter to know that it takes 7,845,000 more BTUs (British Thermal Units of energy) to make a ranched fur than to produce a "fashionable fake." As Brigitte Bardot points out, "Fur is very old-fashioned. We wore it when we didn't know any better. Now, who wants to appear like a cavewoman?" Not the 78 percent of readers who responded to a recent Fashion Police poll, saying animals should not be killed for their pelts.

HUMANS IN SHEEP'S AND
SNAKE'S CLOTHING

Twiggy, one of the guest judges on *America's Next Top Model* and the fabulous and famous first "supermodel," wrote to all the top couturiers in the world on PETA's behalf, asking them to stop using exotic animal skins like alligator, boa, Siberian Steppe pony, and crocodile. Twiggy's kindness contrasts sharply with US *Vogue's* ice maiden editor, Anna Wintour, who still advocates wearing anything that moves and even sings the praises of french fries cooked in pony lard, although it is hard to see how eating them would give anyone that "model look."

Some skins even come from supposedly protected species. In years gone by, the US Fish and Wildlife Service has fined Chanel, Saks Fifth Avenue, Gucci, and Fendi for illegal use of endangered species for shoes, handbags, and watch straps. An estimated 25 to 30 percent of imported crocodile shoe leather and other wildlife items are made from poached animals.

According to Beauty Without Cruelty (BWC), which keeps track of the trade in exotic skins from India, the most common way snakes are skinned is simply to nail them, alive, to a tree and run a knife down their bellies, then strip the skin away and toss the writhing body aside.

Alligators and crocodiles are hard to kill, so their deaths are agonizingly slow. A PETA investigator who visited the back rooms of a Florida "alligator farm" that runs a gift shop jam-packed with alligator purses, belts, and knickknacks found the 'gators kept in half-sunken tin-sided tubs in the dark. The room reeked of rancid meat, alligator waste, and stagnant water.

He videotaped teenage employees wading into the water, armed with metal baseball bats. The kids smashed the young animals repeatedly on the head. Wounded alligators tried to crawl away as fast as they could and were chased down and struck again.

The investigator wrote, "The animals continued to move and writhe minutes after they had been struck. The workers then took out switchblade knives and slit the base of the alligators' necks. Still some of the alligators moved. One had enough strength left in him to slowly edge himself over the door sill and onto the ground below."

British herpetologist Clifford Warwick studied slaughter methods used at another alligator farm that were even worse, although they are described as "humane" by industry standards. This scenario involved three workers: one stood on the alligator's mouth, another on her tail, and another attempted to slice through her spinal cord with a steel chisel and hammer. Warwick says it took five to eight blows for the chisel to break through the vertebra, and even then, the spinal cord was not always completely severed. Of course, severing the spinal cord doesn't kill. It paralyzes. Some alligators remained conscious for two hours.

Nearly all crocodile skin comes from animals taken from the wild. Crocodile hunters typically catch these massive animals with huge hooks and wires, reeling them in when they become weak from blood loss or drown. One eyewitness account describes how men with hammers and picks smashed with all their might at a group of cornered crocs.

Like alligators, these animals are thought of as ugly and frightening, although they are excellent and skilled mothers and have actually enjoyed the company of people when raised with them from hatchlings. The Pedersons of Illinois lived for forty-two years with a six-footer named Alice. They called her "an ideal companion" who had a personality of her own, who sat and smiled beside them while they watched television, and who was particularly fond of bubble baths. Who isn't?

HANNAH SURVIVES

If there is no justification for picking on fierce animals with thick skin, how can there be any for hurting a gentle sheep? I remember Patty Mark, an Australian campaigner and sheep rescuer, telling me, without thinking how odd it sounded, about a sheep "sitting ever so politely" on the seat of her car as she drove about town. I could easily imagine it, having myself ridden in my car with a very polite goat (who stuck her head out of the window, as dogs do, and sat on her haunches when we came to a stop sign, as if it was the most natural thing in the world).

Wool producers love to mock prosheep people for "objecting to the sheep getting nicked during shearing," as if that is the only problem. The truth is, millions of sheep used in the wool trade suffer cruelties that would make any decent person pale.

No matter where you buy it, most wool comes from Australia, where about 148 million sheep are kept in flocks of many thousands each, making individual attention to a sick animal a silly proposition. A mind-boggling eight million mature sheep there die every year from untreated illnesses, heat exhaustion (most are imported European merinos with very thick wool, and so they have a hard time coping with summer temperatures), lack of shelter in winter and shade from the blistering sun in summer, and other forms of plain out-and-out negligence. Up to 40 percent of lambs born each year die at birth or before they reach the ripe old age of eight weeks. If they do live, the lambs have their tails and the *skin* (not the wool, the flesh) cut off the backs of their rumps with a pair of gardening shears to try to keep flies from laying eggs in the folds of their wool. The wounds are staunched with tar, and the pain is so great that the little lambs, when they can rise to their feet, walk sideways like crabs for days. There are other more sensible and painless ways to prevent fly-strike, like using "bare breech" sheep breeds, but the flesh-cutting procedure, called "mulesing," costs almost nothing, and that is why so many farmers choose it.

The next assault occurs when the lambs are sheared. This happens before they would naturally shed their winter coats and results in about one million deaths a year from exposure. Shearing is not a gentle art when there are so many sheep to deal with. It is quick and dirty, and the electric machines sometimes slice off a nipple or a tumor. I have seen freshly sheared sheep standing like quivering blobs of jelly outside the shearing shed, cut marks littering their bodies.

Many of the older sheep—and "meat sheep"—are shipped to the Middle East for slaughter. To get there, they must travel huge distances overland to the coast, sometimes going without water for as long as seventy-two hours at a stretch, before being herded aboard enormous fourteen-tier-high ships. The journey takes about three weeks, the whole time spent standing—and slipping—in their own waste. It would be a terrifying ordeal even for a healthy sheep, given the weather at sea and the motion of the boat, and few are that robust after the life experiences they've already endured. The sick and newborns are left among the living or weeded out and thrown overboard during the journey. When the ship docks, the rest of the sheep are prodded down the ramp and sold at market. They are bundled into trunks of cars in the heat or onto open bed trucks and eventually have their throats slit while fully conscious.

Hannah is a sheep who didn't make it as far as Tehran or Kuwait. She collapsed in the field where she was born and where she gave birth. A caring member of Animal Liberation in Australia spotted her lying about twenty feet from the fence, clearly visible from the road. She stopped the car, crawled through the fence, walked over, and knelt down beside her. The sheep was not even aware of the woman's presence.

The ewe had given birth to twin lambs. One was lying behind her, still covered with afterbirth, dead. The other was cuddled up to her flank, also dead. The woman lifted the sheep's head gently. Both of her eyes were sealed with thick crusts of pus. One ear was full of maggots, as was one of her hind legs. The woman had seen this so many times before. This poor animal needed help. Immediately. Her life was hanging by a thread.

There was a house close by. The resident said that she rented the house from the farmer who owned the sheep. The farmer lived some distance away, and the resident said it was pointless calling him, as he would not come out for "just one sheep." She had told him three days before that the sheep was down, but he had done nothing.

Thankfully, there was a gate nearby. The woman who had stopped for the sheep lifted the animal into the back of her car. She was light as a feather, nothing but skin and bones. The woman picked up the two dead baby lambs and placed them on the seat beside her. They would be buried on her plantation, along with many others, and would have a tree planted for them.

Before driving away, the woman looked back over the paddock. It was dotted with the remains of more than a dozen dead ewes and lambs. She wondered what kind of monster would allow this to happen. She wondered why the law didn't protect sheep from such appalling neglect.

After driving a few kilometers, she turned onto a side road. She managed to clean out most of the maggots in the ewe's ear and scrape those from her leg. She lifted the sheep's head and poured a trickle of water into her mouth. The sheep swallowed and tried to raise her head but was too weak. The ligaments along her neck were so taut that, when the woman removed her hand, the sheep's head was jerked to one side or the other.

The plantation was a good hour's drive away. "Please, hold on. We will help you, sweetheart. No one will hurt you anymore. Please don't give up." The woman spoke these words out loud, over and over, all the way home, giving way to tears, as she had done so many times before.

When she arrived home, she placed the ewe on some old blankets on the living room floor and gave her some electrolyte solution. It was a start. She cleaned out her ears with fly repellent and warm paraffin oil, and bathed the sheep's eyes with boric acid and warm water. It was impossible to find sufficient muscle mass for an intramuscular injection of penicillin, so the woman injected it under her skin.

When the sheep became more comfortable, the family went on a "medicine hunt" around the grounds, returning with a bucketful of grasses and weeds. It must have seemed like a smorgasbord to the sheep, for suddenly she showed life. At that moment, the family realized the ewe—they decided to call her Hannah—had a chance, but there was still a long way to go.

Over the following weeks, her caretakers gradually increased Hannah's food intake and introduced her to such goodies as apples, fresh alfalfa from the garden, willow leaves, whole oats, grass, and the occasional biscuit. She began to improve and was soon able to hold her head up. A mattress was placed on the floor, and her rescuer slept alongside her every night, changing her position every few hours and replacing wet towels (because Hannah was too weak to get up to urinate).

After fourteen days, Hannah could be held up and helped with her feeble attempts to walk. It was almost three weeks before she could stand, supporting her own weight for a couple of minutes before collapsing into waiting arms.

When Hannah was able to rise unassisted, she was moved into the laundry room and the door was left open. Hannah came and went as she pleased. She wore a coat to protect her bare skin from the sun. Her wool had fallen away in tufts, a result of extreme stress.

There was also an orphaned lamb called Babby on the farm. Babby had lost her mum. Hannah had lost her babies. They adopted each other and grazed together by the house. Whenever Babby came to the laundry for a bottle, Hannah would come too, for an apple or a biscuit.

Eventually, Babby was weaned and Hannah's instinct to join the flock returned. They would wait at the gate each morning to be let out with the other rescued sheep, always returning in the evening for their treats and settling down by the house for the night.

But the picture of Hannah lying totally helpless and slowly dying still remains vivid in her rescuer's mind.

SISTERS UNDER THE SKIN

The thought of wearing bits of Hannah or any other animal brings back to me the song from *Dr. Doolittle* that goes:

> *When you dress in suede or leather*
> *Or some fancy fur or feather*
> *Do you stop and wonder whether,*
> *Are you wearing someone's brother,*
> *Perhaps it's someone's mother.*

With suede and leather, should you see a sale of cheap goods, couches perhaps or jackets, you may be looking at rain forest leather. This is the hide of cows grazed in South and

Central America to make cheap burgers for the international meat market. To create grazing land, the forests must come down, and when the multinational corporations bring in their bulldozers to fell the trees, along with them go the homes of countless birds, insects, mammals, and reptiles.

Vegetarians are sometimes asked, "What about your shoes?" Well, we may not eat our shoes, but there is no denying that leather supports the meat industry, and skin accounts for a whopping 50 percent of the by-product value of cattle. To stop supporting the cruelties of factory farming and the slaughterhouse, one must stop making any leather purchases, which subsidize their existence.

If you have ever priced a "fancy" pair of leather boots and calculated how many pairs it would take to rebuild a cow, you know how much money the leather "side business" puts in a farmer's pockets. Even the veal calf can be squeezed for a few dollars. His skin is made into high-priced calfskin gloves, wallets, and car seat linings.

Tanneries use a variety of substances to treat the hide, including antidecomposition chemicals, mineral salts (aluminum, iron, chromium, and zirconium), formaldehyde, coal, tar derivatives (phenol, cresol, and naphthalene), and various oils and dyes, some of them cyanide based. The incidence of leukemia among residents near one Kentucky tannery has been found to be five times the US average, and one study found that more than half of all testicular cancer victims work in tanneries.

Other animals made into clothing and accessories include lizards, ostriches (whose beautiful eyelashes are—believe it or not—made into false ones for human use), and, in Australia, approximately five million kangaroos every year. The kangaroos are killed by purposely poisoning their water supply, or by hunters running them down in jeeps, where the kangaroos are impaled on sticks embedded in the ground. Their leather is made into everything from dog collars to sneakers.

FOES TO FINE FEATHERED FRIENDS

Our trappings spare no animals, from those who swim to those who fly. Just over one hundred years ago, a spot check of the hats worn in New York by women out for a stroll showed that 542 out of 700 of them were decorated with the mounted heads of birds! Kathryn Lasky wrote a book about this phenomenon, called *She's Wearing a Dead Bird on Her Head!*, pointing out that whatever tiny shreds of power women may have had at that time in politics or the community were easily swept away by their ludicrous getup. Says Lasky, "Who is going to listen to a woman with a dead bird on her head?"

The designer Jean Paul Gautier often sends his models down the runway in Paris wearing whole bird bodies on their shoulders and hats. Perhaps this is a sign of progress at least as far as hats go, for feathered headdresses have left the street and only appear onstage in fashion's latest shock theater.

As for the use of feathers for other purposes, the news for birds is still bleak. When North Korea's former president, Kim Il-sung, celebrated his eightieth birthday, the occasion caused a panic in the land as his hangers-on tried to pick the perfect presents for a man who already had everything. The *Wall Street Journal* reported that the North Korean government sent citizens into the countryside to collect ginseng root, live frogs and ducks, as well as snapping turtles, whose blood is thought to be an aphrodisiac. The piéce de resistance, however, was a quilt. Seven hundred thousand tiny sparrows were killed for the feathers that filled it. Today, larger birds bear the brunt of our desire for old-fashioned stuffing material for comforters, jackets, and pillows. The softest and warmest down is supposed to be that of the Eider duck, who uses her breast feathers to line her nest and cover her eggs. Other down and feathers may come from birds killed for meat, as with feather dusters and boas made from chicken feathers, but perhaps the greatest horror of the down industry is in the way feathers are plucked from live geese and ducks.

Most down comes from Hungary and other East European countries where birds are force-fed for foie gras production. These geese and ducks suffer live plucking as a second major insult, and their lives, albeit short, are extraordinarily miserable. Feathers are ripped from the birds' bodies then allowed to grow back four or five times before they are slaughtered. After being restrained (their legs are "hogtied" and they are strung upside down) and having their feathers pulled out of their flesh by hand, the birds make a pathetic sight. They huddle together or scrunch up against a fence or stall, seeking isolation in their pain, their bodies shaking uncontrollably from shock. They are so physically distressed that it takes days for them to recover.

Down is for the birds. Or it should be. For spoiled human beings living in this century, alternatives are easy to find—just as there are alternatives for silk, which is acquired by immersing silkworms in scalding water, steaming them, electrocuting them, or drying them in a hot oven or by microwaving the cocoons (the threads of about nine hundred of which go into one shirt).

THE FINISHING TOUCH

Watch out for fashion accessories. Some bracelets and earrings are made from the "old man of the sea," the turtle. How many shoppers realize that the traditional method of separating turtles from their shells was to suspend the turtles, alive, over a furnace until the heat peeled the plates off their bodies? There is no card at the jewelry counter that advises you that, even today, no anesthetic or courtesy blow is delivered to turtles before their shells are cut away from their flesh, the oil squeezed from them for ointment and creams, and their bodies macheted into steaks. One has to wonder if helping mother turtles find a safe place to hatch eggs is really a service, given that a fair number of the hatchlings will be killed in vile ways *if* they reach adulthood. In fact, they will more than likely end up in parts; a foot clunking around in the bottom of a soup tureen, or a bangle worn to the disco.

All this gives extra meaning to the phrase "Buyer beware!"

WHAT YOU CAN DO

Make Your Closet Cruelty-Free

Speak up. When you see cruelly produced clothing and accessories in stores, please let the clerks and managers know you object to the sale of animal parts.

Write letters. When businesses advertise fur, exotic leathers, and other animal-derived fabrics in your local papers, write letters to the editor and blog comments explaining how the products are obtained and urging readers not to buy them.

If your local hardware store sells steel leg traps, ask to meet with the owners and show them footage of animals suffering in the traps (including companion animals, who are often mistakenly caught), and ask that the traps be removed from their shelves.

Buy nonleather products. Purchase only nonleather shoes, clothing, and accessories (including watchbands, soccer balls, upholstery, belts). There are many comfortable, well-made, and fashionable nonleather options, such as satin dress shoes, synthetic running shoes, and canvas recreation shoes. (Get a current list of companies that make non-leather clothing and accessories at CowsAreCool.com.)

Choose nonanimal fabrics. Avoid eelskin, ivory, pearls, feathers, angora, and felt, which is usually made from animal hair. Choose instead canvas, ramie, cotton, vinyl, nylon, linen, rayon, straw (hats and bags), faux pearls, plastic, rubber, pleather, or hemp.

Avoid down. Choose cotton, cotton corduroy, natural fibers, satin evening coats, parkas, and quilts stuffed with cruelty-free synthetics like Fiberfill II, Polarguard, and Thinsulate.

Don't buy silk. Silk is used in cloth (including taffeta), silkscreening, and as a coloring agent in some face powders, soaps, and other cosmetics. It can cause severe allergic skin reactions, as well as systemic reactions if inhaled or ingested. Alternatives include rayon, milkweed seed-pod fibers, kapok (silky fibers from the seeds of some tropical trees), and synthetic silks.

If you're shopping and notice that a store sells fur, gather some expensive merchandise and ask a clerk to hold it while you continue shopping. After a few minutes, ask to speak to the manager and inform him or her that you won't be purchasing anything because you've noticed that the store sells fur items.

Never buy ivory. Ivory comes from elephants and from marine mammals such as whales, walruses, and narwhals. It is often carved into figurines, curios, or jewelry.

Avoid tortoiseshell products. Don't buy tortoiseshell jewelry or combs; leather, eggs, or food products from turtles; or creams or cosmetics made with turtle flesh extract. Twenty thousand endangered sea turtles are slaughtered every year in Mexico, many as they are crawling back to sea, exhausted, after laying their eggs.

Reject imports. Reject rugs, hunting trophies, and articles such as handbags, compacts, coats, wallets, and key cases made from the skins and fur of jaguars, leopards, snow leopards, tigers, ocelots, margays, and small tiger cats. Earth Island Institute reports that more than 90 percent of Nepal's fur shop coats are made from "protected" species. Approximately four rare snow leopards are killed to make coats that sell for $3,200 apiece; and it takes at least thirty "common" leopard cats to make one full-length coat.

Never let fur-wearers pass by without kindly asking if they know about the cruelty that goes into every coat, hat, and bit of trim.

Protect birds. Don't wear feathers or buy mounted birds. Up to 70 percent of "exotic" birds imported into the United States die during capture, transit, and the required thirty-day quarantine.

Speak up! Tell merchants, catalog companies, vendors, and hotels why they should never order such goods again.

Put on a bloodied fur coat and pass out leaflets to fur-wearers on a busy street corner, or dress up in a tutu and stand outside the ballet to remind patrons that fur is "tutu cruel!"

Protest politely. Always write and call in protest when you see an ad for fur in a newspaper or magazine or hear one on the radio.

Call or e-mail the producers of television shows, especially soap operas, and tell them that, if a character must wear fur, it should be an obvious fake fur and be announced in the credits. Keep your eyes open for sweepstakes and beauty pageants that still offer fur prizes, and charities that feature fur in fund-raising. Call and e-mail the promoters of such events and ask them to join the twenty-first century.

Be a squeaky wheel. Complain if mall managers include fur in fashion shows.

Create a mobile "billboard" by dressing up old jackets or furs (a new fake would do as well) with catchy animal rights slogans and colorful designs and wearing them around town.

Talk loud. Strike up a "casual" conversation, perhaps on your cell phone, within hearing distance of a fur-wearer about the gruesome facts of fur.

Wear a button. Make an antifur button a permanent part of your winter wardrobe.

Dig out that old Santa costume during the holidays and encourage people to "Ho, Ho, Faux" for the holidays—you can pass out candy canes with antifur leaflets attached as an enticement to passersby.

Give to charity. Convince others to donate their furs to PETA. If one of your relatives still has a fur stashed in the back of her closet, use your powers of persuasion to convince her to make a tax deductible contribution of it to PETA, or give it to a wildlife rehabilitator to use as a cuddly "surrogate mother" for orphaned wild babies to snuggle up to.

Give so they can live. Donate to a local campaign action group or national organization to help fund antifur billboards and ads.

Join a planned protest. Contact your local animal rights organization or PETA for fur demonstrations near you, or organize your own.

Use your plates. Turn every rush hour and trip to the store into an educational opportunity by sporting a NO FURS or BAN FUR car license plate.

Build a cow. Build a life-size cow out of a collection of cast-off leather goods and display it in a library, school, art gallery, town square, or even in your front yard. Price the components and then add a price tag to the exhibit in dollars and animals' lives.

Dress up. Jeanie Brown got the last laugh when she won a Halloween "Elvira Look-Alike" contest in which the prize was a fur coat. Brown and other activists were disgusted when the prize was announced, particularly given Cassandra "Elvira" Peterson's support of animal rights. (Cassandra's personalized license plate reads BAN FUR.) Brown donated the coat to PETA for use in educational presentations and demonstrations.

Dress down. Outside the Seattle Fur Exchange, baseball manager Tony La Russa led activists in a "fur funeral." Dressed in black and bearing a fur-laden coffin, they captured media attention while, inside, the price of the pelts of hundreds of thousands of animals of furs slumped, due to "cruelty consciousness" worldwide.

Bare it all. Activists all over the world have "gone naked" to protest fur. From Paris to Tokyo, Italy to the United States, animal rights activists have grabbed international headlines, telling the world loud and clear they'd rather go naked than wear fur!

❓ FREQUENTLY ASKED QUESTIONS

Aren't the cows going to be slaughtered for meat anyway?

Leather is not simply a slaughterhouse by-product, it's a "co-product," meaning that when you buy leather, you make it more profitable to raise and kill cows and other animals. According to industry sources, the skins of the animals represent "the most economically important by-product of the meat packing industry."

When "dairy" cows' production declines, for example, their skin is made into leather, and the hides of their offspring, calves raised for veal for instance, are made into high-priced calfskin. Thus the economic success of the slaughterhouse and the factory farm is directly linked to the sale of leather goods. Decreasing demand for both animal hide and flesh will reduce the number of cows and other animals, like pigs, hurt and killed in the trade. There are so many alternatives to leather that it's easy to stop supporting unnecessary cruelty. To read more about leather and the great alternatives to animal skins that are available, visit CowsAreCool.com.

Isn't leather better for the environment than synthetics?

Contrary to industry propaganda, leather production is actually more harmful to the environment than producing synthetics, and it is certainly more harmful than processing natural fibers like cotton. Tanning prevents leather from biodegrading so it can't rot back into the ground as, say, linen can. Animal skin is turned into finished leather using a variety of harsh chemicals, including mineral salts, formaldehyde, coal, and tar derivatives, and various oils, dyes, and finishes, some of which are cyanide based.

Most leather produced in the United States is chrome tanned, and the Environmental Protection Agency considers all waste that contains chromium to be hazardous. In addition to the toxic substances mentioned above, tannery effluent also contains large amounts of other pollutants, such as protein, hair, salt, lime sludge, sulfides, and acids.

Among the disastrous consequences of this noxious waste is the threat to human health from the highly elevated levels of lead, cyanide, and formaldehyde in the groundwater near tanneries. And think what this effluent does to wildlife in nearby rivers and streams!

*I don't have the time to search high and low
for nonleather shoes and accessories.*

Nonleather products are readily available. Many department stores and shoe stores offer beautiful, practical, fashionable, comfortable, snazzy, you-name-it nonleather shoes, belts, bags, and other products. In fact, many products that look like leather are actually synthetic (pleather)—so check the label for those magic words: ALL MAN-MADE MATERIALS or SYNTHETIC. A great place to find low-priced nonleather shoes is Payless ShoeSource—look no farther than your local mall! For other ideas, consult PETA's Guide to Cruelty-Free Clothes and Accessories or go to PETAMall.com

What's wrong with wearing wool?

As with other industries in which animals are raised for profit, the interests of the animals used in the wool industry are not considered important in and of themselves. Flocks usually consist of many thousands of sheep, so providing individual attention to their needs is out of the question. Some people believe that shearing sheep helps animals who might otherwise be burdened with too much wool, but without human interference, sheep grow just enough wool to protect themselves from temperature extremes.

Most wool comes from Australia. Just weeks after birth, lambs' ears are hole punched, their tails are chopped off, and males are castrated—all without painkillers. Many lambs die from exposure or starvation before they are eight weeks old, and many mature sheep die from disease, lack of shelter, and neglect.

To prevent "fly-strike," many Australian ranchers perform a crude and cheap operation called "mulesing," which involves carving huge strips of flesh off the backs of lambs' legs with gardening shears. When shearing, speed is everything. Shearers are usually paid by volume, not by the hour, which encourages quick and careless work. Says one eyewitness, "The shearing shed must be one of the worst places in the world for cruelty to animals. I have seen shearers punch sheep with their shears or fists until the sheep's noses bled. I have seen sheep with half their faces shorn off." Sheep leave the shearing shed with cuts and stand outside, shaking from their ordeal.

Is the fur industry really as cruel as people make it out to be?

Indeed it is. PETA's investigations at fur farms have found that some animals are killed by anal electrocution, meaning that an electrically charged steel rod is inserted into their rectums, literally frying their insides. Exposed broken bones, upper respiratory infections, and cancerous tumors are among the wounds and diseases that animals have endured—without veterinary treatment—on fur farms we investigated.

Animals caught in steel-jaw leg traps are in so much pain that some actually bite off their limbs in order to escape. Unable to eat, keep warm, or defend themselves against predators, many die horrible deaths before the trapper arrives to stomp them to death or strangle them, sometimes days later.

Whether enduring the excruciating pain of a steel trap or being driven mad in a tiny cage, the animals suffer immensely. To read what PETA is doing to help, visit FurIsDead.com.

Why does PETA give fur coats to the homeless?

Donating unwanted furs to homeless people not only helps needy people keep warm, but it also allows us to show that we are receiving more fur donations than ever from people who are appalled by the cruelty involved in fur ranching and trapping. "Fur kitchens" allow us to point out that after using hundreds of furs in educational displays, dumping them at museums and outside furriers' stores, painting them for floats, dragging them through the streets, burying and burning them, and even donating them to wildlife rehabilitators for use as animal bedding, we still have plenty of coats left over, each representing dozens of animals who were killed for vanity.

Fur giveaways also counteract furriers' efforts to portray fur as status symbols. In fact, the overwhelming influx of fur into our office means that fur has hit rock bottom.

How is down obtained?

Typically, ducks and geese are lifted by their necks, their legs are tied, and their feathers are ripped out. The struggling birds often sustain injuries during plucking. They are then returned to their cages until they are ready to be plucked again. This process begins at about nine weeks of age and occurs every six weeks until the birds go to slaughter.

Feathers are often plucked out of ducks and geese who are raised for food. Those raised for foie gras, especially, suffer terribly in other ways too. These birds are force-fed up to six times a day with a funnel that is inserted into their throats, and up to six pounds of a salty, fatty corn mash is pumped into each bird's stomach each day—until the birds' livers have ballooned to many times their normal size.

Synthetic alternatives to down are not only cruelty-free, but they are also cheaper and, unlike down, retain their insulating capabilities in all weather conditions.

Cruelty-Free Clothing Alternatives

The following companies are either vegan or sell alternatives to leather and fur:

ATHLETIC SHOES	BAGS	
Active Soles	All Vegan	Gravis Footwear
Adidas	Alternative Outfitters	Helen Powers
Asics	Bagg Lady Handbags	Hot Topic
AVIA	Bello Iris	Jack Spade
Converse	Bourgeois Bohème	JCPenney
Etonic	Bulge	Jeanne Lottie
Fila	Cedar Key Canvas	Karen Lukacs
Fogdog Sports	Charlotte Russe	Kate Spade
Gravis Footwear	Chrome Bags	Kathy Van Zeeland
Keds	Crystalyn Kae	Kohl's
New Balance	Diesel	Little Packrats
Nike	DSW	matt & natt
Payless ShoeSource	Ecolution	M. Avery Designs
Puma	Eddie Bauer	Studio & Boutique
Reebok	Fast & Furless Skinless	MuchachaK Handbags
Road Runner Sports	Fashion	Nedra Made It
Saucony, Inc.	Faux	Never Leather Land
Sketchers	FredaLA.com	Nine West
Teva	Freerangers	NY Artificial
Tretorn	Gloria Gerber	Off Broadway Shoes
Vans, Inc.	GoodGoth.com	olsen Haus
		1154 Lill

Pangea

Parapette

Paul Frank

Payless ShoeSource

Queen Bee Creations

Rack Room Shoes

R.E. Load Baggage

   Inc.

Seat Belt Bags

Slim Pawn Handmade

   Handbags

Sparkle Craft

Splaff Flops

Stella McCartney

Susan Nichole

Target

Timberland

Timbuk2 Designs

Tom Bihn

Tomorrow's World

Truth

Used Rubber USA

Vegan Essentials

Vegan Wares

Vegetarian Shoes and

   Bags

TheVegetarianSite

   .com

Vereschagin Designs

Vamp Bags

Vulcana Bags

XOXO

BALLS

Fogdog Sports

Spalding Sports

V Sports

Wilson Sporting Goods

   Company

BASEBALL GLOVES

Carpenter Trade

   Company

Heartland Products

BELTS

All Vegan

Alternative Outfitters

Atticus Clothing

Bourgeois Bohème

Crystalyn Kae

Dress

Ethical Wares

Fast & Furless Skinless

   Fashion

Freerangers

Heartland Products

Hot Topic

Moo Shoes

Mudd Jeans

99x

Nine West

NoBull Footwear

Pangea

Paul Frank

REI

Sparkle Craft

Splaff Flops

Tomorrow's World

Truth

Vegan Essentials

Veganline

Vegan Wares

Vegetarian Shoes

Vegetarian Shoes

   & Bags

BIKING GLOVES

REI

BOWLING SHOES

Dexter Shoes

CLEATS

Adidas

Dexter Shoes

Nike

Puma

Reebok

COMPANION-ANIMAL ACCESSORIES

Morrco Pet Supply

Nedra Made It

Pumpkin & Lulu

Vegan Wares

CYCLING SHOES

Northwave

SiDi USA

DANCE SHOES

Capezio

Cynthia King Dance

Grishko

Vegan Wares

DRESS/CASUAL SHOES

Aerosoles

Alloy

All Vegan

Alternative Outfitters

Anywhere Shoes

À Propos . . .

   Conversations

Beyond Skin

Birkenstock Footwear

Bourgeois Bohème

Charlotte Russe

Charmone Shoes

Chinese Laundry Shoes

Cloudwalkers

Coldwater Creek

Crocs

Delia's

Diesel

Dragonfly

DSW

Earth

Enzo Angiolini

Ethical Wares

Fantasia Wear

Fashion Bug

Fast & Furless

   Skinless

Fashion

Frederick's of

   Hollywood

Freerangers

Funk e Feet

G.O. Max

GoodGoth.com

Green Shoes

Heartland Products

Heavenly Soles

Hot Topic

JCPenney

Kate Spade

Kmart

Kohl's

L.E.I. Jeans

Life Stride

Liz Claiborne

Madeline Stuart

   Shoes

Masseys

matt & natt

Mink Shoes

Moo Shoes

Mudd Jeans

Natalie Portman for Té

Casan

Naturalizer

99x

Nine West

NoBull Footwear

olsen Haus

Off Broadway Shoes

Pangea

Payless ShoeSource

Prima Royale Shoes

Rack Room Shoes

Ragazzi Vegan

REI

Roaman's

Rocket Dog

Sam & Libby

Santana Canada

   Footwear

Sketchers

Snaz75.com

Splaff Flops

Stella McCartney

Steve Madden

Sunsports

Target

Teva

Tomorrow's World

Vans, Inc.

Vegan Essentials

Veganline

Vegan Wares

Vegetarian Shoes

Vegetarian Shoes &
Bags

TheVegetarianSite.com

Veggies Footwear

Wellington House

Wild Pair

Zappos.com

FAUX FUR

Anything Animals

Bootzwalla

Charlotte Russe

Comfurts by Ken Alan

Coquette Faux Furriers

Dillard's

Fabulous Furs

Faux

Frederick's of
Hollywood

Genuine Fake

Orbific Echos

Pamela McCoy

Perfect Image

Posh Pelts

Premium Furs

Sublime Custom
Designs

Sweet Herb

Vereschagin Designs

GUITAR STRAPS

Couch Guitar Straps

DiMarzio

Këpur

Pangea

Resophonic Outfitters

Sparkle Craft

Vegan Wares

HIKING/WORK BOOTS

Bata Shoe Company

Ethical Wares

Five Ten

Garmont USA

Heartland Products

LaCrosse Boots

Last Resort

NoBull Footwear

Pangea

REI

Santana Canada
Footwear

Vegetarian Shoes

ICE/HOCKEY SKATES

LowPriceSkates.com

Skates.com

MOTORCYCLE APPAREL

Aerostich/Rider
Warehouse

Alpine Stars

Competition
Accessories

Dennis Kirk

Fast Company

Giali USA

Harley-Davidson

Heartland Products,
Ltd.

Joe Rocket Sports
Gear

Marsee Products

MotoLiberty

Motonation

Motoport/Cycleport

Olympia Sports

Road Gear

Teknic

Tour Master

Vegetarian Shoes

Viking Bags

Willie & Max

Yamaha Motor
Corporation

ROCK-CLIMBING SHOES

Evolv

Five Ten

Mad Rock

SADDLES

Thorowgood

Wintec

SKATEBOARDING SHOES

Circa

Emerica

És Footwear

Etnies

Fallen Footwear

Globe

Hawk Footwear

IPath

Macbeth Shoes

Osiris

Vans, Inc.

SNOWBOARDING BOOTS

Airwalk

ThirtyTwo

SNOW BOOTS

Naturalizer

Payless ShoeSource

TAP SHOES

Capezio

TOOL BELTS

Nailers

WALLETS

Alternative Outfitters

Atticus Clothing

Bourgeois Bohème

DB Clay, Inc.

Ductbill

Fast & Furless Skinless Fashion

Jeanne Lottie

matt & natt

Moo Shoes

99x

Nine West

NoBull Footwear

Pangea

Paul Frank

Queen Bee Creations

Target

Used Rubber USA

Vegan Essentials

Vegan Wares

TheVegetarianSite .com

Vulcana Bags

Wal-Mart

XOXO

WEIGHT-LIFTING GLOVES

NewGrip.com

WESTERN-STYLE BOOTS

Heartland Products

Dissection Must Go

*With today's modern alternatives, students can
learn science without sacrificing compassion
for animals*

—JASON HANSTOR, PHD

PETA supporter and actress Alicia Silverstone
promotes modern alternatives to dissection
and deeply believes in the project. Alicia has
recorded a television public-service spot in which
she asks that frogs be respected, not dissected.
She worries where the cats come from (PETA's
investigator found collars and identification tags
on some cats at one supply house) and wonders
what the demand for frogs for "classroom cut-
ups" is doing to the wild populations so important to our ecosystem. Her concerns are well
founded.

The excerpts you are about to read come
from a report made by a PETA investigator who
worked incognito at a leading dissection supply
house, a place where animals, from cats and rab-

bits and frogs and worms, were prepared for shipment to schools throughout North and South America.

The cats were roughly shunted from their transport cages into one large cage for gassing by being jabbed with a hooked metal bar. The cats are so tightly packed that their fur is pushed through the openings in the wire. They are put into a small carbon monoxide chamber and gassed for less than five minutes. This brief time is not always sufficient to kill them.

The rabbits were thrown into a wheelbarrow and covered with water. One rabbit was trying to get away. The man put the rabbit underneath the other rabbits. Soon he started to laugh. "Look, he's trying to crawl out from underneath." He grabbed the rabbit, repeatedly picking him up and dunking him back into the water, holding him under for a few seconds before pulling him out for a few seconds.

The rats are strapped by rubber bands to small boards for processing. This morning, one of the rats was moving and trying to get loose. One of the men pulled the band out of the rat's mouth and laughed. "This one's still alive." He pulled her off the board as she struggled with the band around her belly. Everyone was laughing. They began to toss the live rat around. Someone said, "That thing's gonna *bite* somebody." Another man threw the rat into a bucket of water that contained dead rats. The rat was scrambling to get out of the bucket. A worker held her under until she stopped moving.

A live frog was hopping around the floor by the gas chamber. One of the men laughed and said, " 'Hell, let's just stick a needle in it.' "

The animals described in the investigator's notebook all lost their lives just so a child somewhere could say, "Yuck!"

Of course, the students and their teachers never realize how the animals' deaths take place. All they see is a creepy-looking body in a plastic bag.

Adam Pitre, an eighth-grade student in Ontario, didn't need to witness such scenes to know there is something wrong with dissection. When he was told to slice up frogs, worms, rats, and fish in his biology class, Adam refused. His teacher told him he would have to drop out, but Adam chose to go to the school board instead. Not only did the board permit him to use other learning methods, but it also decided to adopt a policy that requires teachers to inform students of their right to seek alternatives.

Animal experimenters fight vigorously against replacing dissection with more sophisticated teaching methods because they see it as a slippery slope. No doubt they think that if young children can be made to overcome their healthy aversion to cutting into animals, then they may be less likely to object to animal experimentation later.

Luckily, many students are sharp enough to want to use one of the hundreds of teaching methods that are more interesting, more relevant, more technical, and more humane than slicing into a formaldehyde-filled cat's corpse or bull's eye. Proof of student interest in alternatives to dissection, even in the face of resistance, comes in the form of students like Oregonian Julie Grizzel-Meyers, who sued her school when her science teacher told her to pick up her scalpel, "or else"; Erin Sharp, a straight-A student in Flower Mound, Texas, whose honors biology course required dissection until Erin convinced her school to switch its requirements; and Ryan Ugstad, Ceilidh Yurenka, and Ian Hatton, three New Hampshire youngsters who got 73 percent of students to sign a petition that resulted in replacing dissection school-wide. In these instances, the children became the educators and their teachers the students, and everyone learned a great deal, including how to save animals' lives.

NATURE'S BOUNTY ON THE SLAB

There is far more spirit and respect in this poem by an anonymous French Canadian poet than in any dissection lesson:

> *What a wonderful bird the frog are!*
> *When he walk, he fly almost;*
> *When he sing, he cry almost.*
> *He ain't got no tail hardly, either.*
> *He sit on what he ain't got almost*

When you think about it, it makes no sense that so many frogs are destroyed simply so that someone can observe where these little animals' hearts lie in their bodies. Looking at a diagram, a three-dimensional model, or a computer software program would serve the purpose just as well—although what the purpose is, I'm not sure. After all, most students are not going to grow up to be frog doctors! Is there more need to study a frog's skeletal structure than that of a wombat? It's all so arbitrary and archaic. For the most part, the frogs are used simply as "generic animals" to demonstrate where the various organs are.

Cats, rats, sharks, squid, rabbits, starfish, and a host of other animals come ready-to-buy and ship through the mail in sealed packs, but frogs are still the top-selling favorite. They are small, easy to catch and kill, and cheap, but the study of biology should not be based on those factors at all. More properly, it should respectfully study life rather than debase and destroy it. How precious to teach students to watch animals in their natural world, from a distance, without interference, and to be in awe of their ways: to see how carefully and cleverly they fashion a home without power tools, feed themselves without going to a supermarket, and raise their offspring without books or classrooms.

HARDENING YOUNG HEARTS

Does dissection in schools desensitize young minds? To take an extreme case, Jeffrey Dahmer, the serial killer, told television reporters that he had enjoyed dissection and that it was through dissection that he had first experienced the "thrill" of taking life. Obviously, not everyone who dissects is going to go on to lobotomize and cannibalize human beings, but there is certainly enough violence in the world already without encouraging students to contribute to it.

George Angell, founder of the Massachusetts Society for the Prevention of Cruelty to Animals, realized this as far back as in 1884. When he was asked why he was so concerned about preventing cruelty to animals, Mr. Angell replied, "I am working at the roots. Nearly all the criminals of the future, the thieves, burglars, incendiaries, and murderers, are now in our public schools and we are educating them. We can mold them now if we will. We may teach a child to shoot a little songbird in springtime, with its nest full of young, or we may teach him to feed the bird and spare its nest. We may go into the schools now and make neglected boys merciful, or we may let them drift, until, as men, they become lawless and cruel."

Luckily, resources abound, and a new world of learning that does not involve bloodshed or gore is available to any teacher or child who wants access to it.

"The things that are on the market now are just phenomenal," raved one Massachusetts science teacher. "There's so much to choose from, it is mind-boggling." The future belongs to the young, and happily, there are great young pioneers out there, actively changing the world into a kinder place for all forms of life.

THE RIGHT TO BE KIND IN THE CLASSROOM

If you're in any grade from kindergarten through twelfth grade and attend public school, then you are entitled to an alternative to dissection, no ifs, ands, or buts, and in some states there are requirements that the school notify you of that right. Private schools, colleges, and universities are not covered by those laws, but you can still get an alternative. You've just got to ask for it the right way (see following).

For Canadian students, your right to refuse to dissect is protected under the Canadian Charter of Rights and Freedoms. Visit FrogsAreCool.com for more information, including details of the policies currently in place in various provinces.

What If Your Class Requires Dissection?

Here is a step-by-step guide below about how to get yourself a better, gentler education. You can probably get the whole class to stop using animals entirely!

1. Find out as early as possible—preferably a few months before the course—what they say you have to do. Then try to find out what animals the school uses and who supplies them.

2. Meet with the instructor right away and tell him or her that you cannot participate in the dissection because of your "sincerely held moral beliefs about the sanctity of all life" and ask for a nonanimal alternative. These words provide the basis for a possible legal case. (You do not have to belong to any formal religion; the courts have interpreted a belief that animals should not be killed for classroom dissection to be a religious belief, which schools cannot violate.) Do not offer a detailed explanation, and don't get into an argument or try to defend your beliefs—you don't have to. State your position in writing, be calm and polite, and ask for a prompt response. Make it clear that observing other students dissect an animal isn't an acceptable alternative—it's another form of participation in the dissection. Keep copies of all correspondence and detailed notes of conversations; take notes during any meetings.

3. You are in the right! Dissection has got to go. It was first introduced into schools in the early part of the last century, and there are now learning tools that are much more advanced. Offer to research the alternatives and find those that satisfy the objectives of the course. Show that you're willing to spend an equivalent amount of time and effort learning the lesson using a humane way. A number of organizations loan alternatives, including CD-ROMs and virtual dissections, to students and schools. The following organizations have extensive lending libraries and will be glad to help you find a suitable alternative and provide you with additional information and suggestions:

AMERICAN ANTI-VIVISECTION SOCIETY (AAVS)
800-729-2287

THE HUMANE SOCIETY OF THE US (HSUS)
301-258-3046

NATIONAL ANTI-VIVISECTION SOCIETY (NAVS)
800-888-6287

ETHICAL SCIENCE EDUCATION COALITION (ESEC)
(The educational branch of the New England
Anti-Vivisection Society)
617-523-6020

"ALTERNATIVES IN EDUCATION DATABASE"
(Allows keyword searches to identify a wide variety
of alternatives)

*ANIMALS IN HIGHER EDUCATION: PROBLEMS,
ALTERNATIVES AND RECOMMENDATIONS* by
Jonathan Balcombe, PhD (An in-depth overview of
the entire issue)

4. If you're still told "dissect or fail," don't worry, just
keep going, right up the chain of command. If you're
in precollege (kindergarten through twelfth grade)
write to the principal, then the superintendent, and
then the school board. Ask your parents or guardians
to write on your behalf. If you're in college, write to
the department head, then to the dean, and finally to
the president. Persistence pays off!

5. If school officials still think they can violate your rights, try contacting an attorney for assistance. PETA can help you. These cases don't always need to go to court; they can often be settled with just a simple phone call from an attorney. To find an attorney in your area, try doing an online search using one of the services listed below. You can also try calling the service's toll-free number, but conducting an online search may be more effective:

AMERICAN BAR ASSOCIATION LAWYER REFERRAL
SERVICE
    541 N. Fairbanks Ct.
    Chicago, IL 60611
    800-285-2221

LAWYERS.COM*
    800-526-4902, ext. 5095
    salesdev@martindale.com
    *Even though "animal law" is not one of the choices
    listed, you can type "animal" in the "Legal Term"
    field to find attorneys who specialize in animal law.

6. Get your friends on your side! Form a group to demand students' right to a violence-free education. Write letters to the editor of the school and local newspapers. Contact the campus radio station. Meet with the editorial board of the campus newspaper and ask them to editorialize in favor of students' right to choose humane alternatives to dissection. Ask the student government to pass a resolution supporting your efforts. Circulate petitions among students, and gather signatures of support. Hold vigils and demon-

strations and alert the media about your events (contact PETA for help).

7. You can always call PETA for help with any dissection dilemma. We can send you literature and videos, encourage you, and use some PETA know-how to get your school to see things straight! Call 757-622-7382 to speak to a PETA representative if you need assistance.

WHAT YOU CAN DO

Stop Dissection in Your School Science Labs

Don't dissect. If you are a student, refuse to dissect. Put your feelings in writing to your teacher and principal, and try to involve your parents if you can. Parents, support your child's right to nonviolent education. The Dissection Hotline, 800-922-FROG (3764), exists *specifically* to help you protest dissection in the classroom. Don't be afraid to ask for help.

Participate in National "Cut Out Dissection" Month. Begin by downloading and printing out a "Cut Out Dissection" pack from peta2.com with information on dissection and tips on how to start a campaign in your area. Also, e-mail peta2@peta2.com if you have any questions about fighting dissection or about your rights or if you need additional materials, like leaflets or stickers.

Ask questions. The next time you receive a call or letter requesting a donation to your alma mater, ask if the school funds animal experiments. Let them know that you will not contribute until you have a guarantee in writing that animals are not being used.

Find out. If you live near a medical or veterinary school, find out whether or not animals are used in classroom training. If they are, approach the administration and faculty about modernizing their curriculum to exclude animal labs. Educate students about the alternatives to using animals in their training. Visit peta2.com for a list of alternatives.

Persuade local universities. If your local universities use animals to teach physiology, ask if they will work with you to switch to a nonanimal teaching technique. Nassau Community College (NCC) routinely abused turtles in the school's "turtle heart lab." In the experiments, turtles' brains were pithed, their shells were cut, and their hearts were exposed and subjected to varying intensities of electrical stimuli, even though these experiments and the results were documented long ago. With the help of Legal Action for Animals and the New York Turtle and Tortoise Society, PETA determined that New York State public health laws require experimental facilities to prove that their experiments benefit human or animal health before they can be approved. NCC did not have the required certification to experiment on any animals. The New York Department of Health (DOH) moved quickly to prohibit all animal experiments at NCC, and the turtle heart lab was stopped. DOH is considering legal action to prohibit any experiment involving animals when a nonanimal method is available.

Organize meetings. Use your state's "open meetings" or "sunshine" law to open up committee meetings at your local state-funded universities about animal care and how animals are used. These meetings are required by the federal Animal Welfare Act and are supposed to provide a forum for discussing research protocols. Sunshine laws require that all public records and meetings be open to scrutiny from the media and the public. By publicizing meetings on the use of animals, activists have been able to influence the outcome of various research proposals.

Inform medical students. Make sure your local medical students know their rights to refuse. PETA and the Animal Legal Defense Fund will help any student who objects to animal labs. Visit PETALiterature.com and download the "Animals and Experimentation Mini Guide."

Be an ethical medical student. Refuse to use animals. The American Medical Student Association will back you up. Most medical schools in the United States have now decided that animal laboratories are ineffectual and misleading and have eliminated them.

Go on YouTube. Make a free-speech message about your right to refuse to dissect with accompanying photos and place them on YouTube for millions to see.

 FREQUENTLY ASKED QUESTIONS

Am I just being squeamish about dissection?

Feeling that dissection is wrong has nothing to do with being afraid or squeamish; for many students, it is a violation of deeply held principles. It is not only okay but also perfectly normal to feel squeamish about doing something you find morally offensive.

Are students qualified to determine whether or not dissection is a necessary part of the curriculum?

Students are entitled to speak up when asked to do something that violates their ethics. If they are "qualified" enough to participate, they are "qualified" enough to decide whether they object to participation.

*Dissection wouldn't be taught if it weren't
an important part of the curriculum.*

Teaching techniques are constantly evolving and should be reevaluated regularly. Dissection is very old-fashioned. It's a third-world learning tool, and we're in the twenty-first century. Countless students are educated every year at top schools without dissecting animals.

There is no substitute for hands-on experience.

Actually, there are many substitutes for hands-on experience. Detailed models of animal anatomy and computer simulations both provide hands-on experience.

Are there really suitable alternatives?

The Alternatives in Education Database from the Association of Veterinarians for Animal Rights, and the Norwegian Inventory of Audiovisuals (NORINA) contain thousands of alternatives to animal use in education. (Most instructors who use this argument haven't considered any particular alternatives, so ask which specific alternatives the professor has considered and rejected and why.)

*A claim to be a conscientious objector is inconsistent
if the student still eats meat, wears leather,
eats dairy products, etc., isn't it?*

Religious freedom means that you can subscribe to any set of views. Meat-eating Hindus are Hindus nonetheless and cannot be forced to do something else that they believe is forbidden by their religion. If a student believes that it is immoral to wear fur or dissect animals but okay to wear leather shoes, no one can dictate a different set of moral values to that student. Everyone has the right to draw the line where their conscience tells them to.

The school doesn't have enough money in its budget to purchase alternatives.

Many groups make alternatives available on loan to students and schools who need them. And alternatives to dissection are more economical over time; many students can make use of one CD-ROM, for instance, but dissection requires that multiple animals be purchased time after time.

9

Dealing Ethically with "Pests"

In 1910, a crowd gathered at an intersection in Boulder, Colorado. They had spotted a dog running about, white froth coming from his mouth.

"He's mad," someone yelled out, and the police were called.

The dog stood with wide-open eyes, either too mad or too frightened to move. The crowd called for the police officer to shoot. Then a tall woman pushed through and went to pick up the dog. A dozen men yelled at her to stand back, and two or three grabbed her. The police officer was firm.

"Madam," he said, "the dog is mad. He must be shot. Look at the foam coming out of his mouth."

"Foam?" the woman said contemptuously. "That's not foam. That's the cream puff he's just been eating!"

That story, from *The First Pet History of the World*, illustrates nicely how people can overreact to animals. "Pest control" companies like nothing more than a rabies scare that they can use to drum up business. The embarrassing old stereotype of the woman screaming and jumping on a table to avoid a two-ounce mouse in her kitchen did not disappear with women's liberation. It has been joined by general hysteria over the minor inconveniences that are caused by wildlife. It is hard to miss stories of these so-called problems, such as the "animal messes" from goose droppings on golf courses (wouldn't *you* stop migrating and decide to raise your family at the sixteenth-hole pond if people were always shooting at you when you tried to go back north?) and the guano delivered by crows, grackles, and starlings doing nothing more threatening than resting in the corporate fruit and nut orchards planted on their plowed-over ancestral homes.

A "live and let live" ethic might require an occasional broom or scrub brush or the bother of sealing up entrance holes into buildings. But too many people choose the Wyatt Earp approach: "exterminators," sticky glue traps, bait boxes, poisons, and anticoagulants (causing the animals to bleed to death) such as zinc phosphide, aluminum phosphide, and gut-wrenching red squill.

Flying from one coast to the other, it is impossible not to be stunned at how little forest and woodland remains. In fact, in the Pacific Northwest, 1,200 acres of ancient forest, critical to owls, eagles, and as many as forty species of animals who share just one tree, are felled every week for timber. Starlings, foxes, tree frogs, squirrels, and raccoons don't need much: a little nourishing food, some clean water, shelter from the elements, and air to breathe. Humans, on the other hand, are needy and greedy. We want everything, from highways and of-fice blocks to pop-top bottles, plastic trash bags, snack foods, air-conditioning, lounge chairs, and beauty salons. And so it is that the construction of our malls, housing developments, golf courses, and other "necessities" has become the single greatest threat facing wildlife.

In Chevy Chase, Maryland, a pregnant raccoon was trying hard to find just the right spot to make a nest for her babies. She was about to deliver, but the tree in which she had been raised had been felled, together with all the others in that patch of woods. In their place, there were now big houses. She was very tired when she spotted the opening under the eaves of a corner house one night, and she crawled inside and found a huge wooden cavern—she thought it was heaven. Every-thing would be all right, she could give birth here.

Her two babies were beautiful when they were born, and their mother was proud. The den she had found was perfect for them to learn to run and play in, and high enough up and sheltered so well that they were safe from dogs, storms, and, of course, people.

The people below heard the tiny raccoon feet scampering about in the attic and took out the Yellow Pages. A "pest control" man arrived with a box trap and assured the couple he would re-lease any "coons" he caught into the woods. They trusted him because he had a state license and a nicely painted truck that said, YOUR WILDLIFE PROBLEMS SOLVED.

The next morning when the mother raccoon came back from foraging, her babies were gone. Wild-eyed with worry, she ran through the attic, making her click call to them, but there was nothing. Nothing except a metal box that smelled of fish. She entered cautiously, and her second nightmare began. Almost as soon as the cage door slammed behind her, she heard heavy steps, then a piece of wood in the den floor swung back and a man with a flashlight appeared just feet away from her. Still frantic about her babies, and now in fear for her own life, the mother raccoon thrashed at her cage, tearing her paws on the wire as she tried to dig out of the metal box.

There is no happy ending for the mother raccoon and her babies. No matter what they tell people, for the truth would lose them a lot of business, wildlife trappers commonly bludgeon and drown animals or turn the animals over to be killed by animal control agencies. It is a rare "nuisance trapper" who has built a relationship with a wildlife rehabilitator. In many states, a fear of rabies has led to extreme laws that prevent certain species from being released back into the community.

Kevin Happell will never forget seeing a Critter Control employee beat baby raccoons to death in his apartment building. The man used a metal rod and "visibly broke multiple bones in their bodies. The raccoons, being babies, offered no resistance whatsoever."

As we force animals into ever decreasing spaces and plant ornamental shrubs where once there were sheltering trees and berry bushes, what can they do? Smelling food in our vegetable gardens or even our trash cans, and seeing holes in our attic and gables in which to shelter their young, who can blame these displaced families for trying to reclaim a little of the land, tree, and food sources stolen from them? They have no options.

THE TINIEST OF MAMMALS

Rats get bad press, and they really don't deserve it. They are still associated with the plague and biting babies in cribs, although the plague was caused by rats simply *spreading* filth created by a slightly larger animal, *Homo sapiens.* In New York City alone, in any given year, the number of people bitten by rats is only a tiny fraction of the number of people bitten by other human beings.

D. O'Hara recalls looking out of her window on a scorching hot day. She had put water out for a stray cat, but as she watched, she saw a mother rat lay her head on the cool rim of the water bowl and fall fast asleep. O'Hara says the rat had such a look of peace on her little face, she seemed to say, "I've found heaven."

The mother rat had had her babies in a nest of eucalyptus leaves near the O'Haras' porch, and Ms. O'Hara could watch from her window as the mother groomed them and taught them to shell the unsalted peanuts Ms. O'Hara left out for them. The mother rat took impressive care of her brood: dipping their little paws in the cool water and smoothing the fur around their ears and faces. Each baby put his or her arms around the mother's neck and paid attention while being bathed. The mother also taught them to dart and run if danger approached.

Everyone told Ms. O'Hara the rats would become a problem, so she swept out the nest, only to see the mother rat work tirelessly to build another and gather more food to store for them. In her heart, Mrs. O'Hara knew that she was making these small animals' lives very difficult.

Although simple and effective solutions to rodent invasions abound, other common "solutions" are grotesquely cruel. Typical back- and neck-snapping traps do not cause instant death. Death comes from slow suffocation, internal bleeding, or eventual starvation and dehydration. Another wretched death is caused by the sticky glue trap in which the animal's tiny face and limbs get stuck. Animals struggling in these traps pull out their hair and bite off their toes in desperation as they try to escape. The traps can be left unattended for days, so that the exhausted, panicked mouse or other small creature dies of dehydration, or the whole trap, mouse and all, may be tossed into the garbage where, again, the animal dies slowly and miserably.

At PETA, wildlife experts send out information on such humane devices as Havahart box traps, "beaver bafflers" (wire mesh tunnels that allow beavers to remain in their family lodge without flooding houses built on low-lying land), and tips on how easy it is to rodent-proof a home. They hear from landowners who want to get rid of prairie dogs without calling in the pest control companies who vacuum the dogs out of their holes and gas them or sell them to pet shops, and they hear from gardeners who have found nests of snakes or wasps.

Simple, effective, and humane solutions exist for almost any "nuisance" problem. Author Gregg Levoy was raised in a household "equipped with pest spray or rolled-up magazines for every genus and species," where his father would "sometimes crouch in an upstairs window, Luger in hand, and try to pick off tomcats." In *A Better Mousetrap*, Levoy wrote that, after experiencing pain firsthand, he decided to live his life without administering it.

> I don't strip the leaves off twigs anymore as I walk along the sidewalk, and I work around the ant colony when I'm clearing the backyard. Sometimes I feel so isolated from the proverbial web of things, living in the city, that a part of me is even glad to have something resembling an ecosystem about. The spiderwebs in the window do wondrous things with the light that slips in at sunset.
>
> Also, I cannot shake the feeling that somewhere there is a tally being kept of these things—my cruelties, my compassions—and that it will make a difference somewhere down the line when I go to cash in my chips. Besides, there is a slight question, in my mind, of relativity. Who is the pest here, me or the mouse?

As I stand in the checkout line at the hardware store, an elderly man taps me on the shoulder. "Good for you," he says, surveying my $17.50 Havahart boxtrap. "You'll probably come back as a mouse."

LIVING IN HARMONY WITH PIGEONS

The pigeons who inhabit nearly all of North America today were brought to the New World by settlers who kept them as domesticated companions, racers, or couriers. Wild descendants of these bird pioneers adapted quickly to the varied climates across the continent, and they continue to thrive, even as humans modify the landscape.

Pigeons have a long and distinguished record of service as messengers during war, including the Vietnam, the Korean, and the two world wars. Some birds were even awarded medals for their heroism. Pigeons have been used by the CIA for aerial photography, and their service is honored in the CIA Museum. But modern technology has now replaced the need to use pigeons.

ABOUT PIGEONS

Pigeons have been around for several million years. They have a typical life span of about fifteen years, although some can live for thirty years—the oldest known pigeon lived to be thirty-three. Their ideal diet includes grain, seeds, insects, and plants, but they will, and often must, eat almost anything that humans give them. The rising popularity of recreational wildlife feeding and wide varieties of artificial food sources in urban areas cause pigeon populations to skyrocket. The birds live in flocks with an even number of males and females—mated pairs and their offspring. Flock sizes are self-regulating according to food availability. In areas where food sources are abundant, pairs will reproduce more frequently through the spring and fall breeding seasons and sometimes throughout the year. If food is scarce, they will only reproduce as much as their environment can support, from only a few babies per breeding season to none at all.

Mom and Pop Pigeons

Pigeons are family oriented and devoted to their offspring. They are faithful, and mate for life. Both parents care for their young, called "squabs," alternating incubating the eggs and feeding the babies when they hatch. Pigeons flock in large numbers in order to protect themselves against cats, hawks, owls, and rats and are very protective of younger birds. During breeding season, when there are many squabs in the flock, adult birds will feed any hungry baby, not just their own.

Did You Know?

- Pigeons sense Earth's magnetic field through the use of a magnetic "map" in their beaks.
- Reuters News Service was originally created as a line of pigeon posts to bridge gaps in the telegraph system.
- Pigeons can fly as fast as sixty miles per hour.
- A joint coast guard and navy venture called Project Sea Hunt trained pigeons to peck a key when they spotted the bright orange color used for life vests. The birds became adept at spotting the vests floating in the open ocean, saving lives by pinpointing shipwreck victims for rescue teams.

Solving Conflicts Compassionately

When wildlife and humans live close together, problems can arise—but they are easily solved with patience and creative thinking. Humane approaches to pigeon control are cheaper and more effective than lethal methods, which are often bad for the environment and other animals as well. Trapping is not effective because when they are released in another area they often return to their homes, and killing birds only creates a vacancy in the flock that will inevitably be filled by newcomers.

Less Food, Fewer Pigeons

A flock of pigeons will continue to grow as long as a food supply supports the birds. The most effective way of reducing pigeon populations is to eliminate their food sources, which means discouraging people from feeding them and covering trash cans. If food is scarce, pigeons will stop reproducing and may even move away. When it comes to pigeons' eating habits, an ounce of prevention can be a pound of cure.

Humane Pigeon Deterrents

There are a variety of devices that can be used to deny pigeons access to nesting areas or frighten them away. Screens and netting can be used on attics, vents, signs, and even the rafters of barns and warehouses so that birds can't fly up into nooks and crannies. Wire coils or spikes on railings, pipes, or building edges will keep birds from perching there, and boards or sheet metal angled against flat surfaces can be used to make a slope where pigeons can't perch. Effigies of predatory animals can be effective if they are realistic-looking and are moved frequently; pigeons catch on and ignore stationary models. Mylar streamers that blow in the wind and reflect light may startle pigeons but won't always drive them away, and sound repellent devices of predators' calls or other loud noises are generally more disruptive to people than they are to pigeons. Most humane pigeon-deterrent products can be purchased from companies such as Bird Barrier, which can even refer you to professional wildlife control operators in your area who have received expert training on how to install these bird control systems.

Poisons, like the notorious Avitrol and DRC-1339, and sticky polybutene substances, which are sold under product names like Tanglefoot or Hot Foot, should never be used. Poisons and sticky gels are inherently cruel, and when birds die from poisoning and so make more food available to others, the remaining birds will have more babies. Poison is also deadly to nontarget animals, like songbirds and predators who eat birds, including companion animals. Sticky material, meant to make birds feel uncomfortable when landing on surfaces, can trap smaller animals who touch it, causing them to break bones as they struggle, starve to death, or be picked apart by predators.

As natural habitats are turned into skyscrapers and parking lots, animals must try to adapt to their new surroundings. Humans too need to work to find ways to live harmoniously with all species. For more information on living with wildlife, visit HelpingWildlife.com.

LIVING IN HARMONY WITH CANADA GEESE

Few things are more beautiful than a goose family lined up for a morning swim. Few things are more inspiring than a flock of

Canada geese heralding the turn of seasons as they fly their ancient patterns of migration.

Thanks to hunting, geese were almost extinct by the 1950s, so to restore populations, geese were relocated to areas where they had never been found before. As a result, geese have adapted to urban and suburban areas, remaining there year-round. Goose populations have exploded, and today, many states are trying to resolve conflicts between geese and impatient humans.

As their homelands are lost to development, "wild" animals such as Canada geese are forced to live in closer proximity to humans. We owe it to these animals to do all that we can to coexist with them peacefully.

About Geese

Geese possess many of the qualities that humans strive to attain. Devoted to each other, goose couples mate for life, raise and protect their young together, and take care of one another. Geese also use teamwork when flying in formation. They will honk to encourage one another, and if a goose gets sick, wounded, or shot down, two flock mates will stay with the goose until he or she dies or is able to fly again.

Did You Know

- Geese and their babies begin talking to each other while the goslings are still inside the egg.
- Geese pass down their migratory routes from generation to generation.
- Goslings cuddle for warmth and protection.
- Highly emotional, geese mourn the loss of their mates and eggs.

• Geese use thirteen or more different calls to convey warnings, extend greetings, and express emotions such as happiness.

Keep the Peace with Canada Geese

The best solution is for human beings to accept that geese are part of nature and to enjoy their presence and cope with any inconveniences. If "live and let live" is not in the cards, effective, humane methods of waterfowl control can be used that do not target the animals themselves but, rather, the things that attract them to certain areas. Methods such as population stabilization, site aversion, public education, and other deterrents can be used to control waterfowl populations humanely.

For example, thousands of people, with only the kindest of intentions, endanger the health of waterfowl by feeding them. This seemingly benign activity can lead to crowding and competition and encourage migratory waterfowl to stay put. For more detailed information on humane waterfowl control, please visit HelpingAnimals.com.

 WHAT YOU CAN DO

Wildlife

When trees are cut down and fields stripped of natural vegetation, squirrels, skunks, raccoons, and opossums who would never have ventured beyond the edge of the forest are suddenly homeless and hungry. Here is what to do if you must keep them out of your home:

Provide wildlife sanctuary. Leave a good part of your yard natural, with bushes and ground cover. The more diverse your bushes, seeds, and berries, the greater the variety of birds and small mammals you will attract and nurture. Cherish rare, huge, great-granddaddy den trees as well as brushy hedgerows, which are vital homes for wildlife along the edges of woodlands and mowed areas. Three books that can help you attract and nurture wildlife are *The New Gardening for Wildlife: A Guide for Nature Lovers*, by Bill Merilees, *Landscaping for Wildlife*, by Carrol L. Henderson, and *Bringing Nature Home: How Native Plants Sustain Wildlife in Our Gardens*, by Douglas Tallamy.

Keep dead wood. Dead wood is ecological gold and crucial to kicking our pesticide habit. More than 150 species of birds and animals live in dead trees and/or feed on the insects there. Top off, rather than chop down, dead trees twelve inches or more in diameter. Fat dead logs, woody debris, and underbrush are also precious to wildlife. Before cutting any wood, check for nests and dens.

Provide birdbaths. Keep water in a birdbath and in a ground pan all year long. Use heating elements to keep them unfrozen in cold weather. Be sure neither is too close to a bush or other cover where a cat might hide.

Install a martin house. Mosquitoes will disappear from your woodsy yard as elegant swifts, swallows, and purple martins sweep through the air.

Make a ramp. Lean branches or wooden planks in uncovered window wells so creatures who may fall into them can climb out.

Leave them alone. If an animal has a nest of young in an unused part of your house and is doing no significant harm, leave the family alone for a few weeks until the youngsters are grown. They will probably then move out on their own.

Squeals above your fireplace usually mean baby raccoons in your chimney. DON'T light a fire! They will move out in a few weeks. If you can't wait, put a radio tuned to loud talk or rock music in the fireplace and hang a mechanic's trouble light down the chimney. (Animals like their homes dark and quiet.) Leave these in place a few days, to give Mom time to find a new home and move her children. You might also hang a thick, knotted rope down the chimney, secured at the top, in case your tenant is not a raccoon and can't climb out unaided.

Seal up your house. Seal all entry places and cap your chimney (or a relative's)—after making sure no animals are inside. A mother animal will (justifiably) tear your roof apart if you seal her young inside.

Avoid "pest control" companies. Don't capture and kill or relocate an animal by calling in "pest control agents" whose promises of humane destruction or relocation can be a fraud. You may be separating the animals from loved ones and the only food and water sources they know.

Build a bat house. A bat consumes three thousand or more mosquitoes and other insects nightly. Bats won't get in your hair, and the chances of them being rabid are minuscule—less than that of your dog. Bats are responsible for up to 95 percent of the seed dispersal essential to the regeneration of forests. For more information about bats, visit the Bat Conservation International at Batcon .org.

Turn off the lights. If bats should enter your home, turn off all lights and open the doors and windows. If they still don't leave, they can be caught in a large jar or net and released outside. Wear thick gloves, since a frightened bat may bite. Then seal the point of entry, which may be as narrow as three-eighths of an inch.

Get certified. Find out what you need to do to certify your yard in the National Wildlife Federation (NWF) Backyard Wildlife Habitat Programatnwf.org/backyard.

Buy metal. Use metal garbage cans with tightly fitting lids, and latch Dumpsters.

Feed pets inside. Never leave dog and cat food outside.

Be smart. If you must set a mousetrap, use the plastic "Smart Mouse Trap," available at PETACatalog.org. When using these, be sure to check them every few hours, as frightened rodents, with their high rate of metabolism, quickly become stressed, thirsty, and hungry.

Complain. Complain to stores that sell glue traps, explaining how cruel these traps are. Recommend that they sell humane box traps instead.

Set them free. If you encounter an animal stuck to a glue trap, pour a small amount of any kind of cooking or baby oil, or even nail polish remover, onto the stuck areas and gently work them free.

Don't feed them! Don't feed geese (or other wildlife), as tempting and kind as it seems. Feeding wildlife weakens their natural (and necessary!) fear of humans and can cause them to become targeted "pests."

Help out birds. Place hawk silhouettes, wind chimes, or streamers in the window, and close drapes or blinds whenever possible to prevent birds from flying into windows. (They can suffer fatal concussions, internal bleeding, and mandible or eye damage.)

Open a window. If a bird enters your house, wait until dark, then open a window and put a light outside it. Turn out all house lights, and the bird should fly out to the light.

Throw birdseed, blow bubbles. At weddings, throw bird seed or blow bubbles instead of throwing rice, which can swell in birds' stomachs, proving fatal.

Avoid plastic. Refuse all unnecessary plastic products. Buy juice in cardboard cartons, use wax paper instead of plastic wrap, and so on. (Your garbage can be a trap—a potentially lethal picnic for animals in your neighborhood.)

Provide an escape. Put a vertical branch in every Dumpster so animals can escape.

Recycle. Recycle paper, aluminum, plastic, and glass. To help preserve habitat by living more simply yourself, visit the Environmental Defense Fund at EDF.org to learn how to lessen your carbon footprint, how to recycle your car, and much, much more.

Dispose of jars. Crush the open end of cans as flat as possible and rinse out jars and other containers in which a curious or hungry animal could get caught. Screw lids back onto empty jars before recycling them, and put sharp tops and tabs inside empty tin cans so they cannot slice tongues and throats.

Tear up containers. Make sure plastic and cardboard containers have at least two entry/exit ways so that small mammals, such as squirrels and mice, cannot get trapped in them. Many have died, unable to back out of inverted-pyramid yogurt cups.

Cut plastic rings apart. Snip or pull apart plastic six-pack rings, including the inner diamond. The rings are commonly found around the necks of wildlife, ranging from turtles to waterfowl.

Patrol beaches and parks. Join, create, or consider yourself the sole member of a beach brigade or park patrol. Pick up string, fishing line, and all plastic litter (bags, bottles, six-pack rings, lids, and disposable diapers) near streams and woods. Birds, turtles, dolphins, and even whales and otters can get tangled in or swallow such trash, and the result is injury and, often, death. Official beach cleanups are usually held in the fall. For information on where and when one may be held near you, visit the Coastal States Organization Web site (CoastalStates.org).

Be careful! Never dispose of razors and other dangerous items by dropping them loose in with your other garbage. One PETA member recommends placing used razor blades inside empty, rinsed-out, *sealed* cartons.

Clean up antifreeze. Take care to clean up antifreeze spills carefully (and rinse out the rags you use to do so!); it is toxic, and animals are attracted to its sweet taste. Do not wash antifreeze down storm water grates. For more information about disposing of hazardous chemicals, visit the Environmental Protection Agency (EPA) Web site: EPA.gov.

Use your own bags. Carry your own string or canvas bags to the grocery store (go to PETACatalog.org to purchase one today), or at least choose paper bags over plastic. In the kitchen, use only biodegradable or photodegradable food storage bags, such as those available from Green Earth Office Supply (greenearthofficesupply.com.).

Make a directory. In case of an emergency, keep the names, telephone numbers, and e-mail addresses of wildlife rehabilitators handy. (They are available from your local humane society or park authority.)

Be aware. If you find a young animal who appears orphaned, wait quietly at a good distance, to be certain the parents are nowhere nearby. If they are not, take the little one to a professional wildlife rehabilitation center for care.

Volunteer. Volunteer to help local wildlife rehabilitators nurse injured wildlife back to good health and prepare them for release. Wildlife rehabilitation operations and shelters need soft bedding materials, newspapers, and other supplies.

Don't use poisons. Never use poison or sticky repellent caulk to control pigeons, starlings, or other birds. A stretched-out

Slinky, nailed to a board and placed on a window ledge or roof, will keep birds from roosting. If your city or town poisons birds, urge them to substitute humane forms of control. (Visit HelpingAnimals.com to learn how you can prevent this.)

Talk to children. Always politely explain to children, should you see them chasing pigeons or seagulls, that this frightens the birds. Most children understand when told. Approach their parents in a friendly way, as well.

Deter Insect Invasions Humanely

Use spices. Ants invading your home? Pour a line of cream of tartar, red chili powder, paprika, or dried peppermint at the place where ants enter the house—they won't cross it. You can also try washing countertops, cabinets, and floors with equal parts of vinegar and water or a citrus-based cleaner.

Try bay leaves. If cockroaches have moved in, never fear! Simply place whole bay leaves in several locations around the room, including inside kitchen cabinets. Bay leaves must smell like dirty socks to cockroaches!

Get Gentrol. PETA pick: Gentrol, an insect-growth regulator, eliminates the reproductive potential of a cockroach population without killing them. For more information, visit: doyourownpestcontrol.com/gentrolaerosol.htm.

Keep clothes fresh. A humane and great-smelling alternative to mothballs: place cedar chips around clothes or store sachets made out of dried lavender or equal parts dried rosemary and mint in drawers and closets.

Use a jar. Are there spiders sharing your home? If you must move them, carefully trap them in an inverted jar and release them outside. You can also purchase the Katcha Bug Humane Bug Catcher at PETACatalog.org.

Fly away! Hang clusters of cloves in a room, or leave an orange skin out. Both smells repel flies.

Plant chives. Avid gardeners are all too familiar with aphids, those little insects who like roses as much as we do. Planting chives near your rosebushes can help keep them away.

Keep them. If you find predators such as ladybugs, snakes, and praying mantises in your yard or garden, the best policy is to let them stay. They too are part of your ecosystem.

Close holes. Prevent insects from entering your home in the first place by filling holes and cracks in walls with white glue. (It's less toxic than caulk.)

Be tidy. Don't give insects a food supply; keep living areas clean. Be careful to sweep up crumbs, wash dishes immediately, store food in tightly sealed containers, and empty garbage frequently. Often this will be enough to make bugs move on in search of more fertile ground.

Try citronella. Deter flying insects gently with citronella candles or other incense. Forget bug zappers. They kill insects who are essential for pollination of night-flowering plants and for people's aesthetic senses—fireflies and moths are priceless flying jewels.

10

Choosing a Health Charity

Because I give a darn, I don't give a dime,
I give a lick, I buy a seal. I believe in charity
to even the smallest of beings.

—DR. WILLIAM ROBERTS, ON WHY HE SUPPORTS
EASTER SEALS OVER THE MARCH OF DIMES

Like everything else, giving to charity requires thought. In 1997, a group of physicians discovered that the March of Dimes had given donation money to experimenters to sew newborn kittens' eyes shut, wait a year to see how depriving cats of normal vision alters brain development, and then kill them. The doctors felt the experiment was not only cruel, but also a waste of time and money. They decided to take a closer look at the March of Dimes research. They found that the charity was also spending donors' contributions on experiments in which cocaine, nicotine, and alcohol were given to animals, although it is already known that these substances are harmful to developing babies and can cause learning defects and other disabilities.

The Physicians Committee for Responsible Medicine (PCRM) went directly to the March of Dimes with their concerns and findings, pointing out that the charity ought to be using its research funds to track down the causes of birth defects in human populations rather than spending money on rat and mouse tests. But executives there brushed them aside and defended the charity's policies. The doctors grew angry and decided to duke it out with the charity, insisting on an end to cruel tests of dubious value at a time when birth defects are rising. They issued public statements calling on the March of Dimes to reform its practices and commissioned a poll that found that more than half of all Americans prefer to support health charities that avoid funding animal tests.

PETA joined that campaign at its outset. Both groups ask anyone who wishes to support birth defects charities to choose Easter Seals because it has a "no animal tests" policy. However, if someone is determined to give to the March of Dimes, PETA recommends earmarking the donation "not to be used for animal experiments."

What PCRM had uncovered was the tip of an ugly iceberg. Many charities perform animal experiments without their donors' knowledge. A person approached at an intersection by high school students soliciting for the American Heart Association (AHA) probably has no idea that AHA has severed the nerves in dogs' hearts, cut holes in the throats of newborn lambs and obstructed their breathing, and forced chickens to breathe concentrated cigarette smoke—even though scientists have known for years that smoking causes cancer and heart disease.

Even the Red Cross, publicly associated with disaster relief, runs its own animal laboratory—not that you'll find any mention of it in Red Cross public service announcements or news.

It is not only animal-friendly donors who become upset

when they realize what horrors they may be funding when they write a check to a health charity; people who have the very diseases and ailments that these charities profess to be trying to cure are upset too.

Kit Paraventi has had diabetes for more than thirty years. She has experienced debilitating complications, including two years of blindness, dialysis, and a kidney transplant, and she is outspoken in her rejection of animal tests. She regularly writes to the American Diabetes Foundation to ask that it adopt a "no animal tests" policy and feels that, as pressure mounts, the charity will be compelled to switch.

Larry Carter has cerebral palsy and was once a poster child for the campaign to find a cure. He is incensed that animals suffer in his name. "Nobody knows pain and suffering better than those of us who have endured it ourselves," he says, "and we owe it to ourselves and the animals to see that they do not suffer in our supposed behalf. If we are willing to kill innocent animals in our quest to be healthy, then what we lose in the bargain—our sense of compassion and empathy—is much, much greater."

Mr. Carter also wants people to know that the only important breakthroughs in cerebral palsy research have come from human studies, including the finding that pregnant women who receive magnesium supplements have a dramatically reduced risk of having a baby born with mental retardation or cerebral palsy.

Women with breast cancer or whose mothers had breast cancer are uniting to fight charities' animal experiments. Groups of people living with AIDS and families of Alzheimer's disease patients want to stress that animal "models" of human disease only hinder, confuse, and mislead. They want charities to modernize, and they are putting their money where their hearts lie, giving only to charities like the Elton John AIDS Foundation,

Cancer Care, and others on PETA's list of charities that do not test on animals.

Helping hasten that day are youngsters like Harry Grimm, a nine-year-old who refused to collect donations for the American Heart Association through a school program and sent the money he collected to a cruelty-free health charity instead.

 WHAT YOU CAN DO

Ask Questions Before You Donate

Ask questions. Question health charities carefully. When you get a fund-raising appeal or are approached for a donation from a foundation, ask whether your donation could be used to fund animal experiments.

Watch your money. Don't give any money, and tell the charity why you won't, if they fund or conduct animal research. Send copies of any responses to PETA and to the Physicians Committee for Responsible Medicine (PCRM).

PART TWO

Resources

11

Health Charities

HEALTH CHARITIES THAT DO NOT FUND ANIMAL EXPERIMENTS

It is easy to find health charities that have earned a place on PETA's list of "good guys." These charities use human clinical trials, fund patient care, and employ modern alternatives to the old-fashioned animal tests.

A+ HOME CARE, INC.
8932 Old Cedar Ave. South
Bloomington, MN 55425
800-603-7760
AplusHomeCare.org

ACCESS TO INDEPENDENCE, INC.
2345 Atwood Ave.
Madison, WI 53704
608-242-8484
Accesstoind.org

ACHIEVEMENTS, INC.
101 Mineral Ave.
Libby, MT 59923
406-293-8848

ACTION AGAINST HUNGER
247 W. 37th St., Ste. 1201
New York, NY 10018
212-967-7800
212-967-5480
ActionAgainstHunger.org

ADULT ACTIVITY SERVICES
307 E. Atlantic St.
Emporia, VA 23847
434-634-2124
GreensvilleCountyVa.gov

ADULT TRAINING AND HABILITATION CENTER
311 Fairlawn Ave., W.
Winsted, MN 55395
320-485-4191
athc.org

AIDS COALITION OF CAPE BRETON
P.O. Box 177
Sydney, NS B1P 6H1

Canada
902-567-1766
accb.ns.ca

AIM CENTER
1903 McCallie Ave.
Chattanooga, TN 37404
423-624-4800
AIMCenterinc.org

THE ALEXIS FOUNDATION
P.O. Box 916263
Longwood, FL 32779-6263
407-862-8833
AlexisFoundation.org

AMERICAN ACTION FUND FOR BLIND CHILDREN
AND ADULTS
1800 Johnson St., Ste. 100
Baltimore, MD 21230
410-659-9315
ActionFund.org

AMERICAN ASSOCIATION OF THE DEAF-BLIND
8630 Fenton St., Ste. 121
Silver Spring, MD 20910-3803
301-495-4402
aadb.org

AMERICAN ASSOCIATION ON INTELLECTUAL
AND DEVELOPMENTAL DISABILITIES
444 N. Capitol St., N.W., Ste. 846
Washington, DC 20001-1512

800-424-3688

AAIDD.org

AMERICAN BREAST CANCER FOUNDATION

1220B E. Joppa Rd., Ste. 332

Baltimore, MD 21286

410-825-9388

contact@abcf.org

ABCF.org

AMERICAN HOSPICE FOUNDATION

2120 L St., N.W., Ste. 200

Washington, DC 20037

202-223-0204

AmericanHospice.org

AMERICAN KIDNEY FUND

6110 Executive Blvd., Ste. 1010

Rockville, MD 20852

800-638-8299

KidneyFund.org

AMERICAN LEPROSY MISSIONS

One ALM Way

Greenville, SC 29601

800-543-3135

Leprosy.org

AMERICAN PEDIATRIC HEART FUND

115 East 57th St.

11th floor

New York, NY 10022

212-939-7253

212-531-6165
APHFund.org

AMERICAN THYROID SOCIETY
6066 Leesburg Pike, Ste. 650
Falls Church, VA 22041
703-998-8890
Thyroid.org

AMERICAN VITILIGO RESEARCH FOUNDATION
P.O. Box 7540
Clearwater, FL 33758
727-461-3899
AVRF.org

THE ANGEL CONNECTION, INC.
3 Executive Dr.
P.O. Box 9123
Greystone Park, NJ 07950
973-898-0048
973-898-6693
TheAngelConnection.org

AP JOHN INSTITUTE FOR CANCER RESEARCH
3526 Equestrian Ct.
Jacksonville, FL 32223
904-260-1588
877-260-1588
info@apjohncancerinstitute.org
APJohnCancerInstitute.org

APS FOUNDATION OF AMERICA, INC.
P.O. Box 801
La Crosse, WI 54602-0801
608-782-2626
608-782-6569
apsfa@apsfa.org
Apsfa.org

ARTHRITIS RESEARCH INSTITUTE OF AMERICA
300 S. Duncan Ave., Ste. 188
Clearwater, FL 33755
727-461-4054
PreventArthritis.org

ARTHRITIS TRUST OF AMERICA
7376 Walker Rd.
Fairview, TN 37062-8141
615-799-1002
ArthritisTrust.org

ASSOCIATION FOR COMMUNITY LIVING
One Carando Dr., Ste. 2
Springfield, MA 01104-3211
413-732-0531
800-536-2910
Theassn.org

ASSOCIATION FOR PERSONS WITH PHYSICAL
DISABILITIES OF WINDSOR AND ESSEX COUNTIES
2001 Spring Garden Rd.
Windsor, ON N9E 3P8
Canada
519-969-8188

AUTISM TREATMENT SERVICES OF
SASKATCHEWAN, INC.
Saskatoon Community Service Village
#302–506 25th St., East
Saskatoon, SK S7K 4A7
Canada
306-655-7013
306-665-7011
AutismServices.ca

AUTOIMMUNE INFORMATION NETWORK, INC.
4 Cardinal Ave.
Brick, NJ 08723
732-262-0450
autoimmunehelp@aol.com
Aininc.org

AVON BREAST CANCER CRUSADE
Avon Products Foundation, Inc.
1345 Avenue of the Americas
New York, NY 10105
877-WALKAVON
AvonCrusade.com

BE AN ANGEL FUND
2003 Aldine Bender
Houston, TX 77032
281-219-3313
BeAnAngel.org

BEBASHI
1217 Spring Garden St., 1st Fl.
Philadelphia, PA 19123

215-769-3561
Bebashi.org

BETH HAVEN
2500 Pleasant St.
Hannibal, MO 63401
573-221-6000
Bethaven.org

BETTER HEARING INSTITUTE
515 King St., Ste. 420
Alexandria, VA 22314
703-684-3391
BetterHearing.org

BIRTH DEFECT RESEARCH FOR CHILDREN
930 Woodcock Rd., Ste. 225
Orlando, FL 32803
800-313-2232
407-895-0802
BirthDefects.org

BRAIN INJURY ASSOCIATION OF AMERICA
105 N. Alfred St.
Alexandria, VA 22314
703-236-6000
biausa.org

BRAIN INJURY ASSOCIATION OF FLORIDA, INC.
201 E. Sample Rd.
Pompano Beach, FL 33064
954-786-2400

800-992-3442
biaf.org

BRAIN INJURY REHABILITATION CENTRE
300, 815 - 8th Ave., S.W.
Calgary, AB T2P 3P2
Canada
403-297-0100
403-234-8860
birc@brainrehab.ca
brainrehab.ca

BREAST CANCER FUND
1388 Sutter St., Ste. 400
San Francisco, CA 94109-5400
415-346-8223
breastcancerfund.org

BRONX HOME CARE SERVICES, INC.
4377 Bronx Blvd., Ste. 205
Bronx, NY 10466
718-231-6292

BURKE FOUNDATION
P.O. Box 40
20800 FM 150 W.
Driftwood, TX 78619
512-858-4258
burkefoundation.com

BURNT MOUNTAIN CENTER
P.O. Box 337
Jasper, GA 30143
706-692-6016

BUTLER VALLEY, INC.
380 12th St.
Arcata, CA 95521
707-822-0301

CALVARY FUND, INC.
1740 Eastchester Rd.
Bronx, NY 10461
877-4-CALVARY
calvaryhospital.org

CANADIAN RED CROSS
(CROIX-ROUGE CANADIENNE)
National Office
170 Metcalfe St., Ste. 300
Ottawa, ON K2P 2P2
Canada
613-740-1900
613-740-1911
redcross.ca

CANCER CARE SERVICES
623 S. Henderson St.
Ft. Worth, TX 76104-2914
817-921-0653
cancerservices.org

CANCER FUND OF AMERICA, INC.
2223 N. 56th St.
Mesa, AZ 85215
800-578-5284
480-654-4715
info@cfoa.org
cfoa.org

CANCER PROJECT
5100 Wisconsin Ave., N.W., Ste. 400
Washington, DC 20016
202-686-2210
cancerproject.org

CAREER DEVELOPMENT CENTER
2110 W. Delaware
Fairfield, IL 62837
618-842-2691
fairfieldcdc.com

CARROLL COUNTY HEALTH AND HOME CARE
SERVICES
Box 420, 448 White Mt. Hwy
Carroll County Complex
Chocorua, NH 03817
800-499-4171

CARROLL HAVEN ACHIEVING NEW GROWTH
EXPERIENCES
115 Stoner Ave.
Westminister, MD 21157-5443
410-876-2179

CHARLOTTE HIV/AIDS NETWORK, INC. (CHAN)
17506 Brighton Ave., Ste. D
Port Charlotte, FL 33954
941-625-6650
941-625-AIDS
chaninc.org

CHEYENNE VILLAGE, INC.
6275 Lehman Dr.
Colorado Springs, CO 80918
719-592-0200
cheyennevillage.org

CHICAGO HEARING SOCIETY
2001 N. Clybourn Ave.
Chicago, IL 60614
773-248-9121
chicagohearingsociety.org

CHICAGO HOUSE
1925 N. Clybourn, Ste. 401
Chicago, IL 60614
773-248-5200
chicagohouse.org

CHILDREN'S BURN FOUNDATION
5000 Van Nuys Blvd., Ste. 300
Sherman Oaks, CA 91403
818-907-2822
800-949-8898
childburn.org

CHILDREN'S CANCER ASSOCIATION
433 N.W. 4th Ave., Ste. 100
Portland, OR 97209
503-244-3141
childrenscancerassociation.org

CHILDREN'S DIAGNOSTIC CENTER, INC.
2100 Pleasant Ave.
Hamilton, OH 45015
513-868-1562

CHILDREN'S HEALTH ENVIRONMENTAL COALITION
12300 Wilshire Blvd, Ste. 410
Los Angeles, CA 90025
310-820-2030
checnet.org

CHILDREN'S WISH FOUNDATION INTERNATIONAL
8615 Roswell Rd.
Atlanta, GA 30350-4867
800-323-WISH
childrenswish.org

THE CHILDREN'S CIRCLE
P.O. Box 351535
Los Angeles, CA 90035
323-931-9828
mail@childrenscircle.org

CHRISTIAN HORIZONS
4278 King St. East, Ste. 2
Kitchener, ON N2P 2G5
Canada

519-650-3241
christian-horizons.org

COLLIER COUNTY ASSOCIATION FOR THE BLIND
4701 Golden Gate Pkwy.
Naples, FL 34116
239-597-6112
naples.net/social/ccab

COLOSTOMY SOCIETY OF NEW YORK
G.P.O. Box 517
New York, NY 10116
212-903-4713

COMMUNITY OPTIONS
801B Washington St.
P.O. Box 725
Chillicothe, MO 64601
660-646-0109

COMMUNITY SERVICES FOR THE
DEVELOPMENTALLY DISABLED
452 Delaware Ave.
Buffalo, NY 14202-1515
716-883-8888
csdd.info

COMPREHENSIVE ADVOCACY, INC.
4477 Emerald, Ste. B100
Boise, ID 83706-2044
800-632-5125
866-262-3462
users.moscow.com/co-ad

CONCERNED CITIZENS FOR HUMANITY
3580 Main St., Ste. 115, Bldg. 1
Hartford, CT 06120-1121
860-560-0833
concernedcitizensforhumanity.org

CRESTWOOD CHILDREN'S CENTER
1183 Monroe Ave.
Rochester, NY 14620
585-258-7500
hillside.com

DANVILLE CANCER ASSOCIATION, INC.
1225 W. Main St.
Danville, VA 24541
434-792-3700

DARTS
1645 Marthaler Ln.
West St. Paul, MN 55118
651-455-1560
darts1.org

DEAF ACTION CENTER
3115 Crestview Dr.
Dallas, TX 75235
214-521-0407
deafactioncentertexas.org

DEAF INDEPENDENT LIVING ASSOCIATION, INC.
806 Snow Hill Rd.
Salisbury, MD 21804

410-742-5052
dila.org

DEAF-BLIND SERVICE CENTER
16 W. 18th Ave., Ste. 200
Seattle, WA 98122
206-323-9178
seattledbsc.org

DELAWARE VALLEY COMMUNITY HEALTH, INC.
1412–22 Fairmount Ave.
Philadelphia, PA 19130
215-684-5344
dvch.org

DESIGN INDUSTRIES FOUNDATION FIGHTING AIDS (DIFFA)
200 Lexington Ave., Ste. 1016
New York, NY 10016-6255
212-727-3100
diffa.org

DEWITT COUNTY HUMAN RESOURCE CENTER
1150 Rte. 54 W.
Clinton, IL 61727
217-935-9496

DIRECT RELIEF INTERNATIONAL
27 S. La Patera Ln.
Santa Barbara, CA 93117
805-964-4767
info@directrelief.org
directrelief.org

DISABILITY RIGHTS EDUCATION &
DEFENSE FUND (DREDF)
2212 Sixth St.
Berkeley, CA 94710
510-644-2555
dredf.org

DISABLED AMERICAN VETERANS
P.O. Box 14301
Cincinnati, OH 45250
877-I Am A Vet
dav.org

DISABLED RESOURCE SERVICES
424 Pine St., Ste. 101
Ft. Collins, CO 80524-2421
970-482-2700

DOCTORS WITHOUT BORDERS
333 7th Ave., 2nd Floor
New York, NY 10001-5004
1-888-392-0392
212-679-6800
212-679-7016
doctorswithoutborders.org

DOGS FOR THE DEAF, INC.
10175 Wheeler Rd.
Central Point, OR 97502
541-826-9220
dogsforthedeaf.org

DR HADWEN TRUST
84a Tilehouse St.
Hitchen, Herts. SG5 2DY
United Kingdom
+44 1462 436844
info@drhadwentrust.org.uk
drhadwentrust.org.uk

DR. SUSAN LOVE RESEARCH FOUNDATION
875 Via De La Paz, Ste. C
Pacific Palisades, CA 90272
310-230-1712
dslrf.org

EAGLE VALLEY CHILDREN'S HOME
2300 Eagle Valley Ranch Rd.
Carson City, NV 89703
775-882-1188
eaglevalleychildrenshome.org

EASTER SEAL SOCIETY
90 Eglinton Ave., East, Ste. 208
Toronto, ON M4P 2Y3
Canada
416-932-8382
416-696-1035
info@easterseals.ca
easterseals.ca

EASTER SEALS
230 W. Monroe St., Ste. 1800
Chicago, IL 60606

800-221-6827
easterseals.com

THE ELTON JOHN AIDS FOUNDATION
584 Broadway
Suite 907
New York, NY 10012

EMPOWERING OUR CHILDREN
9701 E. Happy Valley Rd., #33
Scottsdale, AZ 85255
480-314-0014
empoweringourchildren.com

ENDOMETRIOSIS RESEARCH CENTER
630 Ibis Dr.
Delray Beach, FL 33444
800-293-7280
845-986-6562
heather@endocenter.org
endocenter.org

THE ERIC JOHNSON HOUSE, INC.
44 South St.
Morristown, NJ 07960
973-326-9636
theericjohnsonhouse.org

EYAS CORPORATION
411 Scarlet Sage St.
Punta Gorda, FL 33950
941-575-2255

FAMILIES HELPING FAMILIES AT THE
CROSSROADS OF LOUISIANA
P.O. Box 3356
Pineville, LA 71361-3356
800-259-7200
familieshelpingfamilies.net

FAMILY SERVICE ASSOCIATION
31 W. Market St.
Wilkes-Barre, PA 18701-1304
570-823-5144

FEDERATION OF FAMILIES FOR
CHILDREN'S MENTAL HEALTH
9605 Medical Center Drive, Ste. 280
Rockville, MD 20850
240-403-1901
ffcmh.org

FIVE ACRES/THE BOYS' AND GIRLS' AID SOCIETY OF
LOS ANGELES
760 W. Mountain View St.
Altadena, CA 91001
626-798-6793
5acres.org

FLOATING HOSPITAL
Grand Central Station
P.O. Box 3391
New York, NY 10163-3391
212-514-7440
info@thefloatinghospital.org
thefloatinghospital.org

FRIENDLY HAND FOUNDATION
(FRIENDLY HOUSE)
347 S. Normandie Ave.
Los Angeles, CA 90020
213-389-9964
friendlyhouse.net

THE FRIENDS
27 Forest St.
Parry Sound, ON P2A 2R2
Canada
705-746-5102
888-746-5102
thefriends.on.ca

GATEWAY FOR CANCER RESEARCH
1336 Basswood Rd.
Schaumburg, IL 60173
847-342-7450
888-221-CTRF
gatewayforcancerresearch.org

GAY MEN'S HEALTH CRISIS
119 W. 24th St.
New York, NY 10011
212-367-1000
212-367-1020
gmhc.org

GETABOUT
770 Main St.
New Canaan, CT 06840
203-972-2318

GILDA RADNER FAMILIAL OVARIAN CANCER REGISTRY
(ROSWELL PARK CANCER INSTITUTE)
Elm & Carlton Sts.
Buffalo, NY 14263-0001
800-682-7426
ovariancancer.com

GRACE HOUSE
2412 Tulip
Carlsbad, NM 88220
505-885-3681
gracehouse.net

GREYSTOKE HOMES AND SUPPORT SERVICES, INC.
316 13th St. South.
Lethbridge, AB T1J 2V6
Canada
403-320-0911

HAMILTON DISTRICT SOCIETY FOR
DISABLED CHILDREN
Box 200, Station A
555 Sanitorium Rd.
Hamilton, ON L9C 7N4
Canada
905-385-5391

HANDICAPPED HOUSING SOCIETY OF ALBERTA
4901 48th St., #302
Red Deer, AB T4N 6M4
Canada
403-346-1455

HARMONY HILL RETREAT CENTER
7362 East SR 106
Union, WA 98592
360-898-2364
harmonyhill.org

HARTVILLE HOMES, INC.
7324 A Whipple Ave., N.W.
North Canton, OH 44720
330-244-0050
hartvillehomes.org

HEALING SPECIES
P.O. Box 1202
Orangeburg, SC 29116-1202
803-535-6543
healingspecies.org

HEALTH CARES EXCHANGE INITIATIVE, INC.
7100 N. Ashland Blvd.
Chicago, IL 60626
617-499-7780
hcei.org

HEARTLAND OPPORTUNITY CENTER
323 N. E St.
Madera, CA 93638
559-674-8828
heartlandopportunity.com

HEBRON COMMUNITY, INC.
P.O. Box 11
Lawrenceville, VA 23868

HEIMLICH INSTITUTE
311 Straight St.
Cincinnati, OH 45219
513-559-2100
heimlichinstitute.org

HELEN KELLER INTERNATIONAL
352 Park Ave. South, 12th Floor
New York, NY 10010
877-535-5374
hkworld.org

HELP HOSPITALIZED VETERANS
36585 Penfield Ln.
Winchester, CA 92596
951-926-4500
hhv.org

HIV NETWORK OF EDMONTON SOCIETY
Ste. 300, 11456 Jasper Ave.
Edmonton, AB T5K 0M1
Canada
780-488-5742
780-488-3735
hivedmonton.com

HODAN CENTER, INC.
941 W. Fountain St.
P.O. Box 212

Mineral Point, WI 53565
608-987-3336
hodancenter.org

HOPE HOUSE FOUNDATION
801 Boush St., Third Floor
Norfolk, VA 23510
757-625-6161
hope-house.org

HORIZONS SPECIALIZED SERVICES, INC.
P.O. Box 774867
Steamboat Springs, CO 80477
973-879-4466

**HUMBOLDT COMMUNITY ACCESS
AND RESOURCE CENTER**
P.O. Box 2010
Eureka, CA 95502
707-443-7077
hcar.us

INDEPENDENCE CROSSROADS, INC.
8932 Old Cedar Ave., S.
Bloomington, MN 55425
952-854-8004

INDIANA REHABILITATION ASSOCIATION
P.O. Box 44174
Indianapolis, IN 46244-0174
317-290-4320
dmrtc.net/~rdidc/indrehab.htm

INSTITUTE FOR REHABILITATION, RESEARCH,
AND RECREATION, INC.
P.O. Box 1025
Pendelton, OR 97801
541-276-2752

INTERNATIONAL EYE FOUNDATION
10801 Connecticut Ave.
Kensington, MD 20895
240-290-0269
iefusa.org

INTERNATIONAL SUICIDE PREVENTION, INC.
1736 E. Charleston Blvd., #301
Las Vegas, NV 89104
supportisp.org

JOSHUA TREE FEEDING PROGRAM, INC.
1601 W. Indian School Rd.
Phoenix, AZ 85015-5223
602-264-0223
joshuatreefeedingprograminc.org

JUNIOR BLIND OF AMERICA
5300 Angeles Vista Blvd.
Los Angeles, CA 90043
323-295-4555
juniorblind.org

KENSINGTON COMMUNITY CORPORATION FOR
INDIVIDUAL DIGNITY
9150 Marshall St.

Philadelphia, PA 19114-2217
215-288-9797

KINSMEN TELEMIRACLE FOUNDATION
2217C Hanselman Ct.
Saskatoon, SK S7L 6A8
Canada
877-777-8979
telemiracle@sasktel.net
telemiracle.com

LAKE WHATCOM CENTER
3400 Agate Hts.
Bellingham, WA 98226
360-676-6000

LEAGUE FOR THE HARD OF HEARING
50 Broadway, 6th Fl.
New York, NY 10004
917-305-7700
lhh.org

LIFEGAINS, INC.
1603 S. Sterling St.
P.O. Drawer 1569
Morganton, NC 28680-1569
704-255-8845
lifegains.org

LIONS EYE BANK OF PA, INC.
5015 Richmond St.
Erie, PA 16509-1949

814-866-3545
paeyebank.org

LITTLE PEOPLE'S RESEARCH FUND, INC.
616 Old Edmenson Ave.
Catonsville, MD 21228
800-232-5773
lprf.org

LIVING SKILLS CENTER FOR VISUALLY IMPAIRED
2430 Road 20, #112B
San Pablo, CA 94806
510-234-4984
livingskillscenter.org

LOVING ARMS
1233 Peabody Ave.
Memphis, TN 38104
901-725-6730

LOWN CARDIOVASCULAR RESEARCH CENTER
21 Longwood Ave.
Brookline, MA 02446
617-732-1318
lowncenter.org

LYMPHOMA FOUNDATION OF AMERICA
1100 N. Main St.
Ann Arbor, MI 48104
734-222-1100
lfa@lymphomahelp.org
lymphomahelp.org

THE MAGIC PATH
7130 La Tijera Blvd.
Los Angeles, CA 90045
310-215-0907
wizardslair@myway.com
themagicpath.org

MAIDSTONE FOUNDATION, INC.
1225 Broadway
New York, NY 10001
212-889-5760
maidstonefoundation.org

MANAV AIDS PREVENTION & CARE SOCIETY
Jagdambay Compley, 5
Jyoti Nagar
Jalandhar 144 001
Punjab, India
0181-5577185
manavaids@yahoo.com
manavfoundationtrust.com

MCDOUGALL RESEARCH AND EDUCATION
FOUNDATION
P.O. Box 14309
Santa Rosa, CA 95402
707-538-8609
drmcdougall.com

MCS REFERRAL AND RESOURCES
(MULTIPLE CHEMICAL SENSITIVITY)
618 Wyndhurst Ave., #2
Baltimore, MD 21210

410-889-6666
410-889-4944
donnay@mcsrr.org
mcsrr.org

MEDICAL ADVANCES WITHOUT ANIMALS
(MAWA TRUST)
  P.O. Box 4203
  Weston Creek ACT 2611
  Australia
  02-6287-1980
  info@mawa-trust.org.au
  mawa.asn.au

MICHIGAN COMMUNITY BLOOD CENTERS
  1036 Fuller NE
  P.O. Box 1704
  Grand Rapids, MI 49501-1704
  1-866-MIBLOOD
  miblood.org

MICHIGAN WHEELCHAIR ATHLETIC ASSOCIATION
  P.O. Box 1455
  Troy, MI 48099
  248-321-2914
  miwheelchairathleticassociation.org

MILESTONE, INC.
(ROCVALE CHILDREN'S HOME)
  4060 McFarland Rd.
  Rockford, IL 61111
  815-654-6100
  milestoneinc.org

MINNESOTA STATE ACADEMY FOR THE DEAF
615 Olaf Hanson Dr.
P.O. Box 308
Faribault, MN 55021
507-332-5400
msad.state.mn.us

MIRACLE FLIGHTS
2756 N. Green Valley Pkwy., Ste. 115
Henderson, NV 89014-2120
702-261-0494
miracleflights.org

MIRACLE HOUSE OF NEW YORK
80 Eighth Ave., Ste. 315
New York, NY 10011
212-989-7790
miraclehouse.org

MISS FOUNDATION
P.O. Box 5333
Peoria, AZ 85385-5333
623-979-1000
888-455-MISS
missfoundation.org

MOBILE MEALS, INC.
1063 S. Broadway
Akron, OH 44311
330-376-7717
mobilemealsinc.org

MOUNTAIN VALLEY DEVELOPMENTAL SERVICES
P.O. Box 338
Glenwood Springs, CO 81602
970-945-2306
mtnvalley.org

MOWER COUNCIL FOR THE HANDICAPPED, INC.
111 N. Main St.
Austin, MN 55912-3404
507-433-9609

MT. ANGEL TRAINING CENTER AND
RESIDENTIAL SERVICES
P.O. Box 78
Mt. Angel, OR 97362
503-845-9214

MULTIPLE SCLEROSIS FOUNDATION
6350 N. Andrews Ave.
Ft. Lauderdale, FL 33309-2130
954-776-6805
msfacts.org

MUSCULAR DYSTROPHY FAMILY FOUNDATION
3951 N. Meridian St., Ste. 100
Indianapolis, IN 46208
317-923-6334
800-544-1213
mdff.org

N.W.T. COUNCIL OF PERSONS WITH DISABILITIES
P.O. Box 1387
Yellowknife, NT X1A 2P1

Canada
248-321-2914
nwtability.ca

NATIONAL ASSOCIATION FOR THE
VISUALLY HANDICAPPED
22 W. 21st St., 6th Fl.
New York, NY 10010
212-255-2804
navh.org

NATIONAL CHILDREN'S CANCER SOCIETY
One So. Memorial Dr.
St. Louis, MO 63102
314-241-1600
nationalchildrenscancersociety.com

NATIONAL CRANIOFACIAL ASSOCIATION
P.O. Box 11082
Chattanooga, TN 37401
800-332-2373
faces-cranio.org

NATIONAL FEDERATION OF THE BLIND
1800 Johnson St., Ste. 300
Baltimore, MD 21230
410-659-9314
nfb.org

NATIONAL STUTTERING ASSOCIATION
119 W. 40th St., Fl. 14
New York, NY 10018
212-944-4050

212-944-8244
tflores@westutter.org
westutter.org

NATURALEZA, INC.
8889 Mentor Ave.
Mentor, OH 44060
440-796-6319
naturalezafoundation.org

NEW OPPORTUNITIES
1510 West 7th St.
Granite City, IL 62040
618-876-3178
newopportunities.us

NIA COMPREHENSIVE CENTER FOR
DEVELOPMENTAL DISABILITIES
1808 S. State St.
Chicago, IL 60616
312-949-1808
800-NIA-1976
niapurpose.org

NORTH BAY AND AREA CENTRE FOR THE DISABLED
P.O. Box 137
409 Main St. E.
North Bay, ON P1B 8G8
Canada
705-474-3851

NORTH COUNTRY CENTER FOR INDEPENDENCE
102 Sharron Ave.
Plattsburgh, NY 12901
518-563-9058
ncci-online.com

OAK HILL
120 Holcomb St.
Hartford, CT 06112-1589
860-242-2274
ciboakhill.org

OPPORTUNITIES UNLIMITED
2393 Niagara Falls Blvd.
L.P.O. Box 360
Niagara Falls, NY 14304
716-297-6400

OPTIONS CENTER FOR INDEPENDENT LIVING
22 Heritage Plz., Ste. 107
Bourbonnais, IL 60914-2503
815-936-0100
optionscil.com

OUTLOOK NASHVILLE, INC.
3004 Tuggle Ave.
Nashville, TN 37211
615-834-7570
outlooknashville.org

OZARKS VALLEY COMMUNITY SERVICE, INC. (OVCS)
P.O. Box 156
Ironton, MO 63650-0156
573-546-2418 .

PALM SPRINGS STROKE ACTIVITY CENTER
P.O. Box 335
2800 E. Alejo Rd.
Palm Springs, CA 92263-0355
760-323-7676
psstrkcntr@aol.com
members.aol.com/psstrkcntr

THE PANAFRICAN ACUPUNCTURE PROJECT
113 Summit Ave.
Brookline, MA 02446
617-277-7444
panafricanacupuncture.org

PARCA
(PENINSULA ASSOCIATION FOR RETARDED CHILDREN
AND ADULTS)
1750 El Camino Real, Ste. 105
Burlingame, CA 94010
650-312-0730
650-312-0737
parca.org

PARKINSON'S RESOURCE ORGANIZATION
74-090 El Paseo
Suite 102
Palm Desert, CA 92260
760-773-5628

760-773-9803
parkinsonsresource.org

PATHFINDER INTERNATIONAL
9 Galen St., Ste. 217
Watertown, MA 02472
617-924-7200
pathfind.org

PHOENIX SHANTI GROUP, INC.
2345 West Glendale Ave.
Phoenix, AZ 85021
602-279-0008
shantiaz.org

PLEASANT VIEW HOMES, INC.
P.O. Box 426
Broadway, VA 22815
540-896-8255
pleasantviewinc.org

PLENTY INTERNATIONAL
P.O. Box 394
Summertown, TN 38483
931-964-4323
plenty@plenty.org
plenty.org

PRAIRIE MISSION RETIREMENT VILLAGE
242 Carroll St., R.R. 1, Box 1Z
St. Paul, KS 66771
620-449-2400

PRIDE YOUTH PROGRAMS
4 W. Oak St.
Fremont, MI 49412
800-668-9277
prideyouthprograms.org

PRIMROSE CENTER
2733 S. Fern Creek Ave.
Orlando, FL 32806-5591
407-898-7201
primrosecenter.org

PROJECT OPEN HAND
730 Polk St.
San Francisco, CA 94109
415-477-2300
openhand.org

PUERTO RICO COMMUNITY NETWORK FOR
CLINICAL RESEARCH ON AIDS
Calle Brumbaugh #1162
Urb. García Ubarri Río Piedras, PR 00927
787-753-9443
prconcra.org

PUERTO RICO DOWN SYNDROME FOUNDATION
P.O. Box 195273
San Juan, PR 00919-5273
787-287-2800
sindromedown.org

QUEST CANCER RESEARCH
Seedbed Business Centre, Unit E3
Coldharbour Rd., Pinnacles E.
Harlow, Essex CM19 5AF
United Kingdom
1279451359
questcancer.org.uk

RADIO INFORMATION SERVICE
2100 Wharton St., Ste. 140
Pittsburgh, PA 15203
412-488-3944
readingservice.org

RAINBOW SOCIETY OF ALBERTA
6604 82nd Ave.
Edmonton, AB T6B 0E7
Canada
780-469-3306
rainbowsociety.ab.ca

RECOVERY PATH FOUNDATION
908 W. Horatio St., Ste. A
Tampa, FL 33606
813-514-0350
recoverypathfoundation.org

REHABILITATION CENTER
1439 Buffalo St.
Olean, NY 14760
716-372-8909
rehabcenter.org

REHABILITATION SOCIETY OF CALGARY
7 11th St., N.E.
Calgary, AB T2E 4Z2
Canada
rehabcalgary@shaw.ca
abilities.ca

REMEDY, INC.
3 TMP, 333 Cedar St.
P.O. Box 208051
New Haven, CT 06520-8051
203-737-5356
203-785-5241
remedyinc.org

RESOURCE CENTER FOR ACCESSIBLE LIVING, INC.
592 Ulster Ave.
Kingston, NY 12401
845-331-0541
rcal.org

RIMROCK FOUNDATION
1231 N. 29th St.
Billings, MT 59101
800-227-3953
comm@rimrock.org
rimrock.org

RIVERFRONT FOUNDATION, INC.
592 Ulster Ave.
La Crosse, WI 54601
608-784-9450

ROCK AGAINST CANCER
PMB 216
4711 Hope Valley Rd.
Durham, NC 27707
rockagainstcancer.org

ROCKINGHAM OPPORTUNITIES
342 Cherokee Camp Rd.
Reidsville, NC 27320
336-342-4761
opportunitiescorp.org

ROYAL FREEMASONS' BENEVOLENT
INSTITUTION OF NSW
171 Castlereagh
Sydney, NSW 2000
Australia
02-9-264-5986

SAMARITAN RECOVERY COMMUNITY, INC.
319 S. Fourth St.
Nashville, TN 37206
615-244-4802
info@samctr.org
samctr.org

SAN ANTONIO STATE SCHOOL
P.O. Box 14700
San Antonio, TX 78241-0700
210-532-9610

SAVE A CHILD'S HEART FOUNDATION, US
10050 Chapel Rd, Ste. 18
Potomac, MD 20854-4141
301-618-4588
saveachildsheart.org

SCHIZOPHRENIA SOCIETY OF ALBERTA
9942-108 St., 5th Fl.
Edmonton, AB T5K 2J5
Canada
800-661-4644
780-422-2800
info@schizophrenia.ab.ca
schizophrenia.ab.ca

SEVA FOUNDATION
1786 Fifth St.
Berkeley, CA 94710
510-845-7382
seva.org

SHARE
1501 Broadway, Ste. 704A
New York, NY 10036
866-891-2392
212-869-3431
shareprograms@sharecancersupport.org
sharecancersupport.org

SHELTERED WORKSHOP
1430 Cost Ave.
Clarksburg, WV 26302-2002
304-623-3757

SKIN CANCER FOUNDATION
149 Madison Ave, Ste. 901
New York, NY 10016
800-754-6490
skincancer.org

SOCIETY FOR HANDICAPPED CITIZENS
4283 Paradise Rd.
Seville, OH 44273
330-722-1900
shc.medina.org

SOUTHWEST CENTER FOR INDEPENDENT LIVING
2864 S. Nettleton Ave.
Springfield, MO 65807-5970
800-676-7245
swcil.org

SOUTHWEST HUMAN DEVELOPMENT
2850 N. 24th St.
Phoenix, AZ 85008
602-266-5976
swhd.org

SOUTHWESTERN INDEPENDENT LIVING CENTER
843 N. Main St.
Jamestown, NY 14701
716-661-3010
ilc-jamestown-ny.org

SPECIALIZED TRAINING FOR ADULT REHABILITATION
(START)
20 N. 13th St.
Murphysboro, IL 62966-0938
618-687-2378
startworks.org

SPINA BIFIDA ASSOCIATION OF AMERICA
4590 MacArthur Blvd., N.W., Ste. 250
Washington, DC 20007-4226
800-621-3141
sbaa.org

SPINAL CORD INJURY NETWORK INTERNATIONAL
3911 Princeton Dr.
Santa Rosa, CA 95405
800-548-CORD
spinalcordinjury.org

ST. JOSEPH HOME, INC.
1226 S. Sunbury Rd.
Westerville, OH 43081-9105
614-890-5682

ST. PAUL ABILITIES NETWORK
4915-51 Ave.
St. Paul, AB T0A 3A0
Canada
866-645-3900
780-645-1885
mail@spanet.ab.ca
stpaulabilitiesnetwork.ca

STATEN ISLAND MENTAL HEALTH SOCIETY, INC.
669 Castleton Ave.
Staten Island, NY 10301
718-442-2225
simhs.org

STROKE SURVIVORS SUPPORT GROUP OF PUEBLO
710 1/2 E. Mesa Ave.
Pueblo, CO 81006
719-583-8498

THE SUNSHINE TERRACE FOUNDATION
225 N 200 W
Logan, UT 84321-3805
435-754-0216
sunshineterrace.com

SWIFT COUNTY DEVELOPMENTAL
ACHIEVEMENT CENTER
2105 Minnesota Ave., Bldg. 1
Benson, MN 56215
320-843-4201

TIMBERLAWN PSYCHIATRIC RESEARCH FOUNDATION
2750 Grove Hill Rd.
Dallas, TX 75227
214-388-0451

TOBIAS HOUSE ATTENDANT CARE, INC.
695 Coxwell Ave., Ste. 611
Toronto, ON M4C 5R6
Canada

416-690-3185
tobiashouse.ca

TOMORROWS CHILDREN'S FUND
Hackensack University Medical Center
30 Prospect Ave.
Hackensack, NJ 70601
201-996-5500
atcfkid.com

TRANSPLANTATION SOCIETY OF MICHIGAN
2203 Platt Rd.
Ann Arbor, MI 48104
800-482-4881
tsm-giftoflife.org

TRAUMA FOUNDATION
San Francisco General
1001 Potrero Ave., Bldg. 1, Rm. 300
San Francisco, CA 94110
415-821-8209
traumaf.org

TURN COMMUNITY SERVICES
850 S. Main
Salt Lake City, UT 84101
866-359-8876
turn.nu

UNICEF
333 E. 38th St.
New York, NY 10016

212-686-5522
unicef.org

UNITED AMPUTEE SERVICES
P.O. Box 4277
Winter Park, FL 32793
407-359-5500
oandp.com/resources/organizations/uasa/

UNITED CANCER RESEARCH SOCIETY
3545 20th St.
Highland, CA 92346-4542
800-443-4224
info@ucrs.org
unitedcancer.org

VICTOR C. NEUMANN ASSOCIATION
5547 N. Ravenswood St.
Chicago, IL 60640
773-769-4313
vcna.org

VIRGINIA FEDERATION OF FAMILIES
(PARENTS AND CHILDREN COPING TOGETHER)
13825 Village Mill Dr.
Midlothian, VA 23114
804-264-8428
800-477-0946
medicalhomeplus.org

VISIONS RESOURCE CENTER
725 W. Rowan St.
Fayetteville, NC 28301
910-483-2719

VISIONS/SERVICES FOR THE BLIND AND
VISUALLY IMPAIRED
500 Greenwich St., Fl. 3
New York, NY 10013-1354
212-625-1616
visionsvcb.org

VOCATIONAL SERVICES, INC.
935 S. Kent St.
Liberty, MO 64068
816-781-6292
vsiserve.org

VOLAR CENTER FOR INDEPENDENT LIVING
8929 Viscount, Ste. 101
El Paso, TX 79925
915-591-0800
volar@volarcil.org
volarcil.org

VULVAR PAIN FOUNDATION
P.O. Drawer 177
Graham, NC 27253
336-226-0704
vulvarpainfoundation.org

WARNER HOUSE
31878 Del Obispo St.
San Juan Capistrano, CA 92675
714-441-2000
warnerhouse.com

WASHINGTON CENTER FOR CLINICAL RESEARCH
5100 Wisconsin Ave, N.W.
Ste. 400
Washington, DC 20016
202-686-2210
vhoover@washingtonccr.org
washingtonccr.org

WASHINGTON VOLUNTEER READERS FOR
THE BLIND
901 G St., N.W.
Washington, DC 20001
202-727-2142

WAUKESHA TRAINING CENTER
300 S. Prairie Ave.
Waukesha, WI 53186
262-547-6821
waukeshatrainingcenter.com

WESLEY HEIGHTS
580 Long Hill Ave.
Shelton, CT 06484
203-225-5000
umh.org

WESTERN CAROLINA CENTER FOUNDATION, INC.
P.O. Box 646
Morganton, NC 28680-0646
704-433-2862
westerncarolinacenter.com

WORKSHOP/NORTHEAST CAREER PLANNING
339 Broadway
Menards, NY 12204
518-273-0818

YOUTH SERVICES FOR OKLAHOMA COUNTY
201 N.E. 50th St.
Oklahoma City, OK 73105-1811
405-235-7537
kids.ysoc.org
ysoc.org

HEALTH CHARITIES THAT STILL
FUND ANIMAL EXPERIMENTS
(AS OF JANUARY 1, 2009)

AARON DIAMOND AIDS RESEARCH CENTER
455 First Ave.
New York, NY 10016
212-448-5000
adarc.org

ALLIANCE FOR LUPUS RESEARCH, INC.
1270 Avenue of the Americas, Ste. 609
New York, NY 10030
212-218-2840
lupusresearch.org

ALZHEIMER'S ASSOCIATION
(ALZHEIMER'S DISEASE AND RELATED
DISORDERS ASSOCIATION)
225 N. Michigan Ave., Fl. 17

Chicago, IL 60601-7633
800-272-3900
info@alz.org
alz.org

ALZHEIMER'S DISEASE RESEARCH
22512 Gateway Center Dr.
Clarksburg, MD 20871
800-437-2423
ghandiboe@ahaf.org
ahaf.org

ALZHEIMER'S SOCIETY OF CANADA
20 Eglinton Ave., W., Ste. 1200
Toronto, ON M4R 1K8
Canada
416-488-8772
alzheimer.ca

AMERICAN BRAIN TUMOR ASSOCIATION
2727 River Rd., Ste. 146
Des Plaines, IL 60018-4110
800-886-2282
info@abta.org
abta.org

AMERICAN CANCER SOCIETY
1599 Clifton Rd., N.E.
Atlanta, GA 30329
404-320-3333
cancer.org

AMERICAN DIABETES ASSOCIATION
1701 N. Beauregard St.
Alexandria, VA 22311
800-342-2383
703-549-1500
membership@diabetes.org
diabetes.org

AMERICAN DIGESTIVE HEALTH FOUNDATION
7910 Woodmont Ave., Ste. 700
Bethesda, MD 20814-3015
301-654-2635

AMERICAN FEDERATION FOR AGING RESEARCH
70 W. 40th St., Fl. 11
New York, NY 10018
212-703-9977
888-582-2327
amfedaging@aol.com
afar.org/

AMERICAN FOUNDATION FOR AIDS RESEARCH
(AMFAR)
120 Wall St., Fl. 13
New York, NY 10005-3902
800-39-amfAR
212-806-1601
amfar.org

AMERICAN HEALTH ASSISTANCE FOUNDATION
22512 Gateway Center Dr.
Clarksburg, MD 20871
800-437-2423

eberger@ahaf.org
ahaf.org

AMERICAN HEART ASSOCIATION
7272 Greenville Ave.
Dallas, TX 75231-4596
800-242-8721
214-373-6300
ncrp@heart.org
americanheart.org

AMERICAN INSTITUTE FOR CANCER RESEARCH
1759 R St., N.W.
Washington, DC 20009
800-843-8114
202-328-7226
aicrweb@aicr.org
aicr.org

AMERICAN LIVER FOUNDATION
75 Maiden Ln., Ste. 603
New York, NY 10038
800-465-4837
liverfoundation.org

AMERICAN LUNG ASSOCIATION
National Headquarters
1740 Broadway
New York, NY 10019
212-315-8700
info@lungusa.org
lungusa.org

AMERICAN PARKINSON'S DISEASE ASSOCIATION
1250 Hylan Blvd., Ste. 4B
Staten Island, NY 10305
800-223-2732
718-981-8001
info@apdaparkinson.com
apdaparkinson.org

AMERICAN RED CROSS
2025 E St., N.W.
Washington, DC 20006
800-435-7669
202-303-4498
info@usa.redcross.org
redcross.org

AMERICAN STROKE ASSOCIATION (A division of the
American Heart Association)
National Center
7272 Greenville Ave.
Dallas, TX 75231
888-4STROKE
strokeassociation.org

AMERICAN TINNITUS ASSOCIATION
P.O. Box 5
Portland, OR 97207-0005
800-634-8978
503-248-9985
tinnitus@ata.org
ata.org

AMERICAN UROLOGICAL ASSOCIATION FOUNDATION
1000 Corporate Blvd, Ste. 410
Linthicum, MD 21090
410-689-3700
afud.org

AMYOTROPHIC LATERAL SCLEROSIS (ALS)
SOCIETY OF CANADA
265 Yorkland Blvd., Ste. 300
Toronto, ON M2J 1S5
Canada
800-267-4257
als.ca

AMYOTROPHIC LATERAL SCLEROSIS ASSOCIATION
27001 Agoua Rd., Ste. 150
Calabasas Hills, CA 91301-5104
800-782-4747
818-880-9007
alsinfo@alsa-national.org
alsa.org

APLASTIC ANEMIA & MDS INTERNATIONAL
FOUNDATION, INC.
P.O. Box 316
Annapolis, MD 21404-0613
800-747-2820
help@aamds.org
aamds-international.org

ARIZONA CANCER CENTER
1515 N. Campbell Ave.
P.O. Box 245013

Tucson, AZ 85724-5013
800-327-CURE
azcc.arizona.edu/whos_who/w_dorr.htm

ARTHRITIS FOUNDATION
1330 W. Peachtree St.
Atlanta, GA 30309
404-872-7100
arthritis.org

THE ARTHRITIS SOCIETY
393 University Ave.
Ste. 1700
Toronto, ON M5G 1E6
Canada
416-979-7228
416-979-8366
info@arthritis.ca
arthritis.ca

AUTISM RESEARCH INSTITUTE
4182 Adams Ave.
San Diego, CA 92116
619-218-7165
autismwebsite.com

AUTISM SPEAKS
2 Park Ave.
11th Floor
New York, NY 10016
212-252-8584
212-252-8676

contactus@autismspeaks.org
autismspeaks.org

BNI FOUNDATION
350 W. Thomas Rd.
Phoenix, AZ 85013
602-406-3041

BOOMER ESIASON FOUNDATION
417 Fifth Ave., 2nd Floor
New York, NY 10016
646-344-3765
esiason.org

BOYS TOWN NATIONAL RESEARCH HOSPITAL
555 N. 30th St.
Omaha, NE 68131
402-498-6511
boystownhospital.org

BRAIN TUMOR SOCIETY
124 Watertown St., Ste. 3H
Watertown, MA 02472
800-770-8287
tbts.org

BREAST CANCER RESEARCH FOUNDATION
654 Madison Ave., Ste. 1209
New York, NY 10021
646-497-2600
bcrf@estee.com
bcrfcure.org

BRITISH COLUMBIA CANCER FOUNDATION
200-601 W. Broadway
Vancouver, BC V5Z 4C2
Canada
888-906-2873
bccancerfoundation.com

**BRITISH COLUMBIA CHILDREN'S HOSPITAL
FOUNDATION**
4480 Oak St., Rm. B321
Vancouver, BC V6H 3V4
Canada
888-663-3033
bcchf.ca

BRITISH COLUMBIA LUNG ASSOCIATION
2675 Oak St.
Vancouver, BC V6H 2K2
Canada
604-731-5864
bc.lung.ca

BUONICONTI FUND
P.O. Box 016960, R-48
Miami, FL 33101
305-243-6001

CANADIAN BLOOD SERVICES
1800 Alta Vista
Ottawa, ON K1G 4J5
Canada
613-739-2300
bloodservices.ca

CANADIAN CANCER SOCIETY
(NATIONAL CANCER INSTITUTE OF CANADA)
10 Alcorn Ave., Ste. 200
Toronto, ON M4V 3B1
Canada
416-961-7223
ccs@cancer.ca
cancer.ca

CANADIAN CYSTIC FIBROSIS FOUNDATION
2221 Yonge St., Ste. 601
Toronto, ON M4S 2B4
Canada
800-378-2233
cysticfibrosis.ca

CANADIAN DIABETES ASSOCIATION
National Life Building
1400-522 University Ave.
Toronto, ON M5G 2R5
Canada
800-226-8464
416-363-0177
info@diabetes.ca
diabetes.ca

THE CANADIAN FUND FOR AIDS RESEARCH
(CANFAR)
165 University Ave., Ste. 901
Toronto, ON M5H 3B8
Canada
800-563-CURE
canfar.ca

CANADIAN HEMOPHILIA SOCIETY
625 President Kennedy Ave., Ste. 1210
Montreal, QB H3A 1K2
Canada
800-668-2686
hemophilia.ca

CANCER RESEARCH FOUNDATION OF AMERICA
(CANCER RESEARCH AND PREVENTION FOUNDATION)
1600 Duke St., Ste. 110
Alexandria, VA 22314-3421
800-227-2732
703-836-4412
jandahazy@crfa.org
preventcancer.org

CANCER RESEARCH INSTITUTE
681 Fifth Ave.
New York, NY 10082
800-992-2623
cancerresearch.org

CANCER RESEARCH SOCIETY
2232 1 Pl., Ville-Marie
Montreal, QB H3B 5C3
Canada
514-861-9227

CHARCOT-MARIE-TOOTH ASSOCIATION
2700 Chestnut St.
Chester, PA 19013-4867
800-606-CMTA

cmtassoc@aol.com
charcot-marie-tooth.org

CHILDREN'S CANCER RESEARCH FUND
11633 San Vicente Blvd., Ste. 106
Los Angeles, CA 90049
310-207-5330
ccrfkids@hotmail.com
ccrf-kids.org

CHILDREN'S HEART FOUNDATION
P.O. Box 244
Lincolnshire, IL 60069
847-634-6474
info@childrensheartfoundation.org
childrensheartfoundation.org

CHILDREN'S HOSPITAL OF PITTSBURGH FOUNDATION
3705 Fifth Ave.
Pittsburgh, PA 15213-2583
412-692-7436
chp.edu

CHILDREN'S MIRACLE NETWORK
4525 S. 2300, E., Ste. 202
Salt Lake City, UT 84117
801-278-8900
801-277-8787
cmn.org

CHILDREN'S TUMOR FOUNDATION
95 Pine St., 16th Floor
New York, NY 10005

212-334-6633
ctf.org

CHRISTOPHER REEVE PARALYSIS FOUNDATION
500 Morris Ave.
Springfield, NJ 07081
800-225-0290
info@crpf.org
http:christopherreeve.org/site/c.geimlpopgjf/
    b.1029229/k.c9

CITY OF HOPE
1500 E. Duarte Rd.
Duarte, CA 91010
800-826-HOPE
626-359-8111
cityofhope.org

CROHN'S AND COLITIS FOUNDATION OF AMERICA
386 Park Ave. South, Fl. 17
New York, NY 10016-8804
info@ccfa.org
ccfa.org

CURE AUTISM NOW
5455 Wilshire Blvd., Ste. 715
Los Angeles, CA 90036-4234
888-828-8476
cureautismnow.org

CURE CHILDHOOD CANCER
1835 Savoy Dr., Ste. 317
Atlanta, GA 30341

800-443-2873
curechildhoodcancer.org

CYSTIC FIBROSIS FOUNDATION
6931 Arlington Rd.
Bethesda, MD 20814
800-FIGHT-CF
301-951-4422
info@cff.org
cff.org/home

DAMON RUNYON CANCER RESEARCH
675 Third Ave. 25th Floor
New York, NY 10017
877-722-6237
drcrf.org

THE DANA FOUNDATION
745 5th Ave., Ste. 900
New York, NY 10151
danainfo@dana.org
dana.org

DANA-FARBER CANCER INSTITUTE
44 Binney St.
Boston, MA 02115
866-408-DFCI
dfci.harvard.edu

DEAFNESS RESEARCH FOUNDATION
1050 17th St., N.W., Ste. 701
Washington, DC 20036
202-289-5850

drf@drf.org
drf.org

DIABETES RESEARCH & WELLNESS FOUNDATION
5151 Wisconsin Ave, N.W., Ste. 420
Washington, DC 20016
202-298-9211
diabeteswellness.net

DISCOVERY EYE FOUNDATION
8733 Beverly Blvd.
Ste. 201
Los Angeles, CA 90048
310-623-4466
discoveryeye.org

DOHENY EYE INSTITUTE
1450 San Pablo St.
DEI-3050
Los Angeles, CA 90033
323-442-7101
doheny.org

DYSTONIA MEDICAL RESEARCH FOUNDATION
One East Wacker Dr., Ste. 2430
Chicago, IL 60601
312-755-0198
dystonia-foundation.org

EHLERS-DANLOS NATIONAL FOUNDATION
3200 Wilshire Blvd.
Ste. 1601, South Tower
Los Angeles, CA 90010

213-368-3800
ednf.org

ELIZABETH GLAZER PEDIATRIC AIDS FOUNDATION
2950 31st St., Ste. 125
Santa Monica, CA 90405
888-499-4673
310-314-1459
info@pedaids.org
pedaids.org

ENDOMETRIOSIS ASSOCIATION
8585 N. 76th Pl.
Milwaukee, WI 53223
800-992-3636
endometriosisassn.org

ENTERTAINMENT INDUSTRY FOUNDATION
11132 Ventura Blvd., Ste. 401
Studio City, CA 91604
818-760-7722
eifoundation.org

EPIDERMOLYSIS BULLOSA MEDICAL
RESEARCH FOUNDATION
130 Sandringham Rd.
Piedmont, CA 94611
510-530-9600
ebmrf@comcast.net
ebkids.org

EPILEPSY FOUNDATION OF AMERICA
4351 Garden City Dr., Ste. 500

Landover, MD 20785
301-459-3700
info@efa.org
epilepsyfoundation.org

FAMILIES OF SPINAL MUSCULAR ATROPHY
P.O. Box 196
Libertyville, IL 60048-0196
800-886-1762
847-367-7620
ama@fsma.org
fsma.org

FONDS DE LA RECHERCHE EN SANTÉ DU QUEBEC
500 Rue, Sherbrooke Quest
Bureau 800
Montreal, QB H3A 3L6
Canada
514-873-2114

FOOD ALLERGY INITIATIVE
41 East 62nd St.
4th Floor
New York, NY 10021
212-572-8428
foodallergyinitiative.org

FOUNDATION FIGHTING BLINDNESS (Formerly
National Retinitis Pigmentosa Foundation)
11435 Cronhill Dr.
Owings Mills, MD 21117-2220
888-394-3937
410-568-0150

info@blindness.org
blindness.org

FOUNDATION TO ERADICATE DUCHENNE
P.O. Box 2371
Alexandria, VA 22301
703-683-7500
duchennemd.org

FRED HUTCHINSON CANCER RESEARCH CENTER
1100 Fairview Ave., N.
P.O. Box 19024
Seattle, WA 98109
206-667-5000
fhcrc.org

G&P FOUNDATION FOR CANCER RESEARCH
770 Lexington Ave., Fl. 16
New York, NY 10021-8165
212-486-2575
gpfoundation.com

GLAUCOMA RESEARCH FOUNDATION
490 Post St., Ste. 1427
San Francisco, CA 94102
888-826-6693
info@glaucoma.org
glaucoma.org

HEART AND STROKE FOUNDATION OF CANADA
222 Queen St., Ste. 1402
Ottawa, ON K1P 5V9
Canada

613-569-4361
hsf.ca

HERA WOMEN'S CANCER FOUNDATION
(CLIMB FOR LIFE)
Box 664
Carbondale, CO 81623
970-948-7360
info@herafoundation.org
herafoundation.org

HOUSE EAR INSTITUTE
2100 W. Third St.
Los Angeles, CA 90057
213-483-4431
hei.org

HUNTINGTON'S DISEASE SOCIETY OF AMERICA
505 Eighth Ave., Ste. 902
New York, NY 10018
800-345-HDSA
212-239-3430
hdsainfo@hdsa.org
hdsa.org

THE INSTITUTE FOR CHILDREN
WITH CANCER AND BLOOD DISORDERS
P.O. Box 109
New Brunswick, NJ 08903
800-231-KIDS

INSTITUTE FOR MYELOMA & BONE CANCER RESEARCH
9201 Sunset Blvd., Ste. 300
West Hollywood, CA 90069
310-623-1210
imbcr.org

INTERNATIONAL AIDS VACCINE INITIATIVE
110 William St., Fl. 27
New York, NY 10038
212-847-1111
iavi.org

THE JACKSON LABORATORY
610 Main St.
Bar Harbor, ME 04609
800-474-9880
jax.org

JIMMY FUND
375 Longwood Ave., W.
Boston, MA 02215-7295
800-52-JIMMY
info@jimmyfund.org
jimmyfund.org

JIMMY V FOUNDATION
(THE V FOUNDATION FOR CANCER RESEARCH)
100 Towerview Ct.
Cary, NC 27513
919-380-9505
800-4-JIMMYV
info@jimmyv.org
jimmyv.org

JOHN WAYNE CANCER CENTER INSTITUTE AT SAINT
JOHN'S HOSPITAL AND HEALTH CENTER
2200 Santa Monica Blvd.
Santa Monica, CA 90404
800-262-6259
310-315-6111
jwci@jwci.org
jwci.org

JOHNS HOPKINS CHILDREN'S CENTER
One Charles Center
100 N. Charles St., Ste. 200
Baltimore, MD 21201
410-516-4581
hopkinschildrens.org

JOSLIN DIABETES CENTER
One Joslin Place
Boston, MA 02215
617-732-2400
joslin.harvard.edu

JUVENILE DIABETES RESEARCH FOUNDATION
INTERNATIONAL
120 Wall St.
New York, NY 10005-4001
800-JDF-CURE
info@jdrf.org
jdrf.org

KIDNEY FOUNDATION OF CANADA
15 Gervais Dr., Ste. 700
Toronto, ON M3C 1Y8

Canada
800-378-4474
kidneycob.on.ca

LANCE ARMSTRONG FOUNDATION
P.O. Box 161150
Austin, TX 78716-1150
512-236-8820
donations@laf.org
livestrong.org

THE LANKENAU INSTITUTE FOR MEDICAL RESEARCH
100 Lancaster Ave.
Wynnewood, PA 19096
610-645-8400
limr.org

LES TURNER ALS FOUNDATION
8142 N. Lawndale Ave.
Skokie, IL 60076
888-ALS-1107
lesturnerals.org

THE LEUKEMIA & LYMPHOMA SOCIETY
(THE LEUKEMIA SOCIETY OF AMERICA)
1311 Mamaroneck Ave.
White Plains, NY 10605
800-955-4572
914-949-5213
914-949-6691
leukemia-lymphoma.org | leukemia.org

LEUKEMIA RESEARCH FOUNDATION
2700 Patriot Blvd., Ste. #100
Glenview, IL 60026
847-424-0600
888-558-5385
info@lrfmail.org
leukemia-research.org

LEUKEMIA RESEARCH FUND OF CANADA
110 Finch Ave., W., Ste. 220
Toronto, ON M3J 2T2
Canada
800-268-2114

LIFE EXTENSION FOUNDATION
P.O. Box 229120
Hollywood, FL 33022-9120
800-544-4440
lef.org

LOMBARDI CANCER CENTER
New Research Bldg., Rm. E501
3970 Reservoir Rd., N.W.
Washington, DC 20007
202-687-2956
lombardi.georgetown.edu

LOVELACE RESPIRATORY RESEARCH INSTITUTE
2425 Ridgecrest Dr., S.E.
Albuquerque, NM 87801
888-315-9156
lrri.org

LUPUS FOUNDATION OF AMERICA, INC.
2000 L St., N.W., Ste. 710
Washington, DC 20036
800-558-0121
202-349-1155
202-349-1156
lupus.org

THE LUSTGARTEN FOUNDATION FOR
PANCREATIC CANCER RESEARCH
1111 Stewart Ave.
Bethpage, NY 11714
866-789-1000
lustgarten.org

LYMPHOMA RESEARCH FOUNDATION
111 Broadway, 19th Floor
New York, NY 10006
800-235-6848
lymphoma.org

MACULAR DEGENERATION RESEARCH (a program
of the American Health Assistance Foundation)
22512 Gateway Center Dr.
Clarksburg, MD 20850
800-437-2423
eberger@ahaf.org
ahaf.org

MANITOBA MEDICAL SERVICES FOUNDATION
100A Polo Park Centre
Winnipeg, MB R3G 0W4
Canada

MARCH OF DIMES BIRTH DEFECTS FOUNDATION
1275 Mamaroneck Ave.
White Plains, NY 10605
888-663-4637
914-997-4504
marchofdimes.com

MARY KAY ASH CHARITABLE FOUNDATION
P.O. Box 799044
Dallas, TX 75379-9044
877-652-2737
mkacf.org

MASONIC MEDICAL RESEARCH LABORATORY
2150 Bleecker St.
Utica, NY 13501
315-735-2217
mmrl.edu

MASSACHUSETTS LIONS EYE RESEARCH FUND
(formerly Lions Club International Foundation)
118 Allen St.
Hampden, MA 01036
mlerf.com

McLAUGHLIN RESEARCH INSTITUTE
1520 23rd St. South
Great Falls, MT 59405
406-452-6208
montana.edu/wwwmri

MEMORIAL SLOAN-KETTERING CANCER CENTER
1275 York Ave.
New York, NY 10021
212-639-2000
publicaffairs@mskcc.org
mskcc.org

MESOTHELIOMA APPLIED RESEARCH FOUNDATION (MESO FOUNDATION)
3944 State St., Ste. 340
Santa Barbara, CA 93105
805-563-8400
marf.org

MIAMI PROJECT TO CURE PARALYSIS
P.O. Box 016960, R-48
Miami, FL 33101
800-STANDUP
305-243-6001
mpinfo@miamiproject.med.miami.edu

MICHAEL J. FOX FOUNDATION FOR PARKINSON'S RESEARCH
Grand Central Station
P.O. Box 4777
New York, NY 10163
800-708-7644
michaeljfox.org

MINNEAPOLIS MEDICAL RESEARCH FOUNDATION
600 Shapiro Building
917 South 8th St.
Minneapolis, MN 55404

612-347-7672
mmrf.org

MOLECULAR CARDIOLOGY RESEARCH INSTITUTE
Tufts-New England Medical Center
750 Washington St.
Boston, MA 02111
617-636-5000
nemc.org

MONELL CHEMICAL SENSES CENTER
3500 Market St.
Philadelphia, PA 19104
215-898-6666
monell.org

MORRIS ANIMAL FOUNDATION
45 Inverness Dr., E.
Englewood, CO 80112
800-243-2345
morrisanimalfoundation.org

THE MULTIPLE MYELOMA RESEARCH FOUNDATION
383 Main Ave., 5th Floor
Norwalk, CT 06851
203-229-0464
multiplemyeloma.org

MULTIPLE SCLEROSIS SOCIETY OF CANADA
250 Bloor St., E., Ste. 1000
Toronto, ON M4W 3P9
Canada

416-922-6065
mssociety.ca/en/default.htm

MUSCULAR DYSTROPHY ASSOCIATION
3300 E. Sunrise Dr.
Tucson, AZ 85718-3208
800-572-1717
mda@mdausa.org
mdausa.org

NATIONAL ALLIANCE FOR AUTISM RESEARCH
99 Wall St.
Research Park
Princeton, NJ 08540
888-777-NAAR
naar@naar.org
naar.org

NATIONAL ALLIANCE FOR RESEARCH OF
SCHIZOPHRENIA AND DEPRESSION
60 Cutter Mill Rd., Ste. 404
Great Neck, NY 11021
800-829-8289
info@narsad.org
narsad.org

NATIONAL ALLIANCE ON MENTAL ILLNESS
RESEARCH INSTITUTE
Colonial Place Three
2107 Wilson Blvd., Ste. 300
Arlington, VA 22201-3042
703-524-7600
nami.org

NATIONAL ALOPECIA AREATA FOUNDATION
14 Mitchell Blvd.
San Rafael, CA 94903
415-472-3780
naaf.org

NATIONAL BREAST CANCER RESEARCH CENTER
(WALKER CANCER RESEARCH INSTITUTE)
18 N. Law St.
Aberdeen, MD 21001-2443
410-272-0775

NATIONAL CANCER CENTER
88 Sunnyside Blvd, Ste. 307
Plainview, NY 11803
516-349-0610
nationalcancercenter.org

NATIONAL CANCER COALITION
757 St. Charles Ave., Ste. 202
New Orleans, LA 70130
504-301-1461
nationalcancercoalition.org

NATIONAL CANCER INSTITUTE OF CANADA
10 Alcorn Ave., Ste. 200
Toronto, ON M4V 3B1
Canada
416-961-7223
416-961-4189
ncic@cancer.ca
ncic.cancer.ca

NATIONAL CANCER RESEARCH CENTER
(WALKER CANCER RESEARCH INSTITUTE)
18 N. Law St.
Aberdeen, MD 21001-2443
410-272-0775

NATIONAL CARDIOVASCULAR RESEARCH INITIATIVE
(ENTERTAINMENT INDUSTRY FOUNDATION)
11132 Ventura Blvd., Ste. 401
Studio City, CA 91604
818-760-7722
eifoundation.org

NATIONAL COLORECTAL CANCER RESEARCH ALLIANCE
(ENTERTAINMENT INDUSTRY FOUNDATION)
11132 Ventura Blvd., Ste. 401
Studio City, CA 91604
818-760-7722
eifoundation.org

NATIONAL FOUNDATION FOR CANCER RESEARCH
4600 East-West Hwy.
Bethesda, MD 20814
800-321-2873
nfcr.org

NATIONAL GLAUCOMA RESEARCH (a program of the
American Health Assistance Foundation)
22512 Gateway Center Dr.
Clarksburg, MD 20871
800-437-2423
eberger@ahaf.org
ahaf.org

NATIONAL HEADACHE FOUNDATION
428 W. St. James Pl., Fl. 2
Chicago, IL 60614-2750
800-NHF-5552
773-525-7357
info@headaches.org
headaches.org

NATIONAL HEART FOUNDATION (a program of the
American Health Assistance Foundation)
22512 Gateway Center Dr.
Clarksburg, MD 20871
800-437-2423
ahaf.org

NATIONAL HEMOPHILIA FOUNDATION
116 W. 32nd St., Fl. 11
New York, NY 10001
800-424-2634
212-328-3777
development@hemophilia.org
hemophilia.org

NATIONAL JEWISH MEDICAL AND RESEARCH CENTER
1400 Jackson St.
Denver, CO 80206
303-388-4461
nationaljewish.org

NATIONAL KIDNEY FOUNDATION
30 E. 33rd St., Ste. 1100
New York, NY 10016
800-622-9010

212-889-2210
info@kidney.org
kidney.org

NATIONAL MULTIPLE SCLEROSIS SOCIETY
733 3rd Ave., Fl. 6
New York, NY 10017-3288
800-344-4867
infor@nmss.org
nmss.org

NATIONAL OSTEOPOROSIS FOUNDATION
1232 22nd St., N.W.
Washington, DC 20037-1292
202-223-2226
bob@nof.org
nof.org

NATIONAL PARKINSON'S FOUNDATION
1501 N.W. 9th Ave.
Miami, FL 33136
800-327-4545
mailbox@parkinson.org
parkinson.org

NATIONAL PSORIASIS FOUNDATION
6600 S.W. 92nd Ave., Ste. 300
Portland, OR 97223-7195
800-723-9166
503-244-7404
getinfo@npfusa.org
psoriasis.org

NATIONAL STROKE ASSOCIATION
9707 E. Easter Ln.
Englewood, CO 80112
800-STROKES
303-649-9299
stroke.org

NATIONAL VITILIGO FOUNDATION, INC.
611 S. Fleishel Ave.
Tyler, TX 75701
903-531-0074
nvfi.org/index.shtml

NATIONAL WOMEN'S CANCER RESEARCH ALLIANCE
(ENTERTAINMENT INDUSTRY FOUNDATION)
11132 Ventura Blvd., Ste. 401
Studio City, CA 91604
818-760-7722
eifoundation.org

NATURAL SCIENCES AND ENGINEERING RESEARCH
COUNCIL OF CANADA
350 Albert St.
Ottawa, ON K1A 1H5
Canada

NEUROSCIENCES RESEARCH FOUNDATION
(THE NEUROSCIENCES INSTITUTE)
10640 John Jay Hopkins Dr.
San Diego, CA 92121
858-626-2000
nsi.edu

NEVADA CANCER INSTITUTE
10000 W. Charleston Blvd., Ste. 260
Las Vegas, NV 89135
702-821-0000
nevadacancerinstitute.org

NINA HYDE CENTER FOR BREAST CANCER RESEARCH
(LOMBARDI CANCER RESEARCH CENTER)
3800 Reservoir Rd., N.W.
Washington, DC 20007
202-687-4597

OKLAHOMA MEDICAL RESEARCH FOUNDATION
825 13th St., N.E.
Oklahoma City, OK 73104
800-522-0211
omrf.ouhsc.edu

ORAL & MAXILLOFACIAL SURGERY FOUNDATION
9700 W. Bryn Mawr Ave.
Rosemont, IL 60018
847-233-4304
omsfoundation.org

ORTHOPAEDIC RESEARCH & EDUCATION
FOUNDATION
6300 River Rd., Ste. 700
Rosemont, IL 60018
847-698-9980
oref.org

OSTEOGENESIS IMPERFECTA FOUNDATION, INC.
804 W. Diamond Ave., Ste. 210
Gaithersburg, MD 20878
800-981-2663
301-947-0456
oif.org

OVARIAN CANCER RESEARCH FUND
1 Penn Plz., Ste. 1610
New York, NY 10119
212-268-1002
800-873-5969
ocrf.org

PANCREATIC CANCER ASSOCIATION NETWORK
2221 Rosecrans Ave., Ste. 131
El Segundo, CA 90245
877-272-6226
info@pancan.org
pancan.org

PARALYZED VETERANS OF AMERICA
801 18th St., N.W.
Washington, DC 20006-3715
800-424-8200
202-872-1300
info@pva.org
pva.org

PARKINSON'S DISEASE FOUNDATION, INC.
710 W. 168th St.
New York, NY 10032-9982
800-457-6676

212-923-4700
info@pdf.org
pdf.org

THE PARKINSON'S INSTITUTE
675 Almanor Ave.
Sunnyvale, CA 94085
800-655-2273
thepi.org

PEDIATRIC AIDS FOUNDATION
1311 Colorado Ave.
Santa Monica, CA 90405
310-395-9051

PEDIATRIC BRAIN TUMOR FOUNDATION
302 Ridgefield Ct.
Asheville, NC 28806
800-253-6530
pbtfus.org

PLASTIC SURGERY EDUCATION FOUNDATION
(AMERICAN SOCIETY OF PLASTIC & RECONSTRUCTIVE
SURGERY [PSEF/ASPS])
444 E. Algonquin Rd.
Arlington Heights, IL 60005
847-228-9900

POLYCYSTIC KIDNEY DISEASE FOUNDATION
9221 Ward Pkwy., Ste. 400
Kansas City, MO 64114-3367
800-PKD-CURE
pkdcure.org

PREVENT BLINDNESS AMERICA
211 West Wacker Dr., Ste. 1700
Chicago, IL 60606
800-331-2020
preventblindness.org

PROJECT ALS
511 Avenue of the Americas
P.M.B. 341
New York, NY 10011
800-603-0272
projectals.org

PROSTATE CANCER FOUNDATION
1250 Fourth St.
Santa Monica, CA 90401
800-757-2873
prostatecancerfoundation.org

RESEARCH TO PREVENT BLINDNESS
645 Madison Ave., Fl. 21
New York, NY 10022-1010
800-621-0026
info@rpbusa.org
rpbusa.org

RETT SYNDROME RESEARCH FOUNDATION
4600 Devitt Dr.
Cincinnati, OH 45246
212-448-5000
rsrf.org

SABIN VACCINE INSTITUTE
113 Summit Ave.
Washington, DC 20006
202-842-5025
sabin.org

SALK INSTITUTE FOR BIOLOGICAL SCIENCES
10010 N. Torrey Pines Rd.
La Jolla, CA 92037
858-550-0472
salk.edu

SAMUEL WAXMAN CANCER RESEARCH FOUNDATION
1150 Fifth Ave.
New York, NY 10128
212-241-1760
waxmancancer.org

SCHEPENS EYE RESEARCH INSTITUTE
20 Staniford St.
Boston, MA 02114
877-724-3736
eri.harvard.edu

SCHIZOPHRENIA SOCIETY OF CANADA
50 Acadia Ave., Ste. 205
Markham, ON L3R 0B3
Canada
905-415-2007
schizophrenia.ca

SCRIPPS RESEARCH INSTITUTE
  10550 N. Torrey Pines Rd.
  TPC-2
  La Jolla, CA 92037
  858-784-9365
  scripps.edu

SEATTLE BIOMEDICAL RESEARCH INSTITUTE
  307 West Lake Ave N., Ste. 500
  Seattle, WA 98109
  206-256-7200
  sbri.org

SHRINERS HOSPITALS FOR CHILDREN
  c/o Shriners International Headquarters
  2900 Rocky Point Dr.
  Tampa, FL 33607
  813-281-0300
  shrinershq.org

SMILE TRAIN
  245 5th Ave., Ste. 2201
  New York, NY 10016
  877-KIDSMILE
  212-689-9199
  info@smiletrain.org
  smiletrain.org

SOCIETY FOR PEDIATRIC PATHOLOGY
  3643 Walton Way Extension
  Augusta, GA 30909
  706-364-3375

socpedpath@degnon.org
spponline.org

ST. BALDRICK'S FOUNDATION
1443 E. Washington Blvd., #650
Pasadena, CA 91104
888-899-BALD
sbinfo@stbaldricks.org
stbaldricks.org

ST. JUDE CHILDREN'S RESEARCH HOSPITAL
National Executive Offices
501 St. Jude Pl.
Memphis, TN 38105
901-495-3300
lin.ballew@stjude.org
stjude.org

STEADMAN HAWKINS RESEARCH FOUNDATION
181 W Meadow Dr., Ste. 1000
Vail, CO 81657
970-479-5809
shsmf.org

STEM CELL RESEARCH FOUNDATION
22512 Gateway Center Dr.
Clarksburg, MD 20871
877-842-3442
stemcellresearchfoundation.org

STRANG CANCER PREVENTION CENTER
428 East 72nd St.
New York, NY 10021

212-794-4900
home.strang.org

SUDDEN INFANT DEATH SYNDROME ALLIANCE
1314 Bedford Ave., Ste. 210
Baltimore, MD 21208
800-221-SIDS
410-653-8709
info@sidsalliance.org
sidsalliance.org

SUNNYBROOK & WOMEN'S FOUNDATION
2075 Bayview Ave.
Toronto, ON M4N 3M5
Canada
416-480-4483
sunnybrookandwomens.on.ca

SUSAN G. KOMEN BREAST CANCER FOUNDATION
5005 LBJ Fwy., Ste. 250
Dallas, TX 75244
800-462-9273
972-855-1600
education@komen.org
komen.org

T.J. MARTELL FOUNDATION
555 Madison Ave., 9th Fl.
New York, NY 10022
212-833-5444
tjmartellfoundation.org

TERRY FOX FOUNDATION
  60 St. Clair Ave., E., Ste. 605
  Toronto, ON M4T 1N5
  Canada
  416-962-7866
  national@terryfoxrun.org
  terryfoxrun.org

TEXAS HEART INSTITUTE
  Development Office MC 3-117
  P.O. Box 20345
  Houston, TX 77225
  832-355-3792
  texasheartinstitute.org

TOURETTE SYNDROME ASSOCIATION
  42-40 Bell Blvd.
  Bayside, NY 11361-2820
  800-237-0717
  718-224-2999
  ts@tsa-usa.org
  tsa-usa.org

UNITED CEREBRAL PALSY
  1660 L St., N.W., Ste. 700
  Washington, DC 20036
  202-776-0406
  ucpnatl@ucpa.org
  ucp.org

UNITED SPINAL ASSOCIATION (formerly Eastern
Paralyzed Veterans Association)
  75-20 Astoria Blvd.

Jackson Heights, NY 11370
718-803-3782
info@unitedspinal.org
unitedspinal.org

UNTIL THERE'S A CURE FOUNDATION
560 Mountain Home Rd.
Redwood City, CA 94062
650-332-3200
info@utac.org
utac.org

V FOUNDATION FOR CANCER RESEARCH
(THE JIMMY V FOUNDATION)
100 Towerview Ct.
Cary, NC 27513
919-380-9505
800-4-JIMMYV
info@jimmyv.org
jimmyv.org

12

Recommended Books and Videos

These books, listed in order of preference, are available through PETACatalog.org, Amazon.com, or through your local bookstore.

VEGAN LIVING

Making Kind Choices by Ingrid E. Newkirk

Quantum Wellness: A Practical and Spiritual Guide to Health and Happiness by Kathy Freston

Skinny Bitch by Rory Freedman and Kim Barnouin

101 Reasons Why I'm a Vegetarian by Pamela Rice

Diet for a New America by John Robbins
Don't Eat This Book by Morgan Spurlock
Vegan Handbook by Debra Wasserman
Vegan: The New Ethics of Eating by Eric Marcus
Vegetarian America: A History by Karen Iacobbo and
　Michael Iacobbo
You Don't Need Meat by Peter Cox

COOKBOOKS

The Compassionate Cook by Ingrid E. Newkirk
Cooking with PETA by PETA
The PETA Celebrity Cookbook by PETA
Skinny Bitch in the Kitch by Rory Freedman and
　Kim Barnouin
The Vegetarian Meat & Potatoes Cookbook by Robin
　Robertson
*The Best in the World: Fast, Healthful Recipes from
　Exclusive and Out-of-the-Way Restaurants* by Neal
　D. Barnard, M.D., Ed.
*The Candle Café Cookbook: Over 150 Enlightened
　Recipes from New York's Renowned Vegan Restaurant*
　by The Candle Café
*Meatless Meals for Working People: Quick and Easy
　Vegetarian Recipes* by Debra Wasserman and Charles
　Stahler
7 Minute Chef by Mark Reinfeld and Bo Rinaldi
150 Vegan Favorites by Jay Solomon
*Quick-Fix Vegetarian: Healthy Home-Cooked Meals
　in 30 Minutes or Less* by Robin Robertson
*Vegan Fire & Spice: 200 Sultry and Savory Global
　Recipes* by Robin Robertson

The Vegan Gourmet by Susann Geiskopf-Hadler and
  Mindy Toomay
Vegan Seafood: Beyond the Fish Schtick for Vegetarians
  by Nancy Berkoff, Ed.D., R.D.
Vegan Meals for One or Two by Nancy Berkoff, Ed. D.,
  R.D.
*Fresh From the Vegetarian Slow Cooker 200 Recipes for
  Healthy and Hearty One-Pot Meals That Are Ready
  When You Are* by Robin Robertson
The Joy of Vegan Baking by Colleen Patrick-Goudreau

HEALTH

Making Kind Choices by Ingrid E. Newkirk
*Breaking the Food Seduction: The Hidden Reasons
  Behind Food Cravings—and Seven Steps to End
  Them Naturally* by Neal D. Barnard, M.D.
*Eat Right, Live Longer: Using the Natural Power of
  Foods to Age-Proof Your Body* by Neal D. Barnard,
  M.D.
Dr. Neal Barnard's Program for Reversing Diabetes
  by Neal D. Barnard, M.D.
Food for Life by Neal D. Barnard, M.D.
Foods That Fight Pain by Neal D. Barnard, M.D.
*A Physician's Slimming Guide for Permanent Weight
  Control* by Neal D. Barnard, M.D.
The Power of Your Plate by Neal D. Barnard, M.D.
Turn Off the Fat Genes by Neal D. Barnard, M.D.
The McDougall Plan for Super Health by
  John McDougall, M.D.
Vegan Nutrition Pure and Simple by Michael Klaper

ANIMAL BEHAVIOR

*The Pig Who Sang to the Moon: The Emotional World
of Farm Animals* by Jeffrey Moussaieff Masson
When Elephants Weep: The Emotional Lives of Animals
by Masson and McCarthy
*Pleasurable Kingdom: Animals and the Nature of Feeling
Good* by Jonathan Balcombe
*Animals Matter: A Biologist Explains Why We Should Treat
Animals with Compassion and Respect* by Marc Bekoff
Listening to Cougar by Marc Bekoff
*The Emotional Lives of Animals: A Leading Scientist
Explores Animal Joy, Sorrow, and Empathy—and Why
They Matter* by Marc Bekoff
*How Animals Talk and Other Pleasant Studies of Birds
and Beasts* by William J. Long, Rupert Sheldrake,
and Marc Bekoff
*Animal Passions and Beastly Virtues: Reflections on
Redecorating Nature* by Marc Bekoff
Encyclopedia of Animal Behavior edited by Marc Bekoff
*The Ten Trusts: What We Must Do to Care for the
Animals We Love* by Marc Bekoff and Jane Goodall
Minding Animals: Awareness, Emotions, and Heart by
Marc Bekoff
Strolling with Our Kin by Marc Bekoff

RELIGION

Animals and Their Moral Standing by Stephen R. L.
Clark
Animal Theology by Andrew Linzey

Judaism and Vegetarianism by Richard H. Schwartz, Ph.D.

The Lost Religion of Jesus: Simple Living and Nonviolence in Early Christianity by Keith Akers

Animals on the Agenda: Questions about Animals for Theology and Ethics by Yamamoto and Andrew Linzey

Diet for Transcendence: Vegetarianism and the World Religions by Rosen, Cerquetti, and Greene

Food for the Gods: Vegetarianism and the World's Religions by Berry

Nonviolence to Animals, Earth and Self in Asian Traditions by Chapple

Animal Sacrifices: Religious Perspectives on the Use of Animals in Science by Thomas Regan

Judaism and Animal Rights: Classical and Contemporary Responses by Roberta Kalechofsky

The Slaughter of Terrified Beasts by Rev. J. R. Hyland

The Souls of Animals by Gary Kowalski

Dominion: The Power of Man, the Suffering of Animals, and the Call to Mercy by Matthew Scully

Eternal Treblinka: Our Treatment of Animals and the Holocaust by Charles Patterson

God's Covenant with Animals: A Biblical Basis for the Humane Treatment of All Creatures by Hyland

Good News for All Creation: Vegetarianism As Christian Stewardship by Stephen R. Kaufman and Nathan Braun

GENERAL

Making Kind Choices by Ingrid E. Newkirk
Free the Animals! by Ingrid E. Newkirk

PETA Book of Cartoons by PETA

Committed: A Rabble-Rouser's Memoir by Dan Mathews

Striking at the Roots: A Practical Guide to Animal Activism by Mark Hawthorne

Animal Liberation by Peter Singer

Generation React by Danny Sea

Animal Equality by Joan Dunayer

Animals Like Us by Mark Rowlands

Inhumane Society: The American Way of Exploiting Animals by Michael W. Fox

Visions of Caliban: On Chimpanzees and People by Dale Peterson and Jane Goodall

Introduction to Animal Rights: Your Child or the Dog? by Gary L. Francione

An Unnatural Order: Why We Are Destroying the Planet and Each Other by Jim Mason

Enemies: A Love Story by I. B. Singer.

Empty Cages: Facing the Challenge of Animal Rights by Tom Regan

The Food Revolution by John Robbins

The Jungle by Upton Sinclair

Mad Cowboy: Plain Truth from the Cattle Rancher Who Won't Eat Meat by Howard F. Lyman

Rattling the Cage: Toward Legal Rights for Animals by Steven M. Wise

Slaughterhouse: The Shocking Story of Greed, Neglect, and Inhumane Treatment Inside the US Meat Industry by Gail A. Eisnitz

Slaughter of the Innocent by Hans Ruesch

ANIMALS IN ENTERTAINMENT

A Different Nature: The Paradoxical World of Zoos and Their Uncertain Future by David Hancocks
Beyond the Bars: The Zoo Dilemma by Virginia McKenna, Will Travers, and Jonathan Wray
The Rose-Tinted Menagerie by William Johnson

HUNTING AND FISHING

The American Hunting Myth by Ron Baker

COMPANION ANIMALS

Let's Have a Dog Party! by Ingrid E. Newkirk
250 Things You Can Do to Make Your Cat Adore You by Ingrid E. Newkirk
The Right Way the First Time by Alana Stevenson
Vegetarian Dogs: Toward a World Without Exploitation by Verona re-Bow and Jonathan Dune
The Compassion of Animals by Kristin von Kreisler
Dr. Pitcairn's Complete Guide to Natural Health for Dogs and Cats by Richard Pitcairn, D.V.M.
The Dog Who Loved Too Much: Tales, Treatments, and the Psychology of Dogs by Nicholas Dodman
Mother Knows Best: The Natural Way to Train Your Dog by Carol Lea Benjamin
Preparing for the Loss of Your Pet by Myrna Milani, D.V.M.

Stolen for Profit by Judith Reitman
Understanding Your Dog by Michael Fox, D.V.M.
Vacationing with Your Pet by Eileen Barish

ANIMAL EXPERIMENTS

Free the Animals! by Ingrid E. Newkirk
Monkey Business by Kathy Snow Guillermo
Animal Liberation by Peter Singer
Future Medical Research without the Use of Animals: Facing the Challenge edited by Nina Natelson and Murry Cohen, M.D.
The Human Cost of Animal Experiments by Dr. Robert Sharpe
Lethal Laws: Animal Testing, Human Health and Environmental Policy by Alix Fano
Slaughter of the Innocent by Hans Ruesch
Naked Empress by Hans Ruesch
Secret Suffering: Inside a British Laboratory by Sarah Kite
The Plague Dogs by Richard Adams
Doctor Rat by William Kotzwinkle
Caught in the Act: The Feidberg Investigation by MacDonald
Animal Experimentation: A Harvest of Shame by Moneim Fadali, M.D.
Natural Progesterone: The Multiple Roles of a Remarkable Hormone by John R. Lee
Health with Humanity by Steve McIvor
The Scalpel and the Butterfly by Deborah Rudacille
Drawing the Line: Science and the Case for Animal Rights by Steven M. Wise

CLOTHING

Trapping Animals for Fur by Tyler and Jordan
Pulling the Wool by Christine Townsend
Jaws of Steel: The Truth about Trapping by Thomas
  Eveland

DISSECTION

*Vivisection and Dissection in the Classroom: A Guide to
  Conscientious Objection* by Gary L. Francione and
  Anna E. Charlton
Animals in Education: The Facts, Issues and Implications
  by Lisa Ann Hepner

WILDLIFE

*Pigeons: The Fascinating Saga of the World's Most
  Revered and Reviled Bird* by Andrew Blechman.
*Wild Neighbors: The Humane Approach to Living with
  Wildlife* by Hodge, Grandy, Hadidian, and Hadidian.
*Living with Wildlife: How to Enjoy, Cope with, and
  Protect North America's Wild Creatures around Your
  Home and Theirs* by Landau and Stump
*The Human Nature of Birds: A Scientific Discovery with
  Startling Implications* by Theodore Barber
Common Sense Pest Control by Olkowski, Daar, and
  Olkowski

CHILDREN

50 Awesome Ways Kids Can Help Animals by Ingrid E.
   Newkirk
One in a Million by Nicholas Read
Animal Place: Where Magical Things Happen
   by Kim Sturla
The Gnats of Knotty Pine by Bill Peet
Diary of a Worm by Doreen Cronin
Uncover a Frog by Aimee Bakken
Conner the Calf by Heather Leughmyer
The Lady and the Spider by Faith McNulty
So You Love the Animals by Zoe Weil
Victor the Vegetarian by Vignola
Victor's Picnic by Vignola
William's Story by Deborah Duel

VIDEOS

These videos are available at PETACatalog.org, or through
Amazon.com.

Nonviolence Includes Animals by PETA President
   Ingrid E. Newkirk, introduction by Dennis Kucinich
*I Am an Animal: The Story of Ingrid Newkirk and
   PETA*, directed by Matthew Galkin
The Animals Film, directed by Myriam Alaux and
   Victor Schonfeld
Behind the Mask, written, directed, and produced by
   Shannon Keith

Earthlings, narrated by Golden Globe Winner
  (best actor, *Walk the Line*) Joaquin Phoenix
Meet Your Meat, by PETA
Eating, by Michael Anderson with Dr. Ruth Heidrich
If This Is Kosher, by Jonathan Safran Foer
The Emotional World of Farm Animals, coproduced by
  Animal Place and Earth View Productions

Organizations That Promote Animal Welfare

GENERAL

PEOPLE FOR THE ETHICAL TREATMENT OF ANIMALS (PETA)
  501 Front St.
  Norfolk, VA 23510
  757-622-PETA (7382)
  PETA.org

PETA EUROPE LTD.
  P.O. Box 36668
  London SE1 1WA
  United Kingdom
  +44 (0)20 7357 9229
  PETA.org.uk

PETA DEUTSCHLAND E.V.
Dieselstr. 21
D-70839 Gerlingen
+49 (0)7156-178-280
PETA.de

PETA INDIA
P.O. Box 28260
Juhu, Mumbai 400 049
India
+91 22-2628-1880
PETAIndia.com

PETA HONG KONG
Hong Kong Office
PETA Asia-Pacific
G.P.O. Box 1700
Hong Kong

PETA PHILIPPINES
176 Salcedo St.
Legaspi Village
Makati 1229
Philippines
+63-2-817-5292
PETAAsiaPacific.com

PHYSICIANS COMMITTEE FOR
RESPONSIBLE MEDICINE (PCRM)
5100 Wisconsin Ave., N.W., Ste. 400
Washington, DC 20016
202-686-2210
PCRM.org

ANIMAL RIGHTS FOUNDATION OF FLORIDA (ARFF)
1431 N. Federal Highway
Fort Lauderdale, FL 33304
954-727-ARFF
AnimalRightsFlorida.org

WORLD SOCIETY FOR THE PROTECTION OF ANIMALS
Lincoln Plaza
89 South St., Ste. 201
Boston, MA 02111
800-883-9772
WSPA-International.org

OVERSEAS GROUPS

PETA EUROPE LTD.
P.O. Box 36668
London SE1 1WA
United Kingdom
+44 (0)20 7357 9229
PETA.org.uk

PETA DEUTSCHLAND E.V.
Dieselstr. 21
D-70839 Gerlingen
+49 (0)7156-178-280
PETA.de

PETA INDIA
P.O. Box 28260
Juhu, Mumbai 400 049
India

+91 22-2628-1880
PETAIndia.com

PETA HONG KONG
Hong Kong Office
PETA Asia-Pacific
G.P.O. Box 1700
Hong Kong

PETA PHILIPPINES
176 Salcedo St.
Legaspi Village
Makati 1229
Philippines
+63-2-817-5292
PETAAsiaPacific.com

ANIMAL AID
The Old Chapel
Bradford St.
Tonbridge
Kent TN9 1AW
United Kingdom
44 (0)1732 364546
AnimalAid.org.uk

COMPASSION IN WORLD FARMING (CIWF)
River Court
Mill Lane
Godalming
Surrey GU7 1EZ
United Kingdom

44 (0)1483 521 950
CIWF.org.uk

LEAGUE AGAINST CRUEL SPORTS
New Sparling House
Holloway Hill
Godalming
Surrey
GU7 1QZ
United Kingdom
+44 0845-330-8486
League.org.uk

ROYAL SOCIETY FOR THE PROTECTION
OF ANIMALS (RSPCA)
Wilberforce Way
Southwater
Horsham
West Sussex RH13 9RS
United Kingdom
+44 0300-1234-555
RSPCA.org.uk

VEGAN SOCIETY
Donald Watson House
21 Hylton St.
Hockley
Birmingham B18 6HJ
United Kingdom
44-121-523-1730
VeganSociety.com

LEGAL

ANIMAL LEGAL DEFENSE FUND
170 East Cotati Ave.
Cotati, CA 94931
707-795-2533
ALDF.org

ANIMAL AID
The Old Chapel
Bradford St.
Tonbridge
Kent TN9 1AW
United Kingdom
44 (0)1732 364546
AnimalAid.org.uk

WILDLIFE

BAT CONSERVATION INTERNATIONAL
P.O. Box 162603
Austin, TX 78716
512-327-9721
BatCon.org

BORN FREE FOUNDATION
3 Grove House
Foundry Lane
Horsham
West Sussex
RH13 5PL

United Kingdom
44-1403-240170
BornFree.org.uk

PERFORMING ANIMAL WELFARE SOCIETY (PAWS)
P.O. Box 849
Galt, CA 95632
209-745-2606
PAWSWeb.org

VETS

ASSOCIATION OF VETERINARIANS FOR
ANIMAL RIGHTS (AVAR)
P.O. Box 208
Davis, CA 95617
530-759-8106
AVAR.org

DISSECTION

DISSECTION HOTLINE
1-800-922-FROG (3764)

ENVIRONMENTAL

EARTH ISLAND INSTITUTE
300 Broadway, Ste. 28
San Francisco, CA 94133
415-788-3666
EarthIsland.org

EARTHSAVE
P.O. Box 96
New York, NY 10108
718-459-7503
EarthSave.org

GREYHOUND ADOPTION

NATIONAL GREYHOUND ADOPTION NETWORK
P.O. Box 638
Homosassa, FL 34487
1-800-446-8637
4GreyHounds.org/Adoption.html

THE GREYHOUND PROJECT
261 Robin St.
Milton, MA 02186
617-333-6655
Adopt-a-Greyhound.org

RELIGION

INTERFAITH COUNCIL FOR THE PROTECTION
OF ANIMALS AND NATURE
2841 Colony Rd.
Ann Arbor, MI 48104
ICPANOnline.org

JEWISH VEGETARIANS OF NORTH AMERICA
49 Patton Dr.
Newport News, VA 23606
JewishVeg.com

COMPANION ANIMALS

SPAY USA
2261 Broadridge Ave.
Stratford, CT 06614
800-248-7729

TATTOO-A-PET
6571 S.W. 20th Ct.
Ft. Lauderdale, FL 33317
800-TATTOOS
Tattoo-a-Pet.com

NATIONAL DOG REGISTRY (NDR)
Box 116
Woodstock, NY 12498-0116
914-679-BELL
NationalDogRegistry.com

NATIONAL GREYHOUND ADOPTION NETWORK
P.O. Box 638
Homosassa, FL 34487
1-800-446-8637
4Greyhounds.org/Adoption.html

THE GREYHOUND PROJECT
261 Robin St.
Milton, MA 02186
617-333-6655
Adopt-a-Greyhound.org

ROYAL SOCIETY FOR THE PROTECTION
OF ANIMALS (RSPCA)
Wilberforce Way
Southwater
Horsham
West Sussex RH13 9RS
United Kingdom
+44 0300-1234-555
RSPCA.org.uk

VEGETARIAN SOCIETIES

PEOPLE FOR THE ETHICAL TREATMENT
OF ANIMALS (PETA)
501 Front St.
Norfolk, VA 23510
757-622-PETA (7382)
PETA.org

AMERICAN VEGAN SOCIETY
56 Dinshah Lane
P.O. Box 369
Malaga, NJ 08328
856-694-2887
AmericanVegan.org

NORTH AMERICAN VEGETARIAN SOCIETY
P.O. Box 72
Dolgeville, NY 13329
518-568-7970
NAVS-online.org

VEGAN SOCIETY
Donald Watson House
21 Hylton St.
Hockley
Birmingham B18 6HJ
United Kingdom
+44 121-523-1730
VeganSociety.com

VEGAN OUTREACH
P.O. Box 30865
Tucson, AZ 85751-0865
520-495-0503
VeganOutreach.org

VEGETARIAN RESOURCE GROUP
P.O. Box 1463, Dept. IN
Baltimore, MD 21203
410-366-VEGE
VRG.org

MARINE LIFE

SEA SHEPHERD CONSERVATION SOCIETY
P.O. Box 2616
Friday Harbor, WA 98250
360-370-5650
SeaShepherd.org

ANIMAL EXPERIMENTATION

BRITISH UNION FOR THE ABOLITION OF VIVISECTION
16a Crane Grove
London N7 8NN
United Kingdom
+44 (0) 20 7700 4888
BUAV.org

EMERGENCY (FLOODS, EARTHQUAKES, FIRES)

UNITED ANIMAL NATIONS
P.O. Box 188890
Sacramento, CA 95818
916-429-2457
UAN.org

FARMED ANIMALS

UNITED POULTRY CONCERNS (UPC)
12325 Seaside Rd.
Machipongo, VA 23405
757-678-7875
UPC-online.org

COMPASSION IN WORLD FARMING (CIWF)
River Court
Mill Lane
Godalming

Surrey, GU7 1EZ,
United Kingdom
+44 (0)1483 521 950
CIWF.org.uk

ANIMALS IN ENTERTAINMENT

PERFORMING ANIMAL WELFARE SOCIETY (PAWS)
P.O. Box 849
Galt, CA 95632
209-745-2606
PAWSweb.org

BORN FREE FOUNDATION
3 Grove House
Foundry Lane
Horsham
West Sussex
RH13 5PL
United Kingdom
44-1403-240170
BornFree.org.uk

NATIONAL GREYHOUND ADOPTION NETWORK
P.O. Box 638
Homosassa, FL 34487
1-800-446-8637
4Greyhounds.org/Adoption.html

THE GREYHOUND PROJECT
261 Robin St.
Milton, MA 02186

617-333-6655
Adopt-a-Greyhound.org

ZOOCHECK CANADA
788 1/2 O'Connor Dr.
Toronto, ON M4B 2S6
Canada
416-285-1744
ZooCheck.com

14

Helpful Businesses

ANIMALRIGHTSTUFF.COM
P.O. Box 9235
Reston, VA 20191
703-860-9633
AnimalRightStuff.com
AnimalRightstuff.com has a huge
  selection of clothing, accessories,
  and activist tools.

DAISY DOG STUDIO
80 Chambers St., Apt. 8E
New York, NY 10007
212-346-9228
DaisyDogStudio.com
Daisy Dog Studio designs porcelain
  tableware for all occasions.

HARBOR CANDY SHOP
P.O. Box 2064
Ogunquit, ME 03907
800-331-5856
HarborCandy.com
Harbor Candy Shop has been creating superior
confections since 1956. It carries a large selection of
vegan treats.

HOLIDAY SYSTEMS INTL.
7690 W. Cheyenne Ave., #200
Las Vegas, NV 89129
702-254-3100
HolidaySystems.com
Holiday Systems International will help you plan the
perfect vacation.

MOO SHOES, INC.
78 Orchard St.
New York, NY 10002
212-254-6512
MooShoes.com
Moo Shoes, Inc., is a vegan-owned business that sells an
assortment of cruelty-free footwear, bags, T-shirts,
wallets, books, and other accessories.

EARTH ISLAND/FOLLOW YOUR HEART
P.O. Box 9400
Canoga Park, CA 91309
818-348-3240
FollowYourHeart.com
Follow Your Heart offers Vegan Gourmet
Dairy Alternatives, Fresh and Natural Dressings,

Organic Dressings, and the Unforgettables Balsamic Sauces.

ORGANIC BOUQUET
750 Lindaro St., Ste. 330
San Rafael, CA 94901
877-899-2468
OrganicBouquet.com
Organic Bouquet is the Internet's first socially and environmentally responsible florist, offering fresh organic flowers for personal and business gift-giving needs.

PANGEA VEGAN PRODUCTS
2381 Lewis Ave.
Rockville, MD 20851
301-652-3181
VeganStore.com
Pangea is the one-stop shop for vegan goods, including nonleather shoes, belts, cosmetics, food, and more!

PETGUARD, INC.
1515 CR 315
Green Cove Springs, FL 32043
904-264-8500
PetGuard.com
PetGuard creates companion animal products free of artificial ingredients, colors, preservatives, sugar, and salt.

THE CLOUTIER AGENCY
1026 Montana Ave.
Santa Monica, CA 90403

310-394-8813
CloutierAgency.com
The Cloutier Agency is *the* agency for hair, makeup, and wardrobe styling.

YOGAFIT TRAINING SYSTEMS WORLDWIDE
2321 Torrance Blvd.
Torrance, CA 90501
888-786-0110
YogaFit.com
The mission of YogaFit is to bring Yoga to the masses.

ALLISON'S GOURMET
P.O. Box 2454
Nevada City, CA 95959
530-265-1992
AllisonsGourmet.com
Allison's offers vegan cookies, luxurious organic chocolates, caramels, and English toffee.

ALTERNATIVE OUTFITTERS
408 S. Pasadena Ave., Ste. 1
Pasadena, CA 91105
866-758-5837
AlternativeOutfitters.com
Alternative Outfitters is your online resource for fashionable leather alternatives and cruelty-free products for the compassionate, fashion-forward girl or guy.

A SCENT OF SCANDAL
1945 Cheremoya Ave.
Los Angeles, CA 90068

323-896-2034

AScentOfScandal.com

A Scent of Scandal is a unique candle line in which the
name of each candle and its scent have a funny or
"scandalous" relationship!

CANDLE CAFÉ

1307 Third Ave., at 75th

New York, NY 10021

212-472-0970

CandleCafe.com

Candle Café in New York City is a completely vegan
restaurant, dedicated to making the best of your
vegetarian dining.

JASON NATURAL COSMETICS

3515 Eastham Dr.

Culver City, CA 90232

877-527-6601

Jason-Natural.com

Their mission at JASON is to make the best and most
effective natural products in the marketplace. Their
unique formulations are infused with botanicals,
plants, roots, herbs, proteins, vitamins, and
minerals—all from the earth.

NATIVE FOODS

2079 Paseo Gracia

Palm Springs, CA 92262

714-751-2151

NativeFoods.com

Native Foods restaurants serve healthy, organic,
scrumptious food in a fun, friendly place.

FABULOUS FURS

25 West Robbins St.

Covington, KY 41011

859-291-3300

FabulousFurs.com

All fake fur is not created equal. At Fabulous Furs, their faux-fur coats, faux-fur jackets, and faux-fur throws are the world's finest because they start with the most luxurious faux-fur fabrics and marry them with their unmatched sewing expertise and faux-fur knowledge.

MESSAGE! CHECKS

P. O. Box 700

Edgewood, MD 21040

800-243-2565

messageproducts.com

By purchasing your bank checks and check products from Message! Products, you are going one step further to helping the environment, while supporting the causes that mean the most to you. Message! Checks provide their customers with quality personal bank checks, address labels, contact cards, and checkbook covers that convey messages and feature images that reflect these issues

15

Companies That Do Not Use Animals to Test Their Companion-Animal Food

Companies that are not on this list either responded to let us know that they do conduct laboratory experiments on animals or failed to respond to our numerous inquiries.

ACTIVE LIFE PET PRODUCTS
1-877-291-2913
ActiveLifePP.com

AMORÉ PET SERVICES, INC.
1-866-572-6673
AmorePetFoods.com

ANIMAL FOOD SERVICES
1-800-743-0322
AnimalFood.com

ARTEMIS PET FOOD
1-800-282-5876
ArtemisCompany.com

AZMIRA HOLISTIC ANIMAL CARE
1-800-497-5665
Azmira.com

BOSTON BAKED BONZ (entirely vegan)
781-752-4040
BostonbakedBonz.com

BRAVO RAW DIET
1-866-922-9222
BravoRawDiet.com

BURNS PET HEALTH, INC.
1-877-983-9651
BurnsPetHealth.com

CANISOURCE
1-888-347-3523
CaniSource.com

CANUSA INTERNATIONAL
519-624-5697
CanusaInt.com

COUNTRYPET PET FOOD
1-800-454-7387
CountryPet.com

DR. HARVEY'S
1-866-362-4123
DrHarveys.com

DRY FORK MILLING CO.
1-800-346-1360

DYNAMITE MARKETING, INC.
208-887-9410
DynamiteMarketing.com

EVANGER'S DOG AND CAT FOOD CO., INC.
1-800-288-6796
EvangersDogFood.com

EVOLUTION DIET, INC. (entirely vegan)
1-800-659-0104
PetFoodShop.com

FELINE'S PRIDE
FelinesPride.com

GOOD DOG FOODS, INC.
732-842-4555
GoodDogFoods.com

GREENTRIPE.COM
831-726-3255
GreenTripe.com

HALO, PURELY FOR PETS
1-800-426-4256
HaloPets.com

HAPPY DOG FOOD
1-800-359-9576
HappyDogFood.com

HARBINGERS OF A NEW AGE (entirely vegan)
406-295-4944
VegePet.com

HOLISTIC BLEND
1-800-954-1117
HolisticBlend.com

THE HONEST KITCHEN
858-483-5995
TheHonestKitchen.com

KNOW BETTER DOG FOOD
1-866-922-6463
KnowBetterDogFood.com

KOSHERPETS, INC.
954-938-6270
KosherPets.com

KUMPI PET FOODS
303-699-8562
Kumpi.com

NATURAL BALANCE PET FOODS, INC.
(has vegan options)
1-800-829-4493
NaturalBalanceInc.com

NATURAL LIFE PET PRODUCTS, INC.
(has vegan options)
   1-800-367-2391
   NLPP.com

NATURE'S VARIETY
   1-888-519-7387
   NaturesVariety.com

NEWMAN'S OWN ORGANICS
   NewmansOwnOrganics.com

OMA'S PRIDE
   1-800-678-6627
   OmasPride.com

ONESTA ORGANICS, INC. (entirely vegan)
   619-295-1136
   OnestaOrganics.com

PET CHEF EXPRESS
   604-916-2433
   PetChef Express.ca

PETGUARD (has vegan options)
   1-800-874-3221
   904-264-8500
   PetGuard.com

PIED PIPER PET & WILDLIFE
   1-800-338-4610
   PiedPiperPet.com

POSHNOSH, INC.
613-747-1542
1-866-893-4006 (Outside Ottawa-Outaouais)
PoshNosh.ca

RAW ADVANTAGE, INC.
360-387-5158
RawAdvantagePetFood.com

SAUDER FEEDS, INC.
260-627-2196
SauderFeeds.com

STELLA & CHEWY'S LLC
718-522-9673
StellaAndChewys.com

TIMBERWOLF ORGANICS, INC.
407-877-8779
TimberwolfOrganics.com

V-DOGFOOD LLC (entirely vegan)
1-888-280-8364
V-DogFood.com

VETERINARY NUTRITIONAL FORMULA
1-800-811-0530
VNFPetFood.com

WOW-BOW DISTRIBUTORS LTD. (has vegan options)
1-800-326-0230
Wow-Bow.com

WYSONG CANADA
1-800-748-0188
WysongCanada.net

WYSONG PROFESSIONAL DIETS (has vegan options)
1-800-748-0188
Wysong.net

16

How to Make
Cruelty-Free Products at Home

D ozens of safe and effective home recipes can
be concocted from substances as inexpensive as baking soda and vinegar, including:

CLEANSERS

Cooking utensils: Let pots and pans soak
in baking soda solution before washing.
Copper cleaner: Use a paste of lemon juice,
salt, and flour; or rub vinegar and salt into
the copper.
Furniture polish: Mix three parts olive
oil and one part vinegar, or one part
lemon juice and two parts vegetable oil.
Use a soft cloth.

General cleaner: Mix baking soda with a small
amount of water.

Glass cleaner: White vinegar or rubbing alcohol
and water.

Household cleaner: Three tablespoons of baking soda
mixed into one quart of warm water.

Linoleum floor cleaner: One cup of white vinegar
mixed with two gallons of water to wash, club soda
to polish.

Mildew remover: Lemon juice or white vinegar and salt.

Stain remover, toilet bowl cleaner: Vinegar.

Wine or coffee stains: Blot the fresh spill with a cloth
soaked with club soda.

INSECT REPELLENTS

Ant control: Pour a line of cream of tartar at the place
where ants enter the house—they will not cross it.

Ant repellent: Wash countertops, cabinets, and floors
with equal parts vinegar and water.

Cockroach repellent: Place whole bay leaves in several
locations around the kitchen.

Flea and tick repellent: Feed flaxseed oil and chopped
garlic or garlic tablets to companion animals. Place
herbs such as fennel, rue, pennyroyal, and rosemary
and/or eucalyptus seeds and leaves where the animal
sleeps to repel fleas.

Mosquito repellent: Take 100 milligrams of vitamin B
complex daily during the summer months.

Mothballs: Place cedar chips around clothes; dried
lavender can be made into sachets and placed in
drawers and closets.

MISCELLANEOUS

Air freshener: Leave an opened box of baking soda in the room, or add cloves and cinnamon to boiling water and simmer. Scent the house with fresh flowers or herbs; or open windows (in the winter, for about fifteen minutes every morning).

Drain opener: Prevent clogging by using a drain strainer or by flushing the drain weekly with about a gallon of boiling water. If clogged, pour one-half cup baking soda, then one-half cup vinegar down the drain and cover it tightly for about a minute.

Odor remover (spills and accidents): On carpet or furniture, blot the fresh stain with a cloth soaked with cider vinegar.

Water softener: One-quarter cup vinegar in the final rinse.

17

Contacting the Media
and the Government

MEDIA ADDRESSES

ABC

500 S. Buena Vista St.
Burbank, CA 91521-4551
818-460-7477
ABC.com

CBS

51 West 52nd St.
New York, NY 10019
212-975-4321
CBS.com

CNN

One CNN Center
Atlanta, GA 30303
404-878-2276
CNN.com

FOX

10201 West Pico Blvd.
Los Angeles, CA 90035
310-369-3553
Fox.com

NBC

30 Rockefeller Plz., # 2
New York, NY 10112
212-315-9016
NBC.com

PBS

2100 Crystal Dr.
Arlington, VA 22202
703-739-5000
PBS.com

GOVERNMENT ADDRESSES

ENVIRONMENTAL PROTECTION AGENCY

Ariel Rios Building
1200 Pennsylvania Ave., N.W.
Washington, DC 20460
202-272-0167
EPA.gov

FOOD AND DRUG ADMINISTRATION
5600 Fishers Lane
Rockville, MD 20857-0001
888-INFO-FDA (463-6332)
FDA.gov

NATIONAL PARK SERVICE
1849 C St., N.W.
Washington, DC 20240
202-208-6843
NPS.gov

US DEPARTMENT OF AGRICULTURE
1400 Independence Ave., S.W.
Washington, DC 20250
202-640-2948
USDA.gov

US DEPARTMENT OF FISH AND WILDLIFE
1849 C St., N.W.
Washington, DC 20240
202-208-4131
FWS.gov

THE HONORABLE (REPRESENTATIVE'S NAME)
US House of Representatives
Washington, DC 20515

THE HONORABLE (SENATOR'S NAME)
US Senate
Washington, DC 20510

To find the name of your US senators or representative, call the congressional switchboard at: 202-224-3121, or visit Senate.gov

SAMPLE LETTERS TO THE EDITOR

Here are two very basic samples of published letters to use as a guide.

Letters to the Editor
[NAME OF NEWSPAPER]
ADDRESS
CITY, STATE ZIP

Dear Editor:

February 26 is Spay Day USA, when many veterinarians offer reduced-cost spaying/neutering. If you're not sure about having your animals sterilized, consider this story.

Several years ago, a neighbor who suddenly had to move begged me to take in her cats three hours before she had to leave because she didn't want them to be euthanized at a shelter. One cat had given birth to six kittens the week before, and the other cat was giving birth that very minute to five more kittens in an empty, dirty litter pan. She was so starved, she immediately ate the food I set out while she was giving birth.

The saddest part of this story is that in the span of eight days, eleven cats were brought into this world—which is already desperately short of homes—from one household because two cats hadn't been spayed. Because there are too many animals, shelters must euthanize three to four million animals each year.

Please, make an appointment today to have your animals sterilized. There aren't enough good homes for them all—and there aren't many neighbors out there willing to give your unwanted animals the love they deserve.

Sincerely,

[Your name]
[Phone number]

Letters to the Editor
[NAME OF NEWSPAPER]
ADDRESS
CITY, STATE ZIP

Dear Editor:

Here is what Philip Anselmo's article, Feb. 18, on trapping ("A Centuries-Old Livelihood Hangs Tough") failed to tell readers:

Animals caught in the steel-jaw traps most often used by trappers endure excruciating pain; those who don't freeze or starve, or die of blood loss or infection, are usually beaten to death or suffocated when the trapper arrives hours or even days later. State regulations on how often trappers must check their traps vary from twenty-four hours to one week. Some states have no regulations at all.

To prevent predators from mutilating trapped animals, trappers often use pole traps, which hoist animals into the air, leaving them to hang painfully by the caught limb until they die or the trapper comes back to kill them.

Conibear traps crush animals' necks, applying ninety pounds of pressure per square inch. Animals caught in these traps slowly suffocate. Animals caught in water-set traps, such as beavers and muskrats, slowly drown.

If you don't want to support this senseless cruelty, don't wear fur. It's that simple. To find out more, please visit www .FurIsDead.com.

[Your name]

[Phone number]

Index

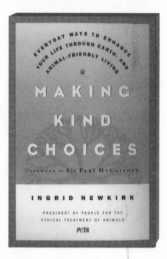